First World War
and Army of Occupation
War Diary
France, Belgium and Germany

58 DIVISION
Divisional Troops
Royal Army Medical Corps
2/1 Home Counties Field Ambulance
23 January 1917 - 13 June 1919

WO95/2997/2

The Naval & Military Press Ltd
www.nmarchive.com
Published in association with The National Archives

Published by

The Naval & Military Press Ltd

Unit 10 Ridgewood Industrial Park,

Uckfield, East Sussex,

TN22 5QE England

Tel: +44 (0) 1825 749494

www.naval-military-press.com

www.nmarchive.com

This diary has been reprinted in facsimile from the original. Any imperfections are inevitably reproduced and the quality may fall short of modern type and cartographic standards.

© Crown Copyright
Images reproduced by permission of The National Archives, London, England, 2015.

Contents

Document type	Place/Title	Date From	Date To
Heading	WO95/2997-2		
Heading	2-1st (H.C) Fld Ambnce 1915 Aug-1916 Feb And 1917 Jan-1919 Jan		
Heading	War Diary Of Lieut Colonel A.T. Falwasser Cmdg 2/1st H.C.F. Ambce From 23rd January 17 To 24th January 17 Volume 1.		
War Diary	Warminster	23/01/1917	23/01/1917
War Diary	Southampton Docks	23/01/1917	23/01/1917
War Diary	Havre	24/01/1917	25/01/1917
War Diary	Abbeville	26/01/1917	26/01/1917
War Diary	Auxi Le Chateau	26/01/1917	26/01/1917
War Diary	Boffles	26/01/1917	03/02/1917
War Diary	Le Souich	03/02/1917	05/02/1917
War Diary	Brevillers	06/02/1917	07/02/1917
War Diary	Sus St Leger	07/02/1917	20/02/1917
War Diary	D.26 Central	20/02/1917	28/02/1917
Heading	58th Division. War Diary Of Lieut Col A.T. Falwasser Cmdg 2/1st Home Counties Fd Ambce From 26.2.17 To 26.3.17 (Volume I.)		
War Diary	D.26 Central	28/02/1917	28/02/1917
War Diary	La Cauchie	28/02/1917	26/03/1917
Heading	War Diary Of Lieut Colonel A.T. Falwasser R.A.M.C. T. Commanding 2/1st Home Counties Field Ambulance From 27.3.17 To 25.4.17 58th Div.		
War Diary	La Cauchie	27/03/1917	29/03/1917
War Diary	Mondicourt	31/03/1917	01/04/1917
War Diary	Pommera	01/04/1917	01/04/1917
War Diary	Beauvoir	01/04/1917	02/04/1917
War Diary	Vaulx	02/04/1917	04/04/1917
War Diary	Frohen Le Grand	04/04/1917	04/04/1917
War Diary	Authieule	04/04/1917	05/04/1917
War Diary	Bertrancourt	05/04/1917	07/04/1917
War Diary	Mailly Maillet	07/04/1917	08/04/1917
War Diary	Achiet Le Grand	08/04/1917	25/04/1917
Heading	War Diary Of Lieut Colonel A.T. Falwasser R.A.M.C. T. Commanding 2/1st Home Counties Field Ambulance From 2.5.17 To 26.5.17 (Volume I.)		
War Diary	Achiet Le Grand	02/05/1917	26/05/1917
Heading	War Diary Of Lieut Colonel A.T. Falwasser R.A.M.C. T. Commanding 2/1st Home Counties Field Ambulance From 23.5.17 To 30.6.17 (Volume I.)		
War Diary	Achiet Le Grand	28/05/1917	27/06/1917
War Diary	Bivouac At L.6.a.5.8	27/06/1917	27/06/1917
Heading	2/1st Home Counties F.A. July 1917		
Heading	War Diary Of Lieut Colonel A.T. Falwasser R.A.M.C. T. Commanding 2/1st Home Counties Field Ambulance From 1.7.17 To 31.7.17 (Volume I)		
Heading	2/1st Home Counties F.A. July 1917		
War Diary	Bivouac At L.6.a.5.8	01/07/1917	05/07/1917
War Diary	Bancourt	05/07/1917	06/07/1917

War Diary	Ruyaulcourt	07/07/1917	27/07/1917
War Diary	Avesnes Le Comte	28/07/1917	28/07/1917
War Diary	Ruyaulcourt	17/07/1917	27/07/1917
War Diary	Avesnes Le-Comte	29/07/1917	30/07/1917
Miscellaneous	Operation Order By Colonel J.W.H. Houghton, A.M.S., A.D.M.S., 56th Division. Appendix I.	04/07/1917	04/07/1917
Operation(al) Order(s)	175th Infantry Brigade. Order No 27. Appendix 2.	04/07/1917	04/07/1917
Miscellaneous	Table 'A'-Issued With 175th Infantry Bde Order No. 27. Of 4/7/17.		
Miscellaneous	Table 'B'-Reliefs To Accompany 175th Infantry Brigade Order No. 27 Of 4/7/17.		
Miscellaneous	175th Infantry Brigade. To Accompany Order No 27 Of 4/7/17.		
Miscellaneous	Appendix 3. O.C. 2/1 H.C. Fd. Amb.	09/07/1917	09/07/1917
Diagram etc	Appendix 4	19/07/1917	19/07/1917
Heading	War Diary Of Lt Colonel A.T. Falwasser R.A.M.C. T.F. Commanding 2/1st Home Counties Field Ambulance From Aug 1st 17 To Aug 31st 17 (Volume I.)		
War Diary	Avesnes Le Comte	01/08/1917	25/08/1917
War Diary	A.23.c.2.9 (Sheet 28)	25/08/1917	26/08/1917
War Diary	A.23.c.2.9	27/08/1917	31/08/1917
Miscellaneous	B.E.F.		
War Diary	Moves and Transfer	25/08/1917	25/08/1917
War Diary	Medical Arrangements	25/08/1917	25/08/1917
War Diary	Moves Detachment	31/08/1917	31/08/1917
War Diary	Moves and Transfer	25/08/1917	25/08/1917
War Diary	Medical Arrangements	25/08/1917	25/08/1917
War Diary	Moves Detachment	31/08/1917	31/08/1917
Heading	War Diary of Lieut Colonel A.T. Falwasser R.A.M.C. T.F. Commanding 2/1st Home Counties Field Ambulance From 1.9.17 to 30.9.17 (Volume I)		
War Diary	Poperinghe Elverdinghe Rd. A.23.c.3.9 (Sheet 28)	01/09/1917	06/09/1917
War Diary	Poperinghe-Elverdinghe Rd. A.23.c.3.9	07/09/1917	30/09/1917
Miscellaneous	B.E.F.		
War Diary	Operations R.A.M.C.	01/09/1917	19/09/1917
War Diary	Casualties	01/09/1917	19/09/1917
War Diary	Casualties Gas	01/09/1917	19/09/1917
War Diary	Operations	20/09/1917	20/09/1917
War Diary	Casualties	21/09/1917	25/09/1917
War Diary	Operations	26/09/1917	26/09/1917
War Diary	Casualties	27/09/1917	28/09/1917
War Diary	Moves and Transfer	29/09/1917	29/09/1917
War Diary	Operations R.A.M.C.	01/09/1917	19/09/1917
War Diary	Casualties	01/09/1917	19/09/1917
War Diary	Casualties Gas	01/09/1917	19/09/1917
War Diary	Operations	20/09/1917	20/09/1917
War Diary	Casualties	21/09/1917	25/09/1917
War Diary	Operations	26/09/1917	26/09/1917
War Diary	Casualties	27/09/1917	28/09/1917
War Diary	Moves and Transfer	29/09/1917	29/09/1917
Operation(al) Order(s)	Operation Order No. 27. By Colonel J.W. Houghton, A.M.S., A.D.M.S., 58th Division. Appendix I.	26/09/1917	26/09/1917
Miscellaneous	Administrative Instructions Issued 58th (London) Division Order No. 60.	26/09/1917	26/09/1917

Type	Description	Date From	Date To
Miscellaneous	173rd Infantry Brigade Administrative Instruction No. 14 Appendix 2	26/09/1917	26/09/1917
Operation(al) Order(s)	173rd Infantry Brigade Order Number 42.	26/09/1917	26/09/1917
Miscellaneous	Move Table "A".		
Miscellaneous	Move Table "B".		
Miscellaneous	Amendments to 173rd Infantry Brigade Order Number 42.	26/09/1917	26/09/1917
Miscellaneous	Table "A"		
Heading	War Diary Of Lt Colonel A.T. Falwasser R.A.M.C. T.F. Commanding 2/1st Home Counties Field Ambulance From October 1.17 to October 31.17 (Volume I)		
War Diary	Lostebarne	01/10/1917	23/10/1917
War Diary	Audruicq	24/10/1917	24/10/1917
War Diary	Gwent Farm	24/10/1917	25/10/1917
War Diary	Duhallow	26/10/1917	31/10/1917
Heading	War Diary Of O.C. 2/1st H.C. Field Ambulance From Nov 1st, 1917 To Nov 30th, 1917. Medical		
War Diary	Duhallow	03/11/1917	14/11/1917
War Diary	Parliament Camp	15/11/1917	25/11/1917
War Diary	Lart	26/11/1917	26/11/1917
War Diary	Brunembert	28/11/1917	28/11/1917
Heading	War Diary Of Lieut Col A.T. Falwasser R.A.M.C. T.F. Commanding 2/1st Home Counties Field Ambce From Dec 1st 17 to Dec 31st 17 (Volume I)		
War Diary	Brunembert	03/12/1917	08/12/1917
War Diary	Lart	08/12/1917	09/12/1917
War Diary	Gwent Farm	09/12/1917	10/12/1917
War Diary	Essex Farm	11/12/1917	31/12/1917
Heading	War Diary Of Lieut Colonel A.T. Falwasser D.S.O. R.A.M.C. T.F. Commanding 2/1st Home Counties F. Ambulance From Jan 1st 1918 to Jan 31st 1918 (Volume 2.)		
War Diary	Essex Farm	01/01/1918	08/01/1918
War Diary	School Camp	09/01/1918	21/01/1918
War Diary	Proven	21/01/1918	21/01/1918
War Diary	Le Paraclet	22/01/1918	31/01/1918
Heading	War Diary of Lieut Colonel A.T. Falwasser R.A.M.C. T. Commanding 2/1st Home Counties Field Ambulance from February 1st 1918 to February 28th 1918 (Volume 2)		
War Diary	Le Paraclet	03/02/1918	05/02/1918
War Diary	Quierzy	07/02/1918	28/02/1918
Heading	War Diary of Lt Colonel A.T. Falwasser R.A.M.C. T.F. Commanding 2/1st Home Counties Field Ambulance From March 1st 1918 to March 31st 1918 (Volume II)		
War Diary	Quierzy	01/03/1918	24/03/1918
War Diary	Varesnes	24/03/1918	25/03/1918
War Diary	La Pommeraye	25/03/1918	25/03/1918
War Diary	Nampcel	25/03/1918	28/03/1918
War Diary	Hautebraye	29/03/1918	31/03/1918
Heading	War Diary of Lieut Colonel A.T. Falwasser R.A.M.C. T. Cmdg 2/1st Home Counties Fd Ambce From 1st April 1918 to 30th April 1918 Volume II		
War Diary	Hautebraye	02/04/1918	03/04/1918
War Diary	Dommiers	03/04/1918	04/04/1918

War Diary	Villers Cotteret	04/04/1918	05/04/1918
War Diary	Longueau	05/04/1918	05/04/1918
War Diary	Amiens	05/04/1918	08/04/1918
War Diary	Longueau	08/04/1918	28/04/1918
War Diary	Hangest sur Somme	28/04/1918	28/04/1918
War Diary	Famechon	29/04/1918	30/04/1918
Heading	War Diary of Lieut Colonel A.T. Falwasser D.S.O. R.A.M.C. T.F. Commanding 2/1st Home Counties Field Ambulance from May 1st 1918 to May 31st 1918 (Volume 2)		
War Diary	Nevilly L'Hopital	01/05/1918	06/05/1918
War Diary	Molliens au Bois	07/05/1918	12/05/1918
War Diary	St Gratien	16/05/1918	31/05/1918
Heading	War Diary of Lieut Colonel A.T. Falwasser R.A.M.C. T.F. Commanding 2/1st Home Counties Field Ambulance From June 1st 1918 To June 30th 1918		
War Diary	St Gratien	01/06/1918	10/06/1918
War Diary	Dreuil-Les-Molliens	10/06/1918	11/06/1918
War Diary	Saissemont	11/06/1918	17/06/1918
War Diary	St Gratien And B.20.b.0.6	17/06/1918	17/06/1918
War Diary	St Gratien Wood	18/06/1918	18/06/1918
War Diary	Montigny	18/06/1918	30/06/1918
Heading	War Diary of Lieut Colonel A.T. Falwasser D.S.O. R.A.M.C. T.F. Commanding 2/1st Home Counties Field Ambulance From July 1.18 to July 31.18 (Volume 2)		
War Diary	Montigny	02/07/1918	31/07/1918
Heading	War Diary of Lieut Col A.T. Falwasser D.S.O. R.A.M.C. T.F. Cmdg 2/1st Home Counties Field Ambulance From Aug 1st 18 to Aug 31st 18 (Volume 2)		
War Diary	Montigny	01/08/1918	03/08/1918
War Diary	Berteaucourt	03/08/1918	04/08/1918
War Diary	Key Wood I.14.a.7.0.	05/08/1918	05/08/1918
War Diary	Key Wood	05/08/1918	06/08/1918
War Diary	Smith's Fm	06/08/1918	12/08/1918
War Diary	Key Wood	12/08/1918	13/08/1918
War Diary	Key Wood I.14.a	14/08/1918	20/08/1918
War Diary	Montigny B.17.b.7.8	20/08/1918	21/08/1918
War Diary	Montigny	22/08/1918	25/08/1918
War Diary	I.30.a.6.6	25/08/1918	30/08/1918
War Diary	I.30.a.6.6 (Sheet 62D)	30/08/1918	31/08/1918
War Diary	L.10.a.5.3 In Bray Maricourt Rd	31/08/1918	31/08/1918
Heading	War Diary of Lieut Col A.T. Falwasser D.S.O. R.A.M.C. T.F. Commanding 2/1st Home Counties Field Ambulance From September 1st 1918 to September 30th 1918 (Volume 2)		
War Diary	L 10.a.3.2	02/09/1918	06/09/1918
War Diary	Maurepas Halte B.13.6.5.4	07/09/1918	07/09/1918
War Diary	C.18.c.9.6	07/09/1918	07/09/1918
War Diary	D22d.0.5	07/09/1918	13/09/1918
War Diary	D22.c.0.3 Gurlu Wood	14/09/1918	24/09/1918
War Diary	Montauban	24/09/1918	25/09/1918
War Diary	Ribemont	26/09/1918	26/09/1918
War Diary	Le Pendu Camp F.1.a.3.9	27/09/1918	29/09/1918
War Diary	Aix Noulette	29/09/1918	30/09/1918

Heading	War Diary Of Lieut Colonel A.T. Falwasser D.S.O. R.A.M.C. T.F. Commanding 2/1st Home Counties Field Ambulance From October 1.18 To October 31.18 (Volume 2)		
War Diary	Aix Noulette R.22.a.2.5	01/10/1918	01/10/1918
War Diary	Aix Noulette	03/10/1918	12/10/1918
War Diary	Lievin	13/10/1918	15/10/1918
War Diary	Montigny	16/10/1918	18/10/1918
War Diary	Ostricourt	18/10/1918	18/10/1918
War Diary	Mons En Pevele	19/10/1918	19/10/1918
War Diary	Auchy	20/10/1918	20/10/1918
War Diary	Lannay H.3.c.7.7	21/10/1918	31/10/1918
Heading	War Diary of Lieut Colonel A.T. Falwasser D.S.O. R.A.M.C. T.F. Commanding 2/1st Home Counties Field Ambulance from November 1st 1918 to November 30th 1918 (Volume 2)		
War Diary	Lannay H.3.c.7.7	02/11/1918	08/11/1918
War Diary	Legis K1.a.5.5	09/11/1918	09/11/1918
War Diary	Peruwelz L3.a.5.6	10/11/1918	10/11/1918
War Diary	Quevaucamp A.23.c.3.8	11/11/1918	11/11/1918
War Diary	Beloeil B.3.a.4.3	12/11/1918	12/11/1918
War Diary	Beloeil	14/11/1918	27/11/1918
War Diary	Bonsecours L.10.c.4.8	30/11/1918	30/11/1918
Heading	War Diary Of Lieut Colonel A.T. Falwasser D.S.O. R.A.M.C. T.F. Commanding 2/1st Home Counties Field Ambulance from Dec 1.18 to Dec 31.18 (Volume 2)		
War Diary	Bonsecours	01/12/1918	29/12/1918
Heading	War Diary of Lieut Colonel A.T. Falwasser D.S.O. R.A.M.C. T.F. Commanding 2/1st Home Counties Field Ambulance from Jan 1st 1919 to Jan 31st 1919. (Volume 3)		
War Diary	Bonsecours	01/01/1919	26/01/1919
Heading	War Diary Of Lieut Colonel A.T. Falwasser D.S.O. R.A.M.C. T.F. Commanding 2/1st Home Counties Field Ambulance from Feb 1st 1919 to Feb 28th 1919 (Volume 3)		
War Diary	Bonsecours	02/02/1919	28/02/1919
Heading	War Diary of 2/1st Home Counties Field Ambulance R.A.M.C. T.F. From 1st March 1919 to 31st March 1919 Volume II.		
War Diary	Bonsecours	01/03/1919	07/03/1919
War Diary	Chapelle a Oie	07/03/1919	31/03/1919
Heading	War Diary Of 2/1st Home Counties Fd Ambce R.A.M.C. T.F. From 1st April 1919 To 30th April 1919		
War Diary	Chapelle a Oie Belgium	01/04/1919	30/04/1919
Heading	War Diary of 2/1st Home Counties Field Ambulance R.A.M.C. (T.F.) From 1-5-1919 to 31.5.1919 (Volume II)		
War Diary	Chapelle-A-Oie Belgium	04/05/1919	31/05/1919
Heading	War Diary of 2/1st Home Counties Field Ambulance R.A.M.C. (T.F.) From 1-6-1919 to 13-6-1919. (Volume II)		
War Diary	Leuze	03/06/1919	07/06/1919
War Diary	Antwerp	13/06/1919	13/06/1919

WO 95/2997/2

58TH DIVISION

2-1ST (H.C) FLD AMBNCE
~~JAN 1917~~ 1918

1915 AUG — 1916 FEB
AND
1917 JAN — 1919 JUN

58 Ken.

Confidential

War Diary
of

Lieut Colonel A.T.FALWASSER

Cmdg 2/1st H.C. Field Amb

from 23rd January 17 to 24th January 17

Volume 1.

COMMITTEE FOR THE
MEDICAL HISTORY OF THE WAR
Date 4 — APR. 1917

WAR DIARY
or
INTELLIGENCE SUMMARY

Army Form C. 2118.

Places	Date	Hour	Summary of Events and Information	Remarks and references to Appendices
WARMINSTER	23.1.17	7.30 a.m	Entrained at WARMINSTER Strength 10 officers 220 other ranks 63 horses 19 vehicles.	
SOUTHAMPTON DOCKS	"	10.20 a.m	Detrained	
"	"	6 p.m	Embarked personnel (less 2 officers 30 other ranks) on S.S. LA MARGUERITE 2 officers 30 other ranks horses & vehicles on S.S. HUNTSCRAFT	
HAVRE	24.1.17	10.45 a.m	Disembarked personnel from S.S. LA MARGUERITE	
"	"	10.30	Proceeded to No 2 Rest Camp	
"	"	11.10 a.m	Remaining personnel with horses & vehicles disembarked from S.S. HUNTSCRAFT & proceeded to No 2 Rest Camp.	
"	"	9 p.m	Orders received from Commandant Rest Camp to march from Rest Camp at 10.30 a.m the following day & entrain at point No. 6 at 12 noon.	
"	25.1.17	10.30 a.m	Marched from Rest Camp complete in personnel, horses & vehicles	
"	"	12 noon	Entrained at Point 6.	
ABBEVILLE	26.1.17	9 a.m	Received verbal orders from O.C. train to detrain at ABBRE AUX1 LE CHATEAU	
AUX1 LE CHATEAU	"	9 a.m	Detrained	
"	"	9.30 p.m	Motor cycl Harr R.T.O. from 173 Inf Bde to proceed by route march to BOFFLES via BOIS D'AUX1 Rd & then billet

Army Form C. 2118.

WAR DIARY
or
INTELLIGENCE SUMMARY

(Erase heading not required.)

Instructions regarding War Diaries and Intelligence Summaries are contained in F. S. Regs., Part II. and the Staff Manual respectively. Title Pages will be prepared in manuscript.

Place	Date	Hour	Summary of Events and Information	Remarks and references to Appendices
ROFFLES	26.1.17	11 pm	Took up billets.	A.D.S

A.D.M.S. ALCL
C.O.Y 41st H.Q. Ambce
R.A.M.C.

WAR DIARY
or
INTELLIGENCE SUMMARY

Army Form C. 2118.

Instructions regarding War Diaries and Intelligence summaries are contained in F. S. Regs., Part II. and the Staff Manual respectively. Title Pages will be prepared in manuscript.

(Erase heading not required.)

Place	Date	Hour	Summary of Events and Information	Remarks and references to Appendices
ROFFLAY	1.2.17	4.30 pm	Battn. recd. orders from AFMS to proceed to LE TOUCH on 2.2.17. Advance Party of Division.	
"	2.2.17	9.0 am	2 Officers & 30 Other ranks forwarded by motor transport to LA CAVERIE to be detailed for instructions to be 1/3 K D Rifles.	
"	"	9.0 pm	Remainder of unit with all horses & vehicles forwarded by route march to LE TOUCH.	
LE TOUCH	"	1.0 pm	Today 1/3 K D Rifles at LE TOUCH handed over to "B" Section to the Reception Depôt in 7 motor lorries on the following day.	A.33
"	"	9.0 pm	Two NCOs & 11 men M.T. A.S.C. reported for duty from Divl. Supply Column with 7 Horse Motor Cars & 10 Motorcycles attached to 1/3 K D Rifles.	A.33
"	4.2.17	10. am	Medl. Reception Station at present established at BREVILLIERS quarters with R. A. field Ambulance in charge.	A.33
"	5.2.17	10.0 am	Personal kits, valises, etc. to field at BREVILLIERS guard station quarters vacated for incoming troops. Inspected etabs/stables 11a.	
BREVILLIERS	6.2.17	4.0 pm	Rec'd orders from AFMS to hand over duties to Sub at LEGER.	A.33
"	7.2.17	10.0 am	Handed over duties to 1/3 H.C.R. and with 30 officers forwarded by motor transport to ON at LEGER.	
ON LEGER	"	10.0 noon	Took of duties.	
"	12.2.17	10.0 am	2 Officers & 30 other ranks forwarded to LA CAVERIE to be attached (instruction) to 1/3 K D Rifles.	
"	"	9.0 pm	2 Officers & 30 other ranks returned from LA CAVERIE on completion of 7 days instruction with 1/3 K D Rifles.	A.33

2449. Wt. W14957/M90 750,000 1/16 J.B.C. & A. Forms/C.2118/12.

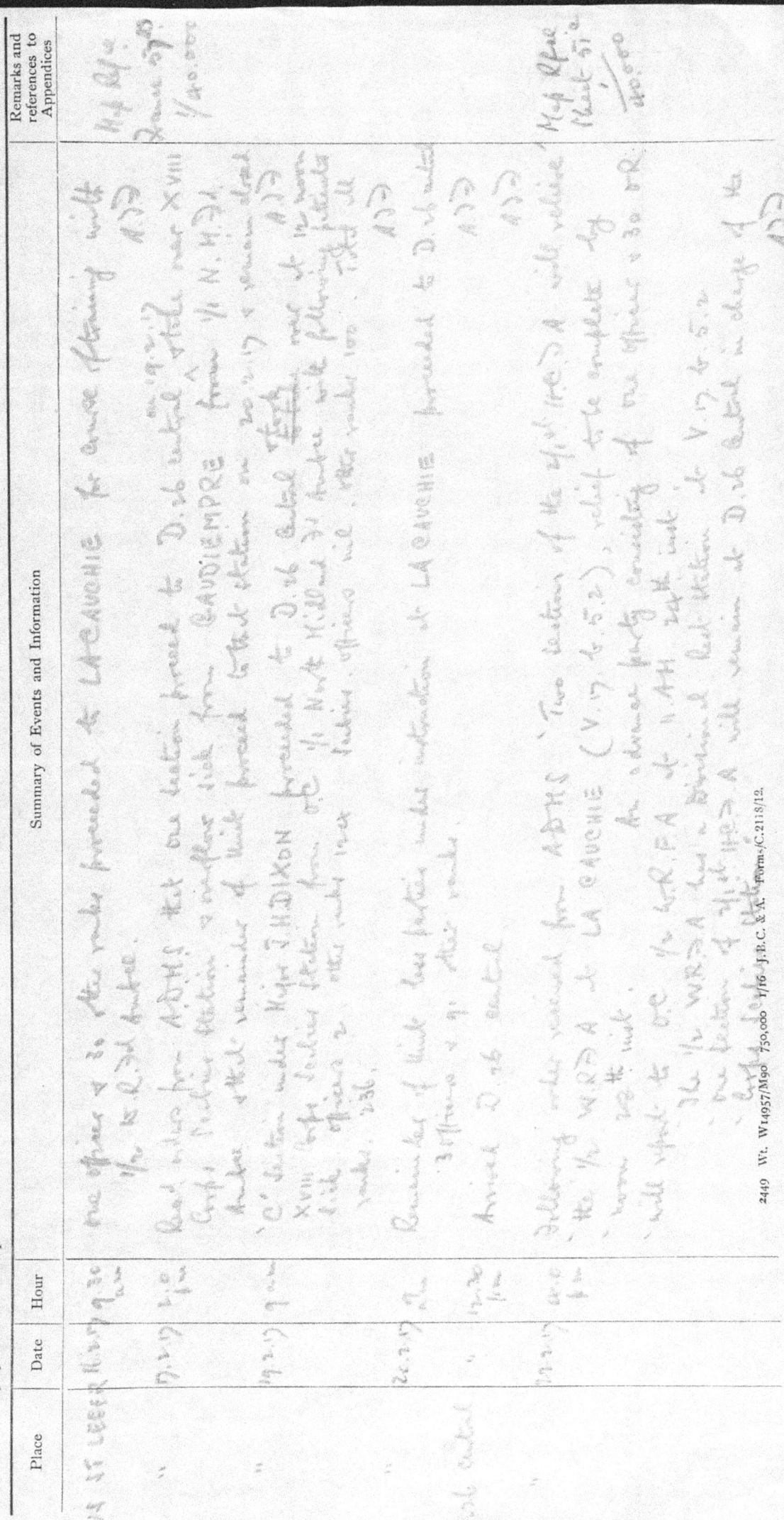

Army Form C. 2118.

WAR DIARY
or
INTELLIGENCE SUMMARY

(Erase heading not required.)

Instructions regarding War Diaries and Intelligence Summaries are contained in F. S. Regs., Part II. and the Staff Manual respectively. Title Pages will be prepared in manuscript.

Place	Date	Hour	Summary of Events and Information	Remarks and references to Appendices
D. to Batral	7.25.17	9.0 a.m.	Capt HUXTABLE & 30 O.R. proceeded to LACAVERIE on return duty to report to O.C. 1/4 K.R.R. there	H.Q. K.R.R. 1/4(2ck 27) D. 1/40,000
			A.D. Labourer Nitye Copy 4/1 H.C.D. Notes 25.2.17	

Medical Vol # 2

140/2042

COMMITTEE FOR THE
MEDICAL HISTORY OF THE WAR
Date 11 MAY 1917

Mar. 1917

58th Division.

Confidential

War Diary
of
Lieut. Col. A.T. FALWASSER
A.D.M.S. 58th Home Counties Dt Antree.

from 26.2.17 to 26.3.17

(Volume 1.)

Army Form C. 2118.

WAR DIARY
or
INTELLIGENCE SUMMARY
(Erase heading not required.)

Instructions regarding War Diaries and Intelligence Summaries are contained in F. S. Regs., Part II. and the Staff Manual respectively. Title Pages will be prepared in manuscript.

Place	Date	Hour	Summary of Events and Information	Remarks and references to Appendices
D.26 Bertel	28.2.17	9.0 am	'X' & 'R' Sections less one Officer & 30 other ranks slowly proceeded to LA CAUCHIE (V.7 t.5.2.) their letters over D.R.S. from duty & proceeded to LA CAUCHIE (V.7 t.5.2.) their letters over D.R.S. from ½ Coy. R. Iny. J. Ack. Strength 3 Officers 174 other ranks 36 horses 17 vehicles. 'C' Section remains at D.26 Central	M.O. Ref. W. Plant Sgt D. ? Plant 51.A Cross
LA CAUCHIE	"	12.0 noon	Took over J.D.R.S. from the M.R.D.A. completed. Patients taken over number 226.	A.D.
"	1.3.17	6.0 pm	Capt. N.M.S. TURNER rejoined from hospital. Lieut. G. THOMSON " " 3rd Army Gas School	
"	2.3.17	2.0 pm	Received orders by A.D.M.S. 58 Div. Sub That Lieut. N. M. Field Ambce will take over from satisfaction of H.Q. 2/1st Home Counties J. Ambce at D.26 Central St-wan-Moh 3rd. D.26 Central.	A.D.
"	"	2.30 pm	Issued orders as above to O.C. 'C' Section to proceed on Completion of hand over to this Station.	A.D.
"	3.3.17	5.30 pm	'C' Section & Major T.H. DIXON commanding, arrived from D.26 Central on completion of hand over to XVIII Corps Advcd Station. 2/1st N.M. Field Ambce. Strength 2 Officers 60 other ranks 14 horses 7 vehicles.	A.D.
"	4.3.17	9.0 pm	Received orders by A.D.M.S. 58 Div. All sick & Injured retain affections will now be treated at 2/1st M.E.J. Ambce at LA CAUCHIE. All patients at present in the Rest hand of the 2/1st M.E.J. Ambce will be transferred to the 2/2nd M.E.J. Ambce.	A.D.

WAR DIARY
or
INTELLIGENCE SUMMARY

Army Form C. 2118.

Place	Date	Hour	Summary of Events and Information	Remarks and references to Appendices
LA CAUCHIE	10.3.17	2.0 p.m.	Transferred to 2/1st H.C.F. Amb. 106 patients, at present in D.R.S. in accordance with following order. Received from 1/1st N.M.F. Amb 20 patients taken over their operation.	Map Ref.
"	10.3.17	6.0 p.m.	Received order by A.D.M.S. 50 Div. The 2/1/1 H.C.F Amb will establish its D.R.S. at V.17 d.5.3. Patients at present in D.R.S. carried on by 2/1st H.C.F. Amb will be transferred to the D.R.S. established by the 2/1st H.C.F. Amb. Transfer to be completed by 4 PM Friday March 16th 1917.	51 C.C. 4000 A.D.S.
"	16.3.17	4.0 p.m.	Admitted to D.R.S. transferred from 2/1st H.C.F. Amb 98 patients. The Unit is now a D.R.S. with accommodation in huts & tents for 7 officers and 190 other ranks & a Nursing Station with accommodation for 30 other officers & other ranks.	A.D.S.
"	17.3.17	9.30 A.M.	Received order by A.D.M.S. 50 Div. "In anticipation of an early advance, the equipment of five Station complete will remain packed & ready to load ... & the station will travel within 2 hours of receipt of order ... for this purpose Ford Lorries will be allotted to 1/4th N.F. F. Amb."	A.D.S.
"	21.3.17	6.0 p.m.	Received instructions that Division is transferred from XVIII to VII Corps. Area is from 6.0 p.m. 22.3.17	A.D.S.
"	"	11.0 p.m.	Received Operation order No. 11 by A.D.M.S. 50 Div notifying new Divisional boundaries.	A.D.S.

Army Form C. 2118.

WAR DIARY
or
~~INTELLIGENCE SUMMARY~~

(Erase heading not required.)

Instructions regarding War Diaries and Intelligence Summaries are contained in F. S. Regs., Part II. and the Staff Manual respectively. Title Pages will be prepared in manuscript.

Place	Date	Hour	Summary of Events and Information	Remarks and references to Appendices
LA CAUCHIE	20.3.17	6.0 p.m.	Received wire of G.H.Q. telegram notifying that summer time will come into force tonight 11.0 p.m. i.e. watches at that moment should will be advanced one hour. Action taken accordingly.	A.D.)
"	25.3.17	11.0 a.m.	Received this o/c 25/3! H.Q. 3rd Army of note by A.D.M.S. 58th Div that, in consequence of his unit being by 65th 3 Amb at 1 p.m. 25/3 it may postpone its present in Yard H.Q. 3 Amb will be transferred to S.R.S. Preville	A.D.) A.D.)
"	"	2.0 p.m.	70 patients from 2/2nd H.C. 3 Amb admitted to S.R.S.	
"	"	7.0 p.m.	Received order by A.D.M.S. 58th Division 21st Division will relief will be completed by 6 a.m. on 29.3.17. 58th Div will concentrate in LUCHEUX area. 2/1st H.C. 3 Amb will be relieved by 64.3. Amb will move to a site and on a date to be notified later.	A.59
"	"	"	Received order by A.D.M.S. to submit name of an officer for duty at No. 62 C.C.S	A.))
"	26.3.17	10.0 a.m.	Submitted to A.D.M.S. name of Capt T. L. BARKIN for duty at No. 43 C.C.S	A.))
"	"	12.0 noon	Number of patients in week 3 D.R.S. received this dinner 56.	E.)) A.))

D. Delamere R.C.R
O/C.
2/1st Home Counties Field Ambee.
R. A. M. C., T.

CONFIDENTIAL 58 Div.

140/2086

Medical

Vol 3

War Diary of
Lieut Colonel A.T. FALWASSER R.A.M.C.T.
Commanding 2/1st Home Counties Field Ambulance

from 27.3.17 to 25.4.17

Volume I.

COMMITTEE FOR THE
MEDICAL HISTORY OF THE WAR
Date -6 JUN.1917

WAR DIARY or INTELLIGENCE SUMMARY

Army Form C. 2118.

Place	Date	Hour	Summary of Events and Information	Remarks and references to Appendices
LA CAUCHIE	27.3.17	9 p.m	Received Operation order No. 13 by A.D.M.S. to send home to MONDICOURT, and to complete by 4 p.m. 29.3.17. An advance party of 1 Officer & 20 other ranks to the new area billets on 28.3.17. Officer i/c advance party to report to Town Major MONDICOURT at 4 pm on 28.3.17. The bat. to start will take over from the 2/1st H.C. 3rd Ant. at LA CAUCHIE on 29.3.17. Patients remaining in the Rest-Camp Section Depot at LA CAUCHIE will be transferred to 64th 3 Ant.	"The 2/1st H.C.3. Ant. will O/C 2/1st H.C. 3rd Ant. Issue 2/D C.B.2 A.D.S.
LA CAUCHIE	28.3.17	9 a.m	Major T.H. DIXON & 20 other ranks proceeded to MONDICOURT as advance party. Details were killed.	
LA CAUCHIE	29.3.17	9 a.m	United one Officer & 20 other ranks advance party and one Officer & 40 other ranks Stretcher Bearer to moving (Bat.), but proceeded to MONDICOURT to billets in 18 Nissen huts.	
	"	9 a.m	Completed hand over of A.D.S. Section Depot to bat. 3 Ant. Patients in A.D.S. 15/5 in 5 others Sept 44, & total of Officers 195 other ranks	A.D.S
MONDICOURT	31.3.17	6 p.m	Received Operation No. 14 by A.D.M.S. to see "The Brigade are billeting will send under the orders of the XIX. Corps at midnight 31/1-4/14 with more later." "ROUGEMAISON area on 1st April" The 3 Field Ambulance will move under orders from the Brigade with which they are brigaded — 2/1st H.C.3. Ant Ant with A.D.S

Army Form C. 2118.

WAR DIARY
or
INTELLIGENCE SUMMARY

(Erase heading not required.)

Instructions regarding War Diaries and Intelligence Summaries are contained in F. S. Regs., Part II. and the Staff Manual respectively. Title Pages will be prepared in manuscript.

Place	Date	Hour	Summary of Events and Information	Remarks and references to Appendices
MONDICOURT	31.3.17	10.0 p.m.	Received 73rd Inf Bde Operation order No. 13 "The Division less Artillery & detached troops will come under the orders of the XIX Corps at midnight 31st/1st. & will move to the BOURGUENAISON area on 1st April & to the FROHEN LE GRAND area on April 2nd." The Brigade will move (a) on April 1st to the B (RUMMERES – BEAUVOIR – BOURGUEMAISON) area. (b) on April 2nd to the E (ROUFFLERS – SELLANDRE – VAULX – VITZ VILLEROY) in accordance with orders which will be issued later. Starting point, April 1st, B.12: a.6.9. ↔ 2/1st-3rd Arts between starting point at 9.27 a.m.	M.4 appx 5) D / 40 000
MONDICOURT	1.4.17	7.30 a.m.	Marched from billets & starting point at POMMERA being billetted & Draught lines (s) and to find Kit-stores (3) we left ground till it appeared at our weight 3 90 tents dumped at billets built party of 10 of the water in charge will return for 3 days, no water cart over QS equipt with one fuel. LD tents also left behind at MONDICOURT.	A))
POMMERA	1.4.17	9.57 a.m.	Halted for 2 hours & found in area of 73rd Bde L'ESPERANCE – LUCHEUX – BOURGUENAISON – MON LE BLOND – BEAUVOIR	A))
BEAUVOIR	1.4.17	2.30 p.m.	Arrived at BEAUVOIR & took up billets	
"	"	10.0 p.m.	Recd 73rd Inf Bde Operation order No. 14 "The Brigade will move tomorrow to the FROHEN LE GRAND area in accordance with Maral table." 2/1st 4 & 2/1st Arts will form the starting point Road Junction & mile due S of	

2449 Wt. W14957/M90 750,000 1/16 J.B.C. & A. Form/C.2118/12.

WAR DIARY or INTELLIGENCE SUMMARY

Army Form C. 2118.

Place	Date	Hour	Summary of Events and Information	Remarks and references to Appendices
BEAUVOIR	2.4.17	9.40 a.m.	R in BONNIERES at 10.45 a.m. Hostile activity took no more offensive in rear of Rla by VILLERS L'HÔPITAL – WAVANS – AUXI LE CHATEAU – LE PONCHEL – VAULX.	Ref. Rs for LENS. A.D. A.D.
VAULX	2.4.17	2.30 pm	Arrival of Gd & Riles.	
"	"	6.20 pm	Rcd. wire from 173 Inf Bde. Bn will be prepared to move tomorrow 3rd or next day at NP's. further orders will be issued later.	A.D.
"	3.4.17	1.30 a.m.	Rcd. orders from 173 Inf Bde. 3rd Field Ambulance will not move until further orders are received, and notifying move of 173 Inf Bde to BEAUMETZ.	A.D.
"	"	12.30 pm	Recd. Operation order No. 15 by ADMS 58 Div. "The D.C. 3/1st H.F.D. after visit with Medical Equipt to proceed by lorry in advance party with Rde split Amy sec. time of starting 3rd/17 with the 173rd Bde. will be arranged direct between the O.C. 3 H.R. 173rd Inf & the accommodation will be advance party will move in the Rde." The 3/1st H.F.D. after bus advance party will march to MAILLY MAILLET, billing for the first night at AUTHIEULE, marches to MAILLY MAILLET 'MEZEROLLES' leaves 1.0 pm on 4/4/17. Field Ambulances will not enter.	A.D.
"	"	5.0 pm	Batches Major J.H. DIXON & 20 other ranks with the advance party proceed thence 4.4.17 to MAILLY MAILLET by two motor with happy return.	A.D.
"	"	6.30 pm	Recd H.Q. 3/2nd Rde for Instructions as to be accommodation arrive of	A.D.

WAR DIARY or INTELLIGENCE SUMMARY

Army Form C. 2118.

Place	Date	Hour	Summary of Events and Information	Remarks and references to Appendices
VAULX	3.4.17	7.30 p.m.	Wire recd. from 174 Inf Bde "Busses will be sent to VAULX at a time to be notified later to convey . . . 2/1/1 S.M.H. to destination. 2/1/1 S.M.H. busses will arrive at VAULX at 1.45 (?)	ADS
"	4.4.17	2.0 a.m.	Wire recd. from 174 Inf Bde. Busses will arrive at VAULX at 1.45 (?)	ADS
"	"	7.0 a.m.	Unit (less advance party of 1 Officer + 20 other ranks, proceeded by route march AUXI LE CHATEAU — WANANS — FROHEN LE GRAND — DOULLENS to AUTHIEULE.	ADS
FROHEN LE GRAND	"	1.30 p.m.	Recd. telephone message from Divl/Adm this O i/c advance party 'to be lorry'. 2 cars were available to follow. Lorry + you will march to AMPLIER until late tonight + march to MAILLY MAILLET tomorrow.	
"	"	1.45 p.m.	Despatched 2 Motor Ambulances with instructions to return to VAULX + collect advance party string to AUTHIEULE.	ADS
AUTHIEULE	"	4.0 p.m.	Arrived at 4 Units	
"	"	5.30 p.m.	Maj— DIXON rejoined his unit with advance party effected by H.Q. Motor Ambulance	ADS
"	5.4.17	10.0 a.m.	Recd. order from ADMS to proceed to BUS LES ARTOIS. Supplies billetting officer to BUS LES ARTOIS. Proceeded by route march AMPLIER — MARIEUX — VAUCHELLES — LOUVENCOURT — BERTRANCOURT — BUS LES ARTOIS in emergence of a village recd. from billetting officer that there was no accommodation in BUS LES ARTOIS	ADS

2449. Wt. W14957/M90 750,000 1/16 J.B.C. & A. Form/C2118/12.

Army Form C. 2118.

WAR DIARY
or
INTELLIGENCE SUMMARY
(Erase heading not required.)

Place	Date	Hour	Summary of Events and Information	Remarks and references to Appendices
BERTRANCOURT	5.4.17	3.30 p.m.	Took up billets & brought site with one large rick well covered from view. No section of 2 ft. fill available	H.Q. Ops. Plate 57 e. A.D.S
"	6.4.17	4 p.m.	Recd. operation order No. 16 by D.R.L.S. The 2/1st H.C. Field Ambulance will move from present billets on 7.4.17 (a) Hd Qrs and one section to Red Huts MAILLY MAILLET now in occupation of 2/1st Field Ambulance. (b) One section to BRICKFIELDS nr ACHIET LE GRAND (c) One section to MIRAUMONT. Additional tentage & transport will be supplied by the O.C. 2/3rd H.C. Field Ambulance. The 2/1st H.C. Field Ambulance will move on 7.4.17 to BERTRANCOURT & the one section now occupied by the 2/1st H.C. 3 Field Ambulance.	A.D.S
"	"	5.0 p.m.	Issued following operation order. "B" & "C" Sections will advanced guard of Major DIXON will proceed by MAILLY MAILLET— will proceed at 9.0 a.m. tomorrow 7.4.17	
"	"	"	AUCHONVILLERS— BEAUMONT HAMEL — BEAUVOIR - MIRAUMONT. "B" Section under command of Capt. SAVAGE will take over MIRAUMONT. "C" section under command of Major DIXON will proceed to ACHIET LE PETIT the Brickfield nr ACHIET LE GRAND and take over occupied by the 2/1st H.C.3 Ambce. 'A' Section will parade at 1.0 p.m. & proceed to the Red Huts MAILLY take over the site now occupied by 2/1 H.C.3 Ambce.	A.D.S
"	7.4.17	9.0 a.m.	"B" & "C" sections marched to MIRAUMONT and ACHIET LE GRAND respectively.	H.Q Ambce A.D.S
"	"	1.0 p.m.	'A' section marched out site to 2/2nd H.C.3 Ambce marched to MAILLY MAILLET	A.D.S

WAR DIARY or INTELLIGENCE SUMMARY

Army Form C. 2118.

Place	Date	Hour	Summary of Events and Information	Remarks and references to Appendices
MAILLY MAILLET	3.4.17	3.0 p.m.	Arrived at Rail Head from 21st Field Ambulance	A.D.M.S. H.Q. Paper Sheet 57D
"	"	3.30 p.m.	Received orders from A.D.M.S. Headquarters of 1/1st H.E.D. Ant. and one Section will move from Rail Head, MAILLY MAILLET to ACHIET LE GRAND on 8.4.17. One section of 1/1st H.E.D. Ant. now at MIRAUMONT will move to ACHIET LE GRAND on 8.4.17. The 1/1st H.E.D. Ant. on completion will occupy the Buildings late 1st ACHIET LE GRAND. Transport to receive Sick. H.E.D. Ant. will transport 5 wagons Hospital ambs from 7th Div. Rail Station at P.17.4.1.7 to ACHIET LE GRAND on 8.4.17 for use of 1/1st H.E.D. Ant.	A.D.S.
"	"	9.0 p.m.	Issued warning Marches orders to O/C 'B' & 'C' Sections	
"	8.4.17	12.0 a.m.	'A' Section marched MAILLY MAILLET — AUCHONVILLERS — BEAUMONT HAMEL — BEAUCOURT — MIRAUMONT — ACHIET LE PETIT — ACHIET LE GRAND.	
ACHIET LE GRAND	"	3.30 p.m.	Arrived ACHIET LE GRAND & preparing Buildings for accommodation of sick.	A.D.S.
"	9.4.17	5.0 p.m.	Three hicheldis each capable of accommodating 60 cases and 5 Hospital marquees in full occupation so patients ready for Reception of 420 sick in all. Admissions to date of sick 250.	A.D.S.

WAR DIARY or INTELLIGENCE SUMMARY

Army Form C. 2118.

Place	Date	Hour	Summary of Events and Information	Remarks and references to Appendices
ACHIET LE GRAND	10.4.17	6.0 p.m.	Admitted total 66 remaining sick 54.	ADS
"	11.4.17	2.0 p.m.	Received order from ADMS that it would be necessary to evacuate to P.7a on 'HAILLY – FORCEVILLE Rd' to carry (sick) Peletons Blankets Hosp.l marquees, & other 'Medical Stores' to give 3. A.3 to 9. ACHIET LE GRAND for your use. "Increase your accommodation to 400".	ADS
"	"	6.0 p.m.	Sick remaining 120.	
"	12.4.17	6.30 a.m.	Despatched 3 C.L. wagons in accordance with the fing orders to collect Med. Hosp.l Stores & equipt.	
"	"	6.0 p.m.	Sick remaining 122.	
"	"		Received 7 Hosp.l marquees 100 stretchers & 350 Blankets from P.7a.	ADS
"	13.4.17	6.0 p.m.	Sick remaining 167. Accommodation now available for 372 > 120 in 3 brick stables & 252 in 12 indl Hosp.l marquees.	ADS
"	14.4.17	6.0 p.m.	Sick remaining 191. Accommodation increased to 400 by erection of 2 strong shell tents	ADS
"	15.4.17	6.0 p.m.	Sick remaining 273.	CCS
"	16.4.17	6.0 p.m.	Sick remaining 307.	ADS
"	17.4.17	6.0 p.m.	Sick remaining 313. Hospital instructed by DMS Third Army	ADS

Army Form C. 2118.

WAR DIARY
or
INTELLIGENCE SUMMARY

(Erase heading not required.)

Instructions regarding War Diaries and Intelligence Summaries are contained in F. S. Regs., Part II. and the Staff Manual respectively. Title Pages will be prepared in manuscript.

Place	Date	Hour	Summary of Events and Information	Remarks and references to Appendices
MONCHY LE GRAND	19.4.17	3.0 PM	D.I. hutments inspected by D.D.M.S. & Capt — intended that number from tentent row by evacuation to C.C.S. standing men to go bns to 2/3rd to bring D.H. up	A(i)
"	19.4.17	6.0 PM	Sick remaining 297.	A(ii)
"	20.4.17	6.0 PM	Sick remaining 220.	A(iii)
"	21.4.17	6.0 PM	Sick remaining 194.	A(iv)
"	22.4.17	6.0 PM	Sick remaining 203.	A(v)
"	23.4.17	9.0 AM	Sick remaining 247.	

Total Admissions of sick during period Apr 9 – 25 (17 days) 902
" Discharged to duty 240
" Evacuated to C.C.S. or other Hospital 445
" Died ..... Nil
Average duration of stay in D.I. hutres from discharged to duty ..... 4 · 6 days
Preventing Causes of admission :—
  I.C.T. ..... 152 cases
  Diarrhoea ..... 150 "
  P.U.O. ..... 92 "
  Scabies ..... 85 "
  Trench Foot ..... 11 "

A.D. Delmege Lt Col
R.A.M.C. T.
Cmdg 2/1st H.C.D. Ambce

Confidential Medical

58th Div.
147/2161
Vol 4

CONFIDENTIAL

War Diary
of
Lieut Colonel A.T. FALWASSER RAMC T.
Commanding 2/1st Home Counties Field Ambulance
from 2.5.17 to 26.5.17

(Volume 1.)

COMMITTEE FOR THE
MEDICAL HISTORY OF THE WAR
Date 10 JUL. 1917

WAR DIARY or INTELLIGENCE SUMMARY

Army Form C. 2118.

Place	Date	Hour	Summary of Events and Information	Remarks and references to Appendices
ACHIET LE GRAND	2.5.17	6.0 pm	Average slightly under of cases in Hospital during week ended today 135 to compared fairly largely of 219 during preceding week, this is due to corresponding decrease in the number of admissions and is due to the fact that the 2/2nd Fd. Amb. are now receiving a small proportion of the sick from Corps area.	A.D.S.
"	5.5.17	11.0 am	Field Ambulance Camp & Hospital inspected by G.O.C. 53 Div.	
"	"	3.0 pm	Following interview from A.D.M.S. 53 Div. "The A.D.M.S. 62nd Division has much pleasure in congratulating Lieut Col FALWASSER and the officers N.C.Os & men of the 2/1st H.C.F.A. at the condition of efficiency displayed by this Field Ambulance at the inspection by the G.O.C. 62nd Division on 5.5.17. The G.O.C. expressed his entire satisfaction with the treatment of the sick & in the excellent work which has been carried out on the Brickfields site by the 2/1st H.C.F.A."	A.D.S. A.D.S.
"	9.5.17	6.0 pm	Average daily number of sick in Hospital during week ended today 132.	
"	11.5.17	9.0 pm	Received 'Medical Arrangements of 52nd Division No 1' by A.D.M.S. 52nd Division. The 2/1st H.C. Fd. Ambulance will establish a Corps Rest Station at the BRICKFIELDS. Received 'Corps Medical Arrangements No 2' by A.D.M.S. V Corps - The personnel of the 62nd Division stationed during duty at the Combined Main Dressing Station at MORY will be withdrawn & replaced by similar personnel for the 52nd Division. Move to be completed by the 12th inst.	

WAR DIARY or INTELLIGENCE SUMMARY

Army Form C. 2118.

Place	Date	Hour	Summary of Events and Information	Remarks and references to Appendices
			Divisional Rest Station will be discontinued. A Corps Rest Station will be established at G.9.c.6.2. By arrangement with ADMS 7 Division. Lt-Col G.H. BROWN DSO OC 23rd Field Ambulance will be in command. Personnel will consist of that of the 23rd Field Ambulance and one Tent Subdivision to be detailed by the ADMS 62nd Division. 'A Corps Scabies Hospital' will be established at the BRICKFIELDS'	Map Ref. Sheet 57c 1/40,000
ACHIET LE GRAND	12.5.17	2.30 pm	2/Lt Stone Counties Field Ambulance .... crew will be shown as transferred to the ADMS 58th Division. ADMS 58th Division will be responsible for the administration & for the provision of the necessary personnel. A.D.S.
Meeting of 58th Div Bde Medical Society at 4 Lt. H.Q. Anker. Paper read on Dental Caries' by Lieut IMLACH Dental Surgeon to 4/5 C.C. Station, 17 Medical Officers of 58 Div. & 62 Div. Div. present.	
"	13.5.17	10 a.m	173 Inf Bde 58 Div took over the line on night 12/13 its front from U.23.c.3.0 to U.20.a.3.6 from 15th Australian Inf Bde. 5th Australian Div. 2 Bdes in line 1 in support & 1 in reserve. A.D.S.	Map Ref. Sheet 57B 1/40,000
"	13.5.17	6 pm	Operation order No 17 by ADMS 58 Division. 'The officer commanding the 2/1st Field Ambulance will take over the site of the enclosed Main Dressing Station at MORY from the OC 2/1 Field Ambulance One Bearer Subdivision from the 62nd Division will be placed	

WAR DIARY or INTELLIGENCE SUMMARY

Army Form C. 2118.

Place	Date	Hour	Summary of Events and Information	Remarks and references to Appendices
ACHIET LE GRAND	15.5.17	6.0 p.m.	...into the orders of the O.C. 2/3rd H.Q. Ankre at MORY. Moved HQ completed by noon 16.5.17.	A.D.S
			Location of Medical Units of 62nd Division as follows: Advanced Dressing Station	
			C.2.a.4.3 (ECOUST)	
			C.9.a.6.3 } 2/2nd H.Q. 3 Ankre	wounded
			Main Dressing Station B.2n.a.2.7 (MORY)	
			BEHAGNIES 2/3rd H.Q. 3 Ankre	sick
			ACHIET LE GRAND 2/1st H.Q. 3 Ankre	gassed A.D.S
"	16.5.17	6.0 p.m.	Average daily number of sick during last week 190. Total sick admissions during past three days 25. Accommodation is now available for 250 cases of sick and 30 sick walking cases. Arrangements have been made to fall back for 35 cases of A.M.DUTHIE tent & store to be taken to MORY infantry for duty.	while
"	17.5.17 12.0 (5.5.17) 5.0 p.m.		Hospital Sitting Capt F.R.CHALMERS & Lieut A.M.DUTHIE Hospital & admin station inspected by D.M.S. 5/th Army Gen Neo & 20 men attached to D.H. H.Q.31 at MORY for billets.	A.D.S A.D.S
"	21.5.17 10.0 a.m.		173 Inf Bde relieved in the line by 175 Inf Bde during the night 20/21st	A.D.S
		3.0 p.m.	Hospital & Medical Station inspected by DD MS V Corps	A.D.S

WAR DIARY
or
INTELLIGENCE SUMMARY

(Erase heading not required.)

Army Form C. 2118.

Place	Date	Hour	Summary of Events and Information	Remarks and references to Appendices
PONCET LE GRAND	21.5.17	5.0 a.m.	Received operation order No 19 by A.D.M.S. detailing time of evacuation of casualties to be followed by one of the H.E.S. Ant. being stuck on BOVIS TRENCH by 7/a 2nd Bde on morning of 21.5.17. Bearers of 2/2 H.E.S. Ant. to be reinforced by one Bearer subdivision of 2/3 H.E.S. before. A.D.S.	
"	22.5.17	10.30 a.m.	Read note from A.D.M.S. to detail one Bearer Subdivision two officers, to attend for the H.E.S. A. at MORY at 10 a.m. 22.5.17.	
"	"	9.15 a.m.	Two NCOs & 37 men detailed in C.S. before in accordance with briefing order one NCO & 10 men also detailed supplementary party sent to MORY on 20 inst.	
"	"	6.0 p.m.	Read operation order No 19 by A.D.M.S. The Beaver division of the 2/3 H.E.S.A. A.D.S. will relieve the Bearer division of the 62nd division the 22/23rd May. Bid. route of evacuation on the night 22/23 May. on the 52th. Bid. route of evacuation	A.D.S.
"	23.5.17	6.0 p.m.	Average daily number of patients sick & schemes during the past week 132. Field Profile admissions for period 14t.—23t. 101 cases	
"	"	9.0 p.m.	Bearer Subdivision 2 NCOs & 37 men who proceeded to MORY yesterday returned. No casualty sustained. Pte. TINSLEY G.W. Butack.	A.D.S.
"	24.6.17	4.0 p.m.	Average daily number of patients during period 27/4 – 26/5 Admissions: 59 Bde. 383 Mar. Inns 809 2/3 Bde 256 235 Detached to duty 300 45 To Opty. Rest station 100 130 Evac. to C.C.S. 140 Sick Admissions 82 Died Total divisions 1022 period 13/5 – 26/5 only Admin. Died on pass	A.D.S.

CONFIDENTIAL

14D/2230

War Diary
of
Lieut Colonel A.T. FALKWASSER R.A.M.C. T.
Commanding 2/1st Home Counties Field Ambulance

from 23.5.17 to 30.6.17

(Volume I)

COMMITTEE FOR THE
MEDICAL HISTORY OF THE WAR
Date -7 AUG 1917

Army Form C. 2118.

WAR DIARY
or
INTELLIGENCE SUMMARY
(Erase heading not required.)

Place	Date	Hour	Summary of Events and Information	Remarks and references to Appendices
ACHIET LE GRAND	30.5.17	10 a.m.	Received operation order by A.D.M.S. "The 58th Division will relieve the 62nd Division (two Artillery) in the left sector of the V Corps front (CRUCIFIX – HENDECOURT ROAD (exclusive) to the CROISILLES – HENDECOURT ROAD (exclusive)) ...... The relief will be carried out by the 173rd Bde will be completed by 9 a.m. May 30th. The 2/3rd M.C.D. there will relieve the 2/2nd W.R.D. Aulnes at ERVILLERS; i.e. will collect & transport all casualties from the left sector of the V Corps front to the M.D.S. at MORY ...... relief to be completed by 9 a.m. May 30th. M.D.S. Aulnes at ERVILLERS. The sick of the 58th Division will be treated by 2/3rd M.C.D. Aulnes at ERVILLERS. Advanced Dressing Stations are established at ECOUST and ST LEGER and casualties are evacuated from these stations to M.D.S. at MORY (2/2 W.R.D. Amb) by 2/1st M.C.D. Aulnes at ACHIET LE GRAND. Sectns, then Cyc, & Dental come to 2/1st M.C.D. Aulnes at ACHIET LE GRAND.	H.A. Refer 51 B 1/20,000 67 C 1/20,000 ADS ADS ADS
"	30.5.17	7.10 p.m.	Average daily number of patients during past week, sick 109, scabies 24. Lieut W.H.ORTON proceeded to MORY for duty with 2/2nd M.C.D. Amb.	ADS
"	2.6.17	12.0 noon	Major J.H.DIXON proceeded to MORY for duty with M.C.D. Amb.	ADS
"	6.6.17	6 p.m.	M.D.S. temporarily moved from MORY to ERVILLERS (B.13.d.1.6) owing to shelling of MORY during H.V. fires in this D.A.E. during past 7 days. Vide 113 Section 51.	ADS

Army Form C. 2118.

WAR DIARY or INTELLIGENCE SUMMARY

(Erase heading not required.)

Place	Date	Hour	Summary of Events and Information	Remarks and references to Appendices
ACHIET LE GRAND	10.6.17	6.0 p.m	"Medical Arrangements" issued by ADMS 7th Division as follows :- M.D.S. (4/1st H.C.F. Amb.) in ERVILLERS. Advanced Dressing Stations are established at ECOUST (for right sector) & at ST LEGER (for left sector). Motor Ambulance evacuate from ECOUST to M.D.S. at times and from ST LEGER to M.D.S. at all times but motor ambulances also work in advance of this letter A.D.S. as far as CROISILLES (T.23.d.2.2.) at all times & in addition horsed ambulance improvised at night as far as sunken road at U.25.d.a.6 A.D.S	Map Ref. 5I.3 1/20.000
"	13.6.17	6.0 p.m	Average daily number of patients in the 3 Ambces. during past 7 days, Sick 116. Festres 55. A.D.S	
"	14.6.17	10.30 p.m	Received Operation Order No 21 by ADMS 7th Division. The 173rd Inf Bde will attack & capture the HINDENBURG front the Support-Lines in U.14 a,c,v,d and U.20.a . . . . The first phase of the attack will take place early of the morning of 16th June. The other Commanding 2/1st H.C.F. Amb. will start one Bearer Sub-Division to work to O.C. 2/3rd H.C.F. Amb. at 10 a.m on 15.6.17 at the ADS ST LEGER. The remaining Bearer Sub-division of the 2/1st H.C.F. Amb. will be held in reserve ready to leave at 2 hours notice. A.D.S	
"	15.6.17	9.0 a.m	Dispatched one Bearer Lieutenant & Sergeant LEANEY & 16 other ranks in 3 G.S. wagons to report to O.C. 2/3rd H.C.F. Amb in accordance with trying order, also 3 water carts also as to report to O.C. 2/3rd H.C.F. Amb. A.J.D	

Army Form C. 2118.

WAR DIARY
or
INTELLIGENCE SUMMARY
(Erase heading not required.)

Instructions regarding War Diaries and Intelligence Summaries are contained in F. S. Regs., Part II. and the Staff Manual respectively. Title Pages will be prepared in manuscript.

Place	Date	Hour	Summary of Events and Information	Remarks and references to Appendices
BILLET LE GRAND	16.6.17	11.00 am	Rec'd order from A.D.M.S. to send Leaney Advn division forwds to report to O.C. 3/1 H.C.F. Amb. at ERVILLERS.	
		12.10 pm	Despatched Leaney Advn division under Sergeant BUDD + 36 other ranks in 3 G.S. wagons in accordance with forgoing order; also 2 additional motor ambulances to 3/1 H.C.F. Amb.	
	19.6.17	n.a.	Hospital inspected by D.M.S. Third Army.	A)
	20.6.17	6.0 pm	Major DIXON + the two Reserve Lieutenants returned. No casualties in personnel. Report from O.C. 3/1 H.C.F. Amb. speaks highly of conduct of all ranks, mentioning especially the hard work carried out by Major DIXON + Sergeant LEANEY. The following names submitted to A.D.M.S. on A.F. W.3121 with recommendations for award of Military Medal: A/93011. Sergeant LEANEY A/93567. Pte. CURD A/93622. " SANDERS A/93632. Pte. BALDWIN A/93393. " READER Pick up, Series 52. Average daily number of patients during the past week,	A)
	21.6.17	6.0 am	Rec'd operation order No 111 by A.D.M.S. The 58th Division (less Artillery) will be relieved by the 2nd Division (less Artillery) on the night. 1st Corps front. Command will pass to G.O.C. 2nd Division at 10 a.m. on 24.6.17. The 1/2nd and 1/3rd H.C.F. Ambces will be relieved by 2 A.C. of the 2nd Division on 23.6.17. The 1/2nd H.C.F. Amb on relief will take over the S.A. site at COURCELLES from the 2/1st 3 Ambs. The 2/3rd H.C.F. Amb on relief will take over the S.A. site at BUCQUOY from the 2/1st 3 Amb.	A)

2449 Wt. W14957/M90 750,000 1/16 J.B.C. & A. Forms/C.2118/12.

Army Form C. 2118.

WAR DIARY
or
INTELLIGENCE SUMMARY
(Erase heading not required.)

Place	Date	Hour	Summary of Events and Information	Remarks and references to Appendices
ACHIET LE GRAND	23.6.17	6.0 pm	The 2/1st H.C.D Ambce will remain at present location. 2/ADMS orders will close at MORY at 10 a.m. on 24.6.17 and re-open at COURCELLES at the same time.	A.D.S
"	24.6.17	6.0 p.m	Lieut R.J.DUTHIE & Lieut W.H.ORTON & 5 Other ranks were attached from 2/2nd H.C.D Ambce in relief of like number of 2/2nd D.Ambce.	A.D.S
"	"	"	Capt A.N.SAVAGE proceeded for temp duty in medical charge of 2/3rd London Regt. Capt A.E.HUXTABLE " " " " " " " " " 2/10th " "	A.D.S
"	25.6.17	12.0 noon	Received 'Medical Arrangements No. 32.' by ADMS 62nd Division. 'The ADMS 62nd Division will arrange to take over the administration of the forward hospital at the Brickfields ACHIET LE GRAND from the ADMS 58th Division & will detail the requisite personnel in relief of that of the 58th Division at present there. The Letter on relief, will come under the orders of ADMS 58th Division & will move & be accommodated under arrangements to be made by him.' 2/1st Horse Counties Fld Ambulance is to be reported to this office for briefing.	A.D.S
"	"	7.30 p.m	Reed. Operation Order No. 23 by ADMS 58th Division be taken over from the 2/1st Horse Counties Field	

Army Form C. 2118.

WAR DIARY
or
INTELLIGENCE SUMMARY
(Erase heading not required.)

Instructions regarding War Diaries and Intelligence Summaries are contained in F. S. Regs., Part II. and the Staff Manual respectively. Title Pages will be prepared in manuscript.

Place	Date	Hour	Summary of Events and Information	Remarks and references to Appendices
ACHIET LE GRAND	26.6.17	9.30 pm	Ambulance taken over by the 2/1st West Riding Field Ambulance. The 2/1st West Riding Sanitary Section Field Ambulance will be retained on relief by the 2/2nd West-R.S. Sanitary Section & proceed to the divisional site at L.6.a.5.9. All ox carts & R.A. lorries stores will be handed over & receipts taken. Detailed arrangements of relief will be made between O/C 2/1st W.R.F.Amb. & O/C 2/2nd W.R.F.Amb. on their site to be reported to this officer.	H.Q. Office Order 67.D 1/6/2000
"	27.6.17	10.0 am	Advance party of 4 N.C.Os men of 2/2nd W.R.3 Amb. reported.	A.D.S.
"	"	12.0 noon	Major T.H.DIXON proceeded to BUCQUOY to take temporary command of 2/3rd West Riding F. Amb. during the absence on leave of Lt.Col J. BARKLEY A.S.C. Officer Commanding. ¾ no section of 2/1st W.R.3 Amb. moved to take over left section Hatfield.	A.D.S.
"	"	2.30 pm	Completed hand over of Capt Nations transfers to 2/2nd W.R.3 Amb. Details handed over 109 Other Ranks Reserves 105 Sick 12 Total 166.	A.D.S.
			2/1st W.R.3 Amb moved to Divisional site at L.6.a.5.9	A.D.S.
Bivouac at L.6.a.5.9.	"	6.0 pm	Bell tents having insufficient quantity & bivouacs have been erected for accommodation of personnel & the necessary sanitary arrangements made.	A.D.Delarkay (?) Lt.Col. R.M.O.T.

Cmdg 2/1st West Riding 3 Amb R.M.O.T.

2449 Wt. W14937/M90 750,000 1/16 J.B.C. & A. Forms/C.2118/12.

COMMITTEE FOR THE
MEDICAL HISTORY OF THE WAR
Date   10 SEP. 1917

21st Home Counties F.A.

Vol 6

CONFIDENTIAL

War Diary
of
Lieut Colonel A.T. FALWASSER   R.A.M.C. T.
Commanding 2/1st Home Counties Field Ambulance

From 1.7.17   to 31.7.17.

(Volume 1)

2/1st Home Counties F.A.

COMMITTEE FOR THE
MEDICAL HISTORY OF THE WAR
Date 10 SEP.1917

WAR DIARY
INTELLIGENCE SUMMARY
(Erase heading not required.)

Army Form C. 2118.

Place	Date	Hour	Summary of Events and Information	Remarks and references to Appendices
Bivouac at L.6.a.5.6.	3.7.17	6.0 p.m.	Field Ambulance closed and in rest.	Map Ref. Sheet 57.D 1/40,000
"	4.7.17	10.0 midnight	Received Operation order No. 24 by A.D.M.S. 5th Division	Appendix 1.
"	"		Received 175th Inf. Bde. order No. 27.	Appendix 2.
"	5.7.17	9.30 a.m.	Capt CUTHBERT, Lieut DUTHIE & 36 other ranks proceeded by Route march to BANCOURT as an advance party to report to Staff Captain 175 Inf Bde at cross roads H.56.8 at 11.0 a.m. in accordance with Bde. operi. order (Appendix 2). This party took with them Bell tents & 1 Officers Mess tents with orders to have these pitched at camp site at BANCOURT by time of arrival of main party of unit. A.S.D.	Map Ref Sheet 57 C 1/40,000
"	"	2.30 p.m.	Remainder of Unit paraded & proceeded to entraining point in accordance with Table "A"4. Appendix 2.	A.S.D
BANCOURT	"	6.30 p.m.	Main party of Unit arrived at I.31.c.5.9., the camp site allotted to Unit, & found tents pitched & necessary arrangements completed by advance party.	Sheet 57 C 1/40,000 A.S.D
"	6.7.17	9.30 a.m.	The above named party under Capt CUTHBERT proceeded to RUYAUCOURT to the Field Ambulance site at P.10.c.9.4. being vacated by the E.Lancs 3 Amb & remain there until 5.45 p.m. at which time they would report to O.C. 1/1st E.Lancs 3 Amb. at P.10.c.9.4 to be posted under his instructions as part relief of the personnel of that unit in the line. An additional party consisting of 1 Capt- CHALMERS and	ditto

WAR DIARY
or
INTELLIGENCE SUMMARY

Army Form C. 2118.

Place	Date	Hour	Summary of Events and Information	Remarks and references to Appendices
			and 7 other ranks proceeded with the above named party to P.10.c.a.4 to take over equipment stores, are handed over by the 1/1st E Rmd Fd Amb & to act as a holding party until the arrival of the main body.	Maps Sheet 57 C. 1/40000 A)
BANCOURT	6.7.17	1.30 pm	Remainder of Unit paraded & proceeded by HAPLINCOURT – BERTINCOURT – ROYAULCOURT – & thing new site vacated at 12.0 noon today by 1/1 E hmr'd Fd Amb @ P.10.c.a.4	A)
ROYAULCOURT	7.7.17	6.0 pm	Completed relief of 1/1 E famd Amb in the line on the front held by 126th & 127th Inf Bdes extending from CANAL DU NORD exclusive (K.31.6 and K.32.a) to TRESCAULT inclusive (Q.14.d) Regimental Aid Posts are established at the following pts T.31.d.9.5. Q.2.c.2.3. Q.3.c.2.0. Q.3.e.9.4 & Q.10.a.3.7. In immediate proximity to each of these is a Bearer post with from 4 to 6 RAMC personnel of this Unit with 1 or 2 wheeled stretchers. Casualties are evacuated from RAPs by these bearers through Bearer Rly Posts at Q.1.a.2.2. Q.2.d.2.6 Q.10.d.5.0. to wagon Posts at P.6.6.0. R.11.6.9.4. P.10.c.a.4. Advanced Dressing Station is established at Q.14.d.0.8 there a casualties are evacuated via ID to Main Dressing Station at P.10.c.a.4. ADS is in charge of Capt. CUTHBERT with Capt. CHALMERS and 30 other ranks. Wagon Post at P.12.6.5.0 is in charge of Lieut DUTHIE with 10 other ranks & casualties from this front are evacuated direct to MDS.	57 C S.E 1/20.000 A) 57 C S.E 1/20.000 A)
"	6.7.17	6.0 pm	Battle casualties during past 24 hours admitted to MDS – 3. No notification of short times & wounded of evacuation.	A)

WAR DIARY
INTELLIGENCE SUMMARY

(Erase heading not required.)

Army Form C. 2118.

Place	Date	Hour	Summary of Events and Information	Remarks and references to Appendices
RUYAULCOURT	9.7.17	6.0 p.m.	Casualties admitted to MDS during past 24 hours 30. Capt. HUXTABLE rejoined for duty from 2/1st London Regt. RAP's at - OXFORD VALLEY Q.3.c.2.5 has been handed over to the fact that front line is held by 2 Battalions only instead of 3 in peace time. Received order No. H.961 by ADMS 58 Division.	Appendix 3. ADD
"	10.7.17	6.0 p.m.	Casualties admitted to MDS – 19. Cases are evacuated to Nos 21 & 48 C.C.S. at YPRES. In accordance with ADMS order (Appendix 3) assumed command of forward 2/3rd H.C.D. Ambulance enjoyed in collection of casualties from right sector of Divisional front TRESCAULT (exclusive) to VILLERS PLOUICH (exclusive) held until 9th inst by 2 Bdes of 59th Division. RAP's for this sector are established at R.13.a.2.7, Q.17.b.2.5 & Q.15.b.1.5 Bearer posts walk Field Ambulance tramcar are established in immediate proximity to all these posts & casualties are evacuated through Relay Bearer Posts at Q.17.d.5.5 Q.23.c.6.3 Q.23.d.5.2 Q.20.d.3.0. This latter is a tramline post from this front evacuation are operated to an ADS at Q.20.d.3.0 are evacuated by wheeled stretcher this relay post. Cars from RAP at Q.15.b.9.5 direct to ADS & thence to MDS RUYAULCOURT. Capt. MATTHEWS with Capt. HEY SMITH with the forward & advanced of our Adv. Ambulance are located at this ADS.	57 C LE 1/20.000
"	11.7.17	6.0 p.m.	Casualties admitted to MDS — or Sorcuville Rleug. Training from ADS at Q.10.x & 0.8 have been running today at 2 PM & 4 PM for conveyance of wounded to MDS & P.10.c.9.9 thence by BUS for conveyance of sick by 4/3rd H.C.D. males thus far will can be returned to their units on return. Major T.H.DIXON posted to 1/3 H.C.A. relieving Major...	A.D.

WAR DIARY
or
INTELLIGENCE SUMMARY

Army Form C. 2118.

Place	Date	Hour	Summary of Events and Information	Remarks and references to Appendices
RUYAULCOURT	12/7/17	6.0 pm	Casualties passed thro' MDS — 12. Route of evacuation on right sector has been shortened by cutting out wagon Post at QUEENS CROSS Q.20.d.5.5 and there are now arrangements for wagons from the right half of this sector to a wagon Post established today at Q.21.b.3.6 & thence to ADS at Q.20.d.3.0. A Medical Officer is located at this new wagon post which is in progress to make increased accommodation at this point to which stretcher bearer is only no cart shelter.	Sheet 57 C S.E. 1/20000 A.D.S.
"	13/7/17	6.0 pm	Casualties thro' MDS — 18. Lieut H. BLYTH joined for duty. Lieut W. HORTON rejoined from 1/w/c 2/5th London Regt.	A.D.S.
"	14/7/17	6.0 pm	Casualties thro' MDS — 13. ADS at METZ Q.20.A.3.0 vacated today & additional accommodation available at wagon post Q.21.b.3.6.	A.D.S.
"	15/7/17	6.0 pm	Casualties thro' MDS — 2. Capt MAXWELL 2/3 H.C.F. Amb. reported for duty at wagon Post Q.21.b.3.6 vice Capt MATTHEWS evacuated sick to No. 48 C.C.S. Capt HEY SMITH to No. 48 C.C.S. for duty.	A.D.S.
"	16/7/17	6.0 pm	Lieut H. BLYTH for duty i/Me 2/3 London Regt. Casualties thro' MDS — 2. Division Operation Order received :- The Divisional front will be held by 2 Brigades each side having 2 Battns in frontline, 1 Battn in support & 1 Battn in Div reserve. The 173 Inf Bde will take over by 7 AM July 17 the half of Div front at present held by AM Inf Bde from QUEENS LANE exclusive was held.	

240M W.W14957/M90 750,000 1/16 J.B.C. & A. Form C.2118/12.

WAR DIARY
or
INTELLIGENCE SUMMARY

Army Form C. 2118.

(Erase heading not required.)

Place	Date	Hour	Summary of Events and Information	Remarks and references to Appendices
			By 174 Inf Bde. The 174 Inf Bde will take over by 9 AM July 19th. Wt. that part of the front now held by 175th Inf Bde from TRESCAULT – RIBECOURT Rd to ASHTON VALLEY exclusive. It is proposed still further to shorten route of evacuation in right sector by transferring Rear Relay Post from its present site at Q.23.c.6.3 to Q.23.a.7.2 v the observing shelter is being erected under R.E. supervision at this latter site.	Map Ref:— 51c SE 1/20,000 A.D.S.
ROYAUCOURT 17.7.17	6.0 p.m		Casualties thro' M.D.S. since 6.0 p.m 16th — 8, includes 1 O.R. who will be shown for previous night.	A.D.S.
"	18.7.17	6.0 p.m	Casualties thro' M.D.S. " " " 17th — 9. Captain L. HADEN GUEST reported 6.30 p.m July 17th for temporary duty with this Unit. Situation of R.A.P.'s; Relays & Wagon Posts remain unchanged except of evacuation at the same 2 work, is Relay Post at Q.23.a.7.2 is nearly completed & the latter should be ready for occupation in extreme situation on the whole front is quite satisfactory for evacuation of wounded by stretcher.	A.D.S.
"	19.7.17	6.0 p.m	Casualties thro' M.D.S. — 11. Capt W.W. MAXWELL i/c Wagon Post at Q.21.6.3.6 proceeded to examine Medical charge of 290 Bde R.F.A. Capt. J.R. CHALMERS detailed to assume this post from A.D.S. Q.14.d.9.8 following minute received from A.D.M.S. 'Capt L. HADEN GUEST will take over command of 1/1st Home Counties 3st Amb. during the absence on leave of Lieut Col FALWASSER.'	Appendix 4 A.D.S.

2449 Wt. W14957/M90 750,000 1/16 J.B.C. & A. Forms/C.2118/12.

Army Form C. 2118.

WAR DIARY
or
INTELLIGENCE SUMMARY
(Erase heading not required.)

Instructions regarding War Diaries and Intelligence Summaries are contained in F. S. Regs., Part II. and the Staff Manual respectively. Title Pages will be prepared in manuscript.

Place	Date	Hour	Summary of Events and Information	Remarks and references to Appendices
ROYAUCOURT	26/7/17	6.0 p.m.	Casualties Kn' H.Q.S. in half returns — B. Period from 20" to midnight 26" recorded & returned by Capt. L. Daden Guest.	
"	27/7/17	8.0 A.M.	Capt L. Daden Guest rejoins his unit; Capt A.H. SAVAGE assumes command at 10 a 2/1st Home Counties Fd Amb; during the absence on leave of Lt. Col. A.T. FALWASSER.	
		9.15. A.M.	CAPT. ORILL proceeded 1/c motor ambulances to new site at AVESNES-LE-COMTE.	dep. Ref. Qud. LENS 11
		9.45. A.M.	Main body of unit (less Newport) marched to YPRES & entrained on the Decauville Ry, proceeding to BAPAUME, arriving at 3 p.m. and	1/100,000
		6.0 P.M.	1" BLYTHE rejoined on unit, from being m/c 2/3rd LONDON REGT. 3d Amb, entrained a broad gauge & departed BAPAUME 6.15 p.m. arriving via ARRAS at AVESNES-LE-COMTE, arriving on at 2.30 a.m. Ecoytion thence marched to	
AVESNES LE-COMTE	28/7/17	2.30 A.M.	main Amb. at AVESNES-LE-COMTE arriving in at 2.30 a.m. Ecoytion had been prepared in advance & to take over from the 1st S. AFRICAN completed. CAPT HUXTABLE reported into the transport.	Map Ref. a LENS 11 1/100,000
		8.0 A.M.	2/1st HOME Counties Fd Amb; opens as D.R.S.	out

2449 Wt. W14957/M90 750,000 1/16 J.B.C. & A. Forms/C.2118/12.

WAR DIARY
or
INTELLIGENCE SUMMARY

Army Form C. 2118.

2/1 H.C. 2nd West

Vol 6

Place	Date	Hour	Summary of Events and Information	Remarks and references to Appendices
ROYAUCOURT	17.7.17	4 pm	Arrived at M.D.C. 2/1 HCFA. Relieve Lt Col FALWASSER of which took over Sp'n	MAPS FRANCE 57c SE (Edition 3) 57c NE (Edit. 3A)
"	18.7.17	9 am	Inspected Advance pts at ROYAUCOURT & made Waffn Posts	
			Left A.D.S. Q14 c & b & Regt'l Pr—mys of HARRINCOURT WOOD & Lt COL FALWASSER	
"	19.7.17	9 am	Visited Waffn Post, M.D.S. & Rely Post in HARRINCOURT	
		11.00	Visited R.A.P. n Bttg hd at Q 36 d 9.5	
"	20.7.17	9 am	Visited R.A.P.s at Q 2 a 33 (RICKET HUBERT) & Q 3 c 9.2 (main)	
			on (COSY CORSE) at Q 10 c 6.5 (TRESCAULT) (Warfr of Infantry) or Q 10 d T.9 (SHERWOOD AVENUE)	
			Over 1000 Ground had in stretchers - R.P. at Q 15 9.5 in company of CAPT CUTHBERT R.A.M.C.	
		5 pm	Took over complete taking taking over balance of stores a/c Shirepher L LT COL FALWASSER	
		10.30	Raid on our trench & Enemy Set machines Sounds Guns L.A.D.S.	Lt Col Elliot Capt. Rogers

WAR DIARY / INTELLIGENCE SUMMARY

Army Form C. 2118.

Place	Date	Hour	Summary of Events and Information	Remarks and references to Appendices
RWA M. CONVT	26.9.17	8.0 a.m.	Arrived convent 2/1st H.L. Field Ambulance. Relieved Lt. Col. A.T. FALWASSER left to go on leave.	
		9.0 a.m. 10.0 a.m.	Lieut. OGSTON left & report for duty to O.C. 2/5 B. Lond. Regt. during absence of M.O. Wounded German prisoner (who captured in attempted raid by enemy in previous evening arrived at M.D.S. - stretcher for examination & Zillybeke (near Pte. Nilson A. 86th Regt.) [Traducteur]	
		12.0 n.	Total casualties from 12.0 n.n. 20.9.17 2 Officers 47 OR wounded 4 OR killed. All casualties caused by enemy barrage. Enemy did not succeed in reaching trench. Attached Front Line - SPOILBANK - OXFORD VALLEY. (K.33)	
		2.0 p.	Inspected Wagon Post P.16.b.9, M.D.S. Q.14 cents Wagon Post at Q.26.b.6 by Lt-Col.	
		3.0 p	C.Q.M.S. killed. Relief arrangements notice spent. On right 92.20., 8.20 discussed - Battalion part are 2/4 2/9 & B" Lond. Regt. 2nd 2/12 B. Lond. Regt. - M.O. ½ A.A. "B" Coy. Regt. (Capt. EUSTACE R.A.M.C.) arr. & detail arranged of relieve R.A.P. Set dressing split receipt & regiment (Beaver Squires Capt. & Lieut. Editor Esplaine)	
		4.30 p	CAPT. H. OXTABLE R.A.M.C. one 2 M.D.S. to relieve CAPT. CYTHBERT. LIEUT. 7TH DIVIS.N.C. Battn reported & 2/13 H.C.A.P. Enfans duty.	

Army Form C. 2118.

WAR DIARY
or
INTELLIGENCE SUMMARY

(Erase heading not required.)

Instructions regarding War Diaries and Intelligence Summaries are contained in F. S. Regs., Part II. and Staff Manual respectively. Title Pages will be prepared in manuscript.

Place	Date	Hour	Summary of Events and Information	Remarks and references to Appendices
RUYAULCOURT	22/7/17	9.0a	Inspected Waggon Posn at P.12.b.50, A.D.S. at Q.14 entres & Waggon Post at Q.2.b.6. Inspected posts of evacuation & arut mounded for 173rd Inf. Bde posts. (Regt-sector Rule) & R.A.P. at BEAUCAMP & VILLERS PLOUICH also Rely. Post at Q.16.a.22 & Q.23.a.54. Arranged relief of Bearer Squads in front posts by Sqds relieved & those in reserve posts. Ambce evacuati units good. Posn of road nr. BEAUCAMP bad & heavy	
		12.0 3.0 3.30	Returned to H.Q. M.O. 1/C 2/12 Rifle Bde & Sgly Officer to O.R. 13 Batt Ladette Regt called re arrangets for Operations on 23rd. Arranged for advance R.A.P. in hostile rate Puffs of chevaux-de-frise into Boches trenches at R.A.P. & R.P. Ford Car at PLACE MORTMARE however when wounded	
		4.30	Capt TINDALL 27th Field Amb. 9th Division reported for preliminary reconnaissance	
		5.0	Accompanied Capt TINDALL on visit to Waggon Post (Left) A.D.S. Waggon Post (Right) & Adv R.P.	

L/Cpl N. Stuart
C/P Royce

2449 Wt. W14957/M90 750,000 1/16 J.B.C. & A. Forms/C.2118/12.

WAR DIARY or INTELLIGENCE SUMMARY

Army Form C. 2118.

Place	Date	Hour	Summary of Events and Information	Remarks and references to Appendices
ROYALLCOURT	23/7/17	9.0 a.m.	Capt TINDALL t/f to A.D.S. & i/c normal evacuation from R.A.P. vice CAPT HUXTABLE. Visited Wagon Post P.12.b.50, A.D.S. Q.14.c.6.0 & Waggon Post Q.2.b.6.6. Quiet. All in order at advance stations. Walter hot + pouring rain. Aeroplane balloons + aeroplanes observing.	6/7/47.45 59 Div Huns in retreat
		11.0 am	Reported whole camp. Total wounded of 12.0 noon 22.7.17. 2 Officers 11 O.R. 1 Officer slight returned to duty. 2 S.I. cases detained pending reports from O.C. unit Casualties from run river last night 2 Officers 5 O.R. wounded 1 O.R. died of wounds in A.D.S.	(Armoured)
		12.0 noon		
		1.0 p.m.	Capt TINDALL leaves to return to his unit t/f with Major HOLLIN without assignment to man Adv Lines 15, 2 M.O. A.D.S. 2O.R. 3 N.R. sn Regt Wag.on Post 6 O.R. & 4 O.R. at 2nd B.S.R R.P. s R.A.P. to HETTI arranged in connection with projected raid on enemy trenches in WIGAN COPSE (K.26.d.3.3). Esta Beavr Squad at Adv Lines R.A.P. in canal Bank (CANAL DU NORD) 2nd Car Station at PLACE MORTUARE (noon)	
		5.0 p.m.	Attack made of reinstation of Divisions took at D.H.Q. (YPRES) + consider nearer locations in rear (FOSSEUX) area	
		9.30 p.m.	C.O No 2.5 & R.O. & I.S. assumed. 59 Div being relieved by 8 & 9 Div. O.O. Armoured 59 Div been C FOSSEUX an transf to XIII Corps to IIIrd Army Reserve.	Lillede-Lizard Captain

Army Form C. 2118.

WAR DIARY
or
INTELLIGENCE SUMMARY
(Erase heading not required.)

Instructions regarding War Diaries and Intelligence Summaries are contained in F. S. Regs., Part II. and the Staff Manual respectively. Title Pages will be prepared in manuscript.

Place	Date	Hour	Summary of Events and Information	Remarks and references to Appendices
HAVRINCOURT	24/11/17	9.a.	Visited Waggon Post on left of HAVRINCOURT WOOD. A.D.S. at Q.14 C.1.1 & Waggon Post on Right of HAVRINCOURT WOOD. Quiet night. Wind was too strong for balloons observed. Arranged relief of Bearers & Stretcher bearers of 2/1 H.F.A. on Right line by 2/1 H.F.A. Relief effected via tread a system that one to front was used by stretcher bearers. Wittibene extra bearers from each & left pastim behind H.Q. 1/c Waggon for left-posts to report for duty at M.D.S. Indeed all Huntingdon Stretchers, splints & stores be returned as soon as possible (Annexure) M.D.S. beyond constant movement for carrying in duties.	① A5/79/17 Estimates Protest in answer to 50 Div. Ord No 4-Final (annexure) ② 175/29 Rd D.I. No 30 (annexure)
		12.0 noon 9.30 hr	Bathes returned from H.Q.'s R.A.P. no casualties & symptoms of the R.A.P. L.B. leaders men. Reference this in unit postcard. Total wounds from 13.10 am - 23. Nov. 17. 7 O.R., but 5 from Raid & none & many Rifle men a Musketry CAPTAIN JACK 2/ Field Ambce reported at D.O.R. on a adv. feet & his men.	③ Ref: R500 B.J.O.O.S (rec'd) ④ 757 Bde
		3.4 p	CAPTAIN JACK & N.C.O. visited right of line & lie guides & Lieut. DISHINGTON R.M.C. Ord 2/1 & 27 F.A. on left Waggon Post.	2 Lieut Ditto R.M.C Ord 2/1 M.C.A. with (annexure)
		9.0.p.	Part of 2/2 H.F.A. Ambce Lie Lephoda at M.D.S. on relief of 2/1 H.F.A. who...	

Army Form C. 2118.

WAR DIARY
or
INTELLIGENCE SUMMARY
(Erase heading not required.)

Instructions regarding War Diaries and Intelligence Summaries are contained in F. S. Regs., Part II. and the Staff Manual respectively. Title Pages will be prepared in manuscript.

Place	Date	Hour	Summary of Events and Information	Remarks and references to Appendices
ROYAUCOURT	25.9.17	9.0 a.m.	Visited A.D.M.S. Office 58 Div'. no instruction for renewed detail. Lieut. Dalington & detail of 2/3 H.C.F.A. to march to 2/3 H.C.F.A. on 26.7.17. Self report for duty to O.C. 2/2 H.F.A. after hand up our front line & M.D.S. to O.C. 2/7 th F.A.	
		10.30 a.m	Detail in hand & Transport to FOSSEUX are arranged to Capt SAVAGE	
			Visited Officers Waggon Part & A.D.S. & arranged last details of	
		5.p.m	Relief by 27 th F.A.	
			Corps Commander, D.D.M.S. Corps, A.D.M.S. 57 th Div'. & D.A.D.M.S. called during absence of self & reve received by Lieuten & Lieut. Ridlington	
	26/9/17		O.C. 27 th F.A. & Capt TINDALL R.A.M.C. 27 th F.A. refused charge of Major Hamb given at 9.0 am 26.9.17 & triplete of Evey 26.9.17 except of parsed details.	
			Lieut. Drillio R.A.M.C. sent sick to Hospital at MARICOURT.	

L. Herden Quest
Capt"

Army Form C. 2118.

WAR DIARY
or
INTELLIGENCE SUMMARY
(Erase heading not required.)

Instructions regarding War Diaries and Intelligence Summaries are contained in F. S. Regs., Part II. and the Staff Manual respectively. Title Pages will be prepared in manuscript.

Place	Date	Hour	Summary of Events and Information	Remarks and references to Appendices
RHAUCOURT	26.7.17	9.00	Relief parties of 27th F.A. go to left Waggon Post, & A.D.S. & right Waggon Post	
		12.0 noon to 1.0 p.m.	2nd Lt. Woodhead arrive 12.0 noon 25.7.17 1 Officer 9 O.R. 3 O.R. wounded transport, namely 2 G.S. limbers, handed off of A BEAUZEVELLE under command of Capt DEHUXTABLE R.A.M.C.	
		2.0 p.m.	Relief of Waggon Post, A.D.S. & front line posts complete	
		2.30	Visited A.D.S. & right Waggon Post with O.C. 27 F.A. all in order. Receipts to take over stores for 27th F.A.	
		5.30 p.m.	A.D.M.S. called & interviewed O.C. 27 F.A. Lt. Col. COSTELLO	
		9.0 p.m.	Right duty taken over by 27th F.A. Relief of 27th F.A. now complete except for Orderly Room Staff	L. Haden Guest Capt RAMC

WAR DIARY or INTELLIGENCE SUMMARY

Army Form C. 2118.

Place	Date	Hour	Summary of Events and Information	Remarks and references to Appendices
ROYAULCOURT	27/7/17	9.0 a.m.	Orderly Room 2/1st N.F.F.A. closed at ROYAULCOURT. Lieut Andrew handed over to CAPT SAVAGE. CAPT SAVAGE moved off en route for retaining centre at BAPAUME. Command of Field Ambulance Personnel of F.A.	

L. Arden Guest
Captain

WAR DIARY or INTELLIGENCE SUMMARY

Army Form C. 2118.

Place	Date	Hour	Summary of Events and Information	Remarks and references to Appendices
AVESNES LE-COMTE	29/7/19	3.0 p.m.	Lt. W.R. REEDS from CHINESE GEN. DEP: } reported for temporary duty. Lt. R.M. BRADLEY " " " }	
"	30/7/19	8.0 a.m.	Nothing fresh to report.	

Harold Savery
Capt. R.A.V.C.
for O.C. 2/1 2ND C.F.A.

Appendix 1.

SECRET.   Copy No. 1

OPERATION ORDER No.24
by
Colonel J.W.H.Houghton, A.M.S.,
A.D.M.S., 58th Division.

---- * ----

4/7/1917.

Reference Map 57 C.
1/40,000.

Information.

The 58th Division will take over the line from the Canal du Nord to VILLERS PLOUICH exclusive, in relief of the 42nd and 59th Divisions (less Artillery) in accordance with the attached move table.

The 174th Infantry Brigade will take over the front now held by the 59th Division with their Headquarters at Q.15.c.7.3.

The 175th Infantry Brigade, that held by the 42nd Division with their Headquarters at Q.15.d.1.9.

The 173rd Infantry Brigade will be in reserve with their Headquarters at NEUVILLE BOURJONVAL.

1. 5he 2/1st H.C.Field Ambulance will accompany the 175th Infantry Brigade Group on the march to the new area on the 5th July. On arrival in the YTRES area on 6th July, Officer Commanding 2/1st H.C.Field Ambulance will take over the Main Dressing Station at RUYAULCOURT and will be responsible for the collection of casualties from the left Brigade of the Divisional front, from 6 p.m. on the 7th July.

2. The 2/3rd H.C.Field Ambulance will accompany the 174th Infantry Brigade Group on the march to the EQUANCOURT area on the 6th July. On arrival in this area, Officer Commanding 2/3rd H.C.Field Ambulance will take over the Field Ambulance site at BUS and also will take over the Advanced Dressing Station at METZ and be responsible for the collection of casualties from the right Brigade of the Divisional front.

3. The 2/2nd H.C.Field Ambulance (less one section) will proceed direct to MARICOURT on 8th July and on arrival take over the III Corps Rest Station.

4. The 2/2nd H.C.Field Ambulance will detail one section to accompany the 173rd Infantry Brigade Group on the march to the new area on 8th July.

This section of the Field Ambulance on arrival in the YTRES area will bivouac at BUS by arrangement with Officer Commanding 2/3rd H.C.Field Ambulance and will rejoin the 2/2nd H.C.Field Ambulance on 10th July at MARICOURT.

5. All sick in the new area will be sent to the 2/3rd H.C. Field Ambulance at BUS.

6. Sick on the march will be admitted to the Field Ambulance at BUS.

7. Advance parties will be sent by each Field Ambulance to take over the new sites.

Detailed arrangements of reliefs will be made between Commanding Officers concerned.

- 2 -

8. The Foden Disinfector will move independently on the 7th July to the new site of the 2/3rd H.C.Field Ambulance at BUS.

9. A.D.M.S., Office, 58th Division, will close at COURCELLES on the 9th July at 10 a.m. and reopen at YTRES at the same hour.

10. Completion of reliefs to be reported to this Office.

11. ACKNOWLEDGE.

S. Soway Beaver

Captain,
for Colonel, A.M.S.,
A.D.M.S., 58th Division.

Issued at 11- 30 p.m.

	Copy No.	
	1.	O.C., 2/1st H.C.Field Ambulance.
	2.	O.C., 2/2nd H.C.Field Ambulance.
	3.	O.C., 2/3rd H.C.Field Ambulance.
	4.	A.D.M.S., 42nd Division.
	5.	A.D.M.S., 59th Division.
	6.	D.D.M.S., III Corps.
	7.	D.D.M.S., IV Corps.
	8.	D.D.M.S., V Corps.
	9.	173rd Infantry Brigade.
	10.	174th Infantry Brigade.
	11.	175th Infantry Brigade.
	12.	"A. & Q" 58th Division.
	13.	"G" 58th Division.
	14.	Signals, 58th Division.
	15.	S.S.O., 58th Division.
	16.	C.R.A., 58th Division.
	17.	C.R.E., 58th Division.
	18.	A.D.V.S., 58th Division.
	19.	A.P.M., 58th Division.
	20) 21)	War Diary.
	22) 23)	File.

SECRET.

Reference Map
Sheet 57-C, 1/40,000.

HEADQUARTERS 4 JUL 1917 175th INFANTRY BRIGADE

Appendix 2.

175th INFANTRY BRIGADE.   Copy No. 9

ORDER No 27.

1. The Brigade will relieve the 126th and 127th Infantry Brigades (42nd Division) in the line on the nights of 7/8th and 8/9th July respectively.

2. On completion of these reliefs the Brigade Sector will extend from Q.5.a.0.0 to the CANAL DU NORD K.26.c.7.0 exclusive.
   South Boundary. Q.5.a.0.0 - Q.4.d.7.0 - Q.9.d.5.0 - Q.14.d.7.3.
   Northern Boundary.
   CANAL DU NORD.
   Inter-Battalion Boundary.
   K.33.c.9.0 - Q.3.a.4.0 - Q.2.d.9.0 - Q.8.b.0.4 - Q.8.a.4.0 - Q.8.c.0.4.

3. The Brigade will move as a Group in accordance with the attached.- Table 'A' shews moves of the Brigade Group from the LOGEAST WOOD AREA to the YTRES - BERTINCOURT area.
   The Reliefs of the line will be carried out as shewn in Table 'B'.

4. All Trench Stores, Defence Schemes, Maps, Aeroplane Photographs, etc, will be taken over and duplicate lists forwarded to Brigade Headquarters in due course.

5. Unit Commanders will pay particular attention to the taking over of work in hand in their areas, and will forward the policy for this to Brigade Headquarters 24 hours after the completion of relief.

6. A detailed disposition list will be forwarded to Brigade Headquarters as soon as possible after completion of relief.

7. Appendix I shews the arrangements made for reconnoitring parties.

8. Command of the line now held by 126th Infantry Bde will pass to G.O.C.175th Bde at 9-0am on 8th instant, and of front now held by 127th Brigade on completion of relief on the 9th instant.

9. Completion of reliefs will be notified to Brigade Headquarters by wire, by the code word 'SLUMBER'.

10. Administrative instructions are issued together with this order; further details will be issued later.

11. All details not provided for in this order will be arranged between Commanding Officers concerned.

12. Brigade Headquarters will close at LOGEAST WOOD at 2-0pm on 5th instant and re-open at BANCOURT at the same hour: it will close at BANCOURT and re-open at YTRES at 2-0 pm on 6th instant.

13. ACKNOWLEDGE.

J. W. G. WYLD, CAPTAIN.
BRIGADE MAJOR.
For distribution - P.T.O.   175th INFANTRY BRIGADE.

Issued to Signals at... 4.45 p.m.

Distribution:-

Copy No	1 to	2/9th London Rgt
	2	2/10th :
	3	2/11th :
	4	2/12th :
	5	215 Coy.M.G.C.
	6	175th L.T.M.Bty.
	7	503rd Coy.R.E.
	8	512 H.T.Coy. A.S.C.
	9	2/1st H.C.Field Amb'ce
	10	Officer i/c Brigade Sigs:
	11	Staff Captain 175th Inf.Bde
	12	58th Division 'G'
	13	: 'A' & 'Q'
	14	A.D.M.S. :
	15	126th Infantry Brigade
	16	127th : :
	17	A. P. M. 58th Division
	18	War Diary.
	19	File.

TABLE 'A' - issued with 175th INFANTRY BDE ORDER No 27. of 4/7/17.

Serial No.	Date.	Unit.	From.	To.	Hour of passing starting point.	Adv: parties report to Staff Captain:— At.	Hour.	ROUTE.	REMARKS.
1	5th July.	2/9th Lon.Regt.	LOGEAST WOOD.	BANJOURT.	* 2-0pm	Cross-rds H.36.b.	11-0am.	ACHIET-LE-G'ND BIHUCOURT - BIEFVILLERS - BAPAUME.	Adv.party to consist of 1 offr & 20 O.R.
2.	-do-	2/10th -do-	-do-	-do-	* 2-10pm	-do-	-do-	-do-	-do-
3.	-do-	2/11th -do-	-do-	-do-	* 2-20pm	-do-	-do-	-do-	-do-
4.	-do-	2/12th -do-	-do-	-do-	* 2-30pm	-do-	-do-	-do-	-do-
5.	-do-	215.M.G.Coy.	-do-	-do-	* 2-40pm	-do-	-do-	-do-	Adv.party 1 offr. 10 OR
6.	-do-	175th LTMBty.	-do-	-do-	* 2-45pm	-do-	-do-	-do-	-do-
7.	-do-	503rd F.Co.RE.	-do-	-do-	* 2-50pm	-do-	-do-	-do-	-do-
8.	-do-	2/1st H.C. F.A.	Present location	-do-	* 3-0 pm	-do-	-do-	-do-	-do-
9.	-do-	512 H.T.Co.ASC.	-do-	ROYAUCOURT G.17.c.1.1.	3-30pm	-do-	-do-	HAPLINCOURT BARASTRE.	?
10.	6th July.	2/9th Lon.Regt.	BANJOURT.	YRES.	∮ 2-0 pm	YRES CHURCH	10-0am.	HAPLINCOURT BARASTRE -BUS.	Adv.party 1 offr. 6 OR.
11.	-do-	2/10th -do-	-do-	-do-	∮ 2-10pm	-do-	-do-	-do-	-do-
12.	-do-	215 M.G.Coy.	-do-	-do-	∮ 2-20pm	-do-	-do-	-do-	-do-
13.	-do-	175th LTMBty.	-do-	-do-	∮ 2-25pm	-do-	-do-	-do-	Adv.party 1 offr. 3 O.R
14.	-do-	503rd F.Co.RE	-do-	-do-	∮ 2-30pm	-do-	-do-	-do-	-do-
15.	-do-	2/11th Lon.Rgt.	-do-	BERTINCOURT	∮ 2-40pm	BERTIN- COURT CH.	11-30am	HAPLINCOURT.	Adv.party 1 offr. 6 O.R
16.	-do-	2/12th -do-	-do-	-do-	∮ 2-50pm	-do-	-do-	-do-	-do-
17.	-do-	2/1st Fld.Amb'ce	-do-	RUYAULCOURT	∮ 3-0pm	RUYAUL- COURT CH.	1-0pm. ?	HAPLINCOURT - BERTINCOURT.	-do-

NOTES.
(a) * Starting point for 5th July - cross-roads G.9.b.3.7.
       ∮   "   "   6th   "   -   "   I.31.a.7.1.
(b) Distances of 200 yds will be maintained between Coys. throughout the march.
(c) First Line Transport will move with their units.

J.W.G. WYLD CAPTAIN.
BRIGADE MAJOR 175th INFANTRY BRIGADE.

TABLE 'B' — RELIEFS.   to accompany 175th INFANTRY BRIGADE ORDER No 27 of 4/7/17.

Meet Guides

Serial No.	Date.	Unit.	From.	To.	Relieving whom	Hour	Rendezvous.	Remarks.
1.	7th July.	2/9th Bn.	YPRES.	Right Sub-Sector.	From right to left, 1 Coy of each in front line. 126th (1/9th Manchesters Infy. (4th E.Lancs. Bde. (5th E.Lancs.	9-50pm	Where railway cuts overland track Q.14.c. 7.8.	Platoons to arrive at rendezvous of guides at intervals of 150 yards.
2.	--do--	2/10th "	--do--	Right Res. position.	10th Manchesters.	Relief to be complete by 5-0 p.m.		By direct arrangements to be made between Battns.
3.	--do--	215 M.G.C.	--do--	Line.	M.G.Coys of 126th and 127th Bdes with 6 & 4 guns respectively.	Details to be settled between Company Commanders concerned.		2 offrs & Nos 1 of Guns to proceed to the line on 6th.
4.	--do--	175th LTMB.	--do--	Line.	LTMB's of 126 & 127th Bdes with 4 & 3 guns respectively.	For right-subsector 9-50pm. Q.14.c.7.8 For left-subsector 10pm. P.12.b.6.7.		Further details to be arranged between C.O's.
5.	--do--	503rd Field Coy. R.E.	--do--	HAVRINCOURT WOOD.	Field Company 42nd Division.	By direct arrangements to be made between Company Commanders.		—
6.	8th July.	2/12th Bn.	BERTIN-COURT.	Left Sub-Sector.	5th Manchesters. (127th Inf.Bde).	10-0pm.	P.12.b.6.7.	Platoons to arrive at rendezvous of guides at intervals of 150 yards.
7.	--do--	2/11th "	--do--	Left Reserve position.	Battalion of 127th Infantry Brigade.	11-0pm	--do--	Arrangements to be made direct between Battns concerned.

J. H. G. WYLD, CAPTAIN.
BRIGADE MAJOR.
175th INFANTRY BRIGADE.

175th INFANTRY BRIGADE.
(To accompany ORDER No 27 of 4/7/17).

DISPOSITIONS OF UNITS ON COMPLETION OF RELIEFS.

Brigade Headquarters   Q.14 central

2/9th London Regt:
- H.Q. - Q.3.d.15.40.
- 3 Coys. - In front line and outpost line.
- 1 Coy. - In Support Line about Q.3.d.1.9.

2/10th :
- H.Q. - Q.14.b.4.3.
- 2 Coys. - In intermediate line about Q.15.c, Q.8.d & a.
- 2 Coys. - In shelters about Q.14.b central.

2/11th :
- H.Q. - K.31.c.0.0.
- 1 Coy. - About Q.1.c.
- 2 Coys. - About Q.1.a.
- 1 Coy. - About K.31.d.

2/12th :
- H.Q. - Q.2.c.8.5
- 3 Coys. - In front and outpost line.
- 1 Coy. - In trench running through Q.2.a & b.

215 Coy.M.G.Corps.
- H.Q. - Q.8.d.2.3.
- 10 guns - in front line.
- 2 guns - in Support.
- 1 Sect. - In Reserve at H.Q.

175th L.T.M.Battery.
- H.Q. - Q.18.d.3.3. with that of 215 Coy.M.G.C.
- 7 guns - In the Line.

J. W. G. WYLD, CAPTAIN.
BRIGADE MAJOR
175th INFANTRY BRIGADE.

Appendix 3.

O.C. 2/1 H.C. Fd Amb

1. O.C. 2/3 H.C. Fd Amb will hand over to O.C. 2/1 H.C. Fd Amb on July 10th the personnel of 1 section of the 2/3 H. Fd Amb.

2. O.C. 2/3 H.C. Fd Amb will hand over to O.C. 2/1 H.C. Fd on July 10th
   Motor Amb. Siddeley Deasy   2
   Motor Amb. Ford   1

3. O.C. 2/1 H.C. Fd will be responsible for the collection of casualties from the whole of the Divisional front from 10 am on July 10th.

9/7/17

Harvey Brown Capt
for Col ADMS 58 Div

Appendix 4

Diagram showing Routes of Evacuation of Casualties from 58th Divisional Front

[Stamp: 2/1st HOME COUNTIES FIELD AMBULANCE, Date 19.7.17, R.A.M.C. T.F.]

- R.A.P. Q2 a 3.3. — 5.
- R.A.P. Q10 a 6.5. — 5.
- R.A.P. R 13 a 2.7. — 8.
- R.A.P. J 36 d.9.2 — 5.
- R.A.P. Q 3 c 9.2. — 4.
- R.A.P. Q 17 b 2.8. — 8.
- R.A.P. Q 15 b.9.5. — 4.
- Relay Post Q 23 a 5.4. — 4.
- Relay Post Q 1 a 2.2. — 4.
- Relay Post Q 8 d.2.6. — 4.
- Relay Post Q 16 c 2.2. — 4.
- Relay Post P 12 a 0.5. — 3.
- Wagon Post P 12 b.5.0. — 9 (10)
- A.D.S. Q 14 d 0.8 — 34 (20 s.)
- Wagon Post Q 21 b 3.6. — 7
- Relay Post P 18 d 3.0. — 4
- M.D.S. P 10 c 4.4

Arrow labels: Hand carriage of Wheeled stretchers; Wheeled stretchers of Breauville; Motor Ambulance of Breauville; Motor Ambulance by night; Motor Ambulance of Breauville through A.D.S.

Figures to right of Posts indicate R.A.M.C. Personnel.

A. S. Delvasses Lt Col R.A.M.C. T.

Andy 2/1st Home Counties Field Ambce.

Map Reference:—
57 c N.E.
57 c S.E. } 1/20000

CONFIDENTIAL

War Diary
of
Lt-Colonel A.T. FALWASSER R.A.M.C. T.F.
Commanding 4/1st. Home Counties Field Ambulance
from Aug 1st '17 to Aug 31st '17

(Volume 1.)

Army Form C. 2118.

WAR DIARY
or
INTELLIGENCE SUMMARY

(Erase heading not required.)

Instructions regarding War Diaries and Intelligence Summaries are contained in F. S. Regs., Part II. and the Staff Manual respectively. Title Pages will be prepared in manuscript.

Place	Date	Hour	Summary of Events and Information	Remarks and references to Appendices
AVESNES LE COMTE	1.9.17	7.0 p.m.	Division in rest with HQ at FOSSEUX P.10.E.7.5. This Unit has found a Divisional Rest Station at AVESNES LE COMTE. T.16.L.4.6. accommodation is available for 300 sick in a shed, fifteen huts and Hospital marquees. Sick nursing 31. I returned today from leave to UK & rr-assumed Command of Unit from Capt A.H.SAVAGE. Capt A.E.HUXTABLE proceeded on leave to UK.	Met. Gr. "Ungoro" A.1.)
"	2.9.17	6.0 p.m.	Admissions 16. Evacuations —. Discharged to duty —. Remaining 47.	A.1.)
"	3.9.17	6.0 p.m.	Lieut W.H.ORTON returned from 1/1m/c 2/5th London Regt. Admissions 12. Evac'n 3. To duty 5. Remaining 51.	A.1.) A.1.)
"	4.9.17	6.0 p.m.	Admissions 20. Evac'n 1. To duty 8. Rem'g 62.	A.1.)
"	5.9.17	6.0 p.m.	Admissions 20. Evac'n —. To duty —. Rem'g 82.	A.1.)
"	6.9.17	6.0 p.m.	Capt J.R.CHALMERS proceeded on leave to UK. Admissions 35. Evac'n 1. To duty 3. Rem'd 113.	A.1.)
"	7.9.17	6.0 p.m.	Admissions 29. Evac'y 1. To duty —. Rem'd 141.	(.1.)
"	8.9.17	6.0 p.m.	Capt A.H.SAVAGE proceeded on leave to UK. Admissions 21. Evac'n 3. To duty 6. Rem'd 153.	A.1.)

Army Form C. 2118.

WAR DIARY
or
INTELLIGENCE SUMMARY
(Erase heading not required.)

Instructions regarding War Diaries and Intelligence Summaries are contained in F. S. Regs., Part II. and the Staff Manual respectively. Title Pages will be prepared in manuscript.

Place	Date	Hour	Summary of Events and Information	Remarks and references to Appendices
NESNES LE COMTE	9.8.17	6.0 pm	Admissions 33. Evac'd 3. To duty 5. Remg. 170.	A)?
"	10.8.17	6.0 pm	Admissions 13. Evac'd 1. To duty 6. Remg. 180.	A)?
"	11.8.17	6.0 pm	Admissions 18. Evac'd —. To duty 1. Remg. 197.	A)?
"	12.8.17	6.0 pm	Capt. A.E. HUXTABLE rejoined from leave to UK	
			Admissions 14. Evac'd 4. To duty 1. Remg. 201.	A)?
			Adv.143. Private PARSONS B.A. absent without leave since 6.30.	
"	13.8.17	6.0 pm	Admissions 9. Evac'd 2. To duty 20. Remg. 188.	A)?
"	14.8.17	6.0 pm	Admissions 21. Evac'd 3. To duty 13. Remg. 213.	A)?
"	15.8.17	6.0 pm	Admissions 12. Evac'd 4. To duty 13. Remg. 217.	A)?
"	16.8.17	6.0 pm	Admissions 20. Evac'd 1. To duty 20. Remg. 220.	A)?
"	17.8.17	6.0 pm	D.R.S. inspected by D.D.M.S. XVII Corps.	
			Admissions 19. Evac'd 3. To duty 33. Remg. 203.	A)?

Army Form C. 2118.

WAR DIARY
or
INTELLIGENCE SUMMARY

(Erase heading not required.)

Instructions regarding War Diaries and Intelligence Summaries are contained in F.S. Regs., Part II. and the Staff Manual respectively. Title Pages will be prepared in manuscript.

Place	Date	Hour	Summary of Events and Information	Remarks and references to Appendices
AESNES LE COMTE	18.3.17	1.30 pm	Rec'd wire from A.P.M. 5th Div. requesting escort to meet to ABBEVILLE to receive AA8183 Private PARSONS detained there in custody by M.P. Escort despatched.	
"	"	6.0 pm	Admissions 30. Evac. 1. To duty 19. Rem R. 213. A.S.→	
"	19.3.17	6.0 pm	Admissions 37. Evac. — To duty 19. Rem. F. 231. A.S.→	
"	20.3.17	6.0 pm	Admissions 43. Evac. 5. To duty 19. Rem. S. 250. A.S.→	
"			Rec'd verbal instructions from A.D.M.S. that the Division will move into a rest area during the present week & that this D.R.S. will be closed that the site will not be handed over to an incoming Medical Unit. All patients unlikely to be fit to return to duty by 23rd inst. to be evacuated to No. 6 Stationary Hospital FREVANT. A.S.→	
"	21.3.17	6.0 am	Received "Warning Order" by A.D.M.S. 5th Division. A.S.→	Appendix 1.
"	"	10.0 am	In compliance of Para 3 of above order Capt. A.E. HUXTABLE with Serjt. R.N. MARCHANT proceeded by Motor Ambulance to IZEL LE HAMEAU and thence to WINNEZEELE.	
			Received D.A.D.R.T. III & arranged that a special train on interruption cycle of a commodity of 16 stretcher & 75 sitting cases is to be at this front siding at two succeeding days at 1.0 pm for transition of sick to No. 6 Stationary Hospital FREVANT. A.S.→	

Army Form C. 2118.

WAR DIARY
or
INTELLIGENCE SUMMARY

(Erase heading not required.)

Instructions regarding War Diaries and Intelligence Summaries are contained in F. S. Regs., Part II. and the Staff Manual respectively. Title Pages will be prepared in manuscript.

Place	Date	Hour	Summary of Events and Information	Remarks and references to Appendices
AVESNES LE COMTE	21.10.17	6.0 p.m	Capt. T.S. WARD R.A.M.C. reported for duty from 4/4/c 2/10th London Regt. taken on strength. Lieut. W.H. ORTON R.A.M.C. proceeded for duty 4/4/c 2/10th London Regt. struck off strength. Admissions 43. Evac. 46. To duty 60. Rem S. 16a. Rem 8. 16a.	
"	22.10.17	11.0 a.m	Capt. HUNTER R.A.M.C. & 6 other ranks R.A.M.C. formerly #4 Division reported under orders of DDMS XIII Corps to take charge of site selected on departure of that Unit & until the arrival of another field Ambulance. Recd. order from ADMS that business of unit completion of move this Unit will be proceeded with. 17th Fd Amb. will be under orders of OC 1/1st Bn. Red J instructions for move of 1/1/st Bn. Admissions 45 Evac. 10a. To duty 40. Rem t. 65.	Appendix 2. ADS ADS
"	"	6.0 p.m	Admissions 37 Evac. 20 To duty 30. Rem t. No A.D.S.	
"	23.10.17	6.0 p.m	Recd. order from ADMS "The officer in charge of No 3 A.D.S will assemble at IZEL LE HAMEAU at 10 noon 24th inst with personnel & transport. Names of Convoy in charge of an Officer to be detailed by OC 4/1st IFO3. Amb. to the Hour are reporting in dressed at ADMS Office A. Bo. & v. 6." Capt. H.C. OKILL detailed for above duty. Recd. 17x 24 Bde order No 54	Map Ref etc Sketches Appendix 3. ADS

Army Form C. 2118.

WAR DIARY
or
INTELLIGENCE SUMMARY

(Erase heading not required.)

Place	Date	Hour	Summary of Events and Information	Remarks and references to Appendices
AVESNES LE COMTE	24/7/17	11.30 a.m	Capt. H.C. O'KILL proceeded in charge of No 6 Motor Ambulance Con to IZEL LE HAMEAU thence to view area in charge of Motor Ambulance Cars of the Division. Field Ambulance is now closed & evacuations are being dealt with by No Section 17th Division.	A.D.?
"	25/7/17	2.30 a.m	Transport paraded marched under command of Capt WARD to ARRAS	A.D.?
"		4.0 a.m	R.A.M.C. paraded marched to ARRAS.	A.D.?
A.23.c.2.9 (Sheet 20)		4.0 p.m	Unit with transport entrained at ARRAS at 9.5 a.m today and detrained at GODEWAERSVELDE at 6.0 p.m, marched by ABEELE - POPERINGHE - ELVERDINGHE Rd. to A.23.c.2.9 XVIII Corps Main Dressing Station, reported on arrival to Capt H.S. MCL RORIE D.S.O. R.A.M.C. at 10.30 p.m. R.A.M.C. personnel accommodated in marquees at C.M.D.S. & transport parked in adjoining field.	Map Reference Sheet 27 & 20.
"	26/7/17	6.0 p.m	Heldinglin equipt. tents have been pitched in field adjoining C.M.D.S. & unit is now accommodated in these. C.M.D.S. is commanded by Lt.Col D. RORIE D.S.O. R.A.M.C. T.F. and staffed by one complete tent division of 45 S Midland 3 Amb (48th Div) two tent sub divisions of 1/2" Highland 3 Amb (51st Div) and one tent sub division of 3 Amb (11th Div) & one tent sub division of ... two complete tent sub divisions in all. Lieut. L.H. RODOLPH reported for duty with unit. Division at A.D.S. at C.25.d.3.3 Re-formed from leave to United Kingdom	Sheet 20. A.D.?

O.32? Wt. W14957/M99. 750,000 1/16 J.B.C. S & A.* Forms/C.2118/12.

Army Form C. 2118.

WAR DIARY
or
INTELLIGENCE SUMMARY

(Erase heading not required.)

Instructions regarding War Diaries and Intelligence Summaries are contained in F. S. Regs., Part II. and the Staff Manual respectively. Title Pages will be prepared in manuscript.

Place	Date	Hour	Summary of Events and Information	Remarks and references to Appendices
A.23.c.2.9	27.8.17	7.0 p.m.	Received operation order No. 26 by RAMS 59th Division.	Appendix 4.
"	26.8.17	2.30 a.m.	Received line from ADMS 59th Division being above order into operation	A.D.→
"	"	12.0 noon	Part personnel of 6th division posted for duty at CMDS to relieve similar number of personnel of 1/3rd S. Midland 3. Amb & Hhligston equivalent changed over.	A.D.→
"	29.8.17	2.0 p.m.	Remainder of personnel posted for duty to CMDS to complete relief of 6th division of 1/3rd S. Midland 3. Amb. Lieut G.H. RODOLPH rejoined from duty with 58th division at ADS at C.25.d.3.0. Bearer subdivisions 3 Officers and rank & file with 3 motorbus wagons, one bit ambulance wagon to report to OC 2/3 1st C3 Amb for duty in the line. OC 2/3 1st C3 Amb > 5 Motor Motor Cars (Sidley-Berry) have reported to OC No 24 MAC at C.HB.T for duty.	Map Refs. Nieuw-... A.D.→
"	30.8.17	4.0 p.m.	Bus dispense to rank & file of Bearer division proceeded en route to 1/1st C3 Amb at C.25.d.3.0 to act as guides to remainder of bearer division when present at a later time today.	
"	"	5.0 p.m.	Remainder of Bearer division proceeded to C.25.d.3.0 to report to OC 1/3 1st C3 Amb for duty.	
"	"	6.0 p.m.	Capt C.P. SYMONDS RAMC (T.C.) posted to this unit, reported for duty.	A.D. 3rd... Any r/f Home quarters > Amb

J. Shallcross Lt Col
RAMC
Comdg

B.E.F.

SUMMARY OF MEDICAL WAR DIARIES OF 2/1st Home Counties F.A. 58th Div.

18th Corps. 5th Army. from 25/8/17.
19th Corps, 29/9/17.

Western Front Operations - Aug-Sept., 1917.

Officer Commanding - Lt. Col. A.T. Falwasser.

SUMMARISED UNDER THE FOLLOWING HEADINGS:-

Phase "D" 1 - Passchendaele Operations - "July-Nov. 1917."
(a) - ### Operations commencing - July 1917.

B.E.F.

1.

<u>2/1st Home Counties F.A. 58th Div.</u>   Western Front.
                                          Aug.-Sept. 1917.
<u>18th Corps. 5th Army.</u>

<u>Officer Commanding - Lt.Col. A.T. FALWASSER.</u>

<u>PHASE "D" 1. Passchendaele Operations - "July-Nov. 1917.</u>

    (a) - <u>Operations commencing - July 1917.</u>

<u>Headquarters at A23.C.2.9. (Sheet 28).</u>

Aug. 25th.   <u>Moves and Transfer.</u>   Unit transferred with 58th Division from 17th Corps, III Army to 18th Corps V. Army and moved to A23. C.2.9 18th C.M.D.S.

<u>Medical Arrangements.</u> Portion of C.M.D.S. taken over.

31st.   <u>Moves Detachment.</u> Bearer Division to 2/3rd H.C.F.A. at C.25.d.3.0. for duty in the line.

B.E.F.

1.

<u>2/1st Home Counties F.A. 58th Div.</u>   Western Front.
                                         Aug.-Sept. 1917.
<u>18th Corps. 5th Army.</u>

Officer Commanding - Lt.Col. A.T. FALWASSER.

<u>PHASE "D" 1. Passchendaele Operations - "July-Nov. 1917."</u>

   (a) - <u>Operations commencing - July 1917.</u>

<u>Headquarters at A23.C.2.9. (Sheet 28).</u>

Aug. 25th.   <u>Moves and Transfer.</u>   Unit transferred with 58th Division from 17th Corps III Army to 18th Corps V. Army and moved to A23. C.2.9 18th C.M.D.S.

<u>Medical Arrangements.</u>   Portion of C.M.D.S. taken over.

31st.   <u>Moves Detachment.</u> Bearer Division to 2/3rd H.C.F.A. C.25.d.3.0. for duty in the line.

11/6
10.11.97

CONFIDENTIAL

War Diary
of
Lieut Colonel A.T. FALWASSER RAMC. T.F.
Commanding 2/1st Wessex Counties Field Ambulance

from 1.9.17 to 30.9.17

(Volume 1)

COMMITTEE FOR THE
MEDICAL HISTORY OF THE WAR
Date -5 NOV.1917

WAR DIARY or INTELLIGENCE SUMMARY

Army Form C. 2118.

(Erase heading not required.)

Place	Date	Hour	Summary of Events and Information	Remarks and references to Appendices
POPERINGHE — ELVERDINGHE A.23.C.3.9 (Sheet 20)	1.9.16	6.0 a.m.	Field Ambulance of this Field Ambulance arrived at XVIII Corps Main Dressing Station which it is running in conjunction with 1/2 Highland F.A. Lt-Col D. RORIE DSO RAMC 1/2 Highland in command. Personnel establishment of the Unit is shared by Highland to that MDS. Acts for duty in the lines. Capts Scott & Bell by 51st (Highland) Division on the night. Two Advanced Dressing Stations are established on the W. front 2 YSER Canal and for each Bde front at respectively ESSEX FARM C.25.a.3.0 and DUNALLON C.20.d.3.3.	M. of Refugees [illeg] 1/40,000
	2.	6.0 p.m.	Casualties of 51st Div. for 24 hours ending 12 noon dealt with at Advanced H. Bns. are Officers 1; Other ranks 11 (including Guard – nil) To CCS. Officers 0; Other ranks 10 [illeg]	
			Casualties Officers Nil. OR 20 (including Guard – nil) To CCS. OR 23. To duty. OR 7. [illeg]	
	3.	6.0 p.m.	Casualties Officers Nil. OR 9 (including Guard 1.) To CCS Officers 1; OR 7. To duty Officers 1; But OR 2. [illeg]	
	4.	6.0 p.m.	Casualties O.1. OR 17 (including Guard OR 10) To CCS OR 17. To duty O.1. Capt C.P. SYMONDS offd to the National change of 290 Bde RFA host H.BLYTH 2/a Hunter Rgt. [illeg]	
	5.	6.0 p.m.	Casualties O.1. OR 12 (including Guard OR 2) To CCS. O.1. OR 11. To duty OR 1. [illeg]	
	6.	6.0 p.m.	Casualties OR 23 (including Guard 2) To C.C.S. OR 23. [illeg]	

Army Form C. 2118.

WAR DIARY
or
INTELLIGENCE SUMMARY

(Erase heading not required.)

Instructions regarding War Diaries and Intelligence Summaries are contained in F. S. Regs, Part II. and the Staff Manual respectively. Title Pages will be prepared in manuscript.

Place	Date	Hour	Summary of Events and Information	Remarks and references to Appendices
POPERINGHE — ELVERDINGHE Rd A.23.c.2.9	Sept 7	6.0 pm	Casualties. O.1. OR 11 (includes Guard OR 2) To CCS. O.1. OR 11.	Map Ref see Sheet 28 A.I.D 1/40000 A.I.D
"	8	6.0 pm	Casualties OR 10. (includes Guard 4) To CCS. OR 10.	A.I.D
"	9	6.0 pm	Capt. E.S. CUTHBERT RAMC promoted to T/3 H.E.D. Nut for duty. Casualties. O.3 OR 39 (includes Guard O.1. OR 22) To CCS. O.3 OR 32	A.I.D
"	10	6.0 pm	Casualties O.1. OR 35 (includes Guard OR 7) To CCS. O.1 OR 35	A.I.(-)
"	11	6.0 pm	Casualties O.3 OR 39 (includes Guard OR 11) To CCS. O.2 OR 30. Died. O.1 OR 1.	A.I.S
"	12	6.0 pm	Casualties OR 27 (includes Guard 16) To CCS. OR 22. Died. OR 5	A.I.D
"	13	6.0 pm	Casualties O.1. OR 60. (includes Guard 16) To CCS. O.1. OR 53. To duty OR 8 Died OR 2.	A.I.D
"	14	6.0 pm	Lieut. G.H. RODOLPH RAMC T.C. proceeded to England on termination of his contract. Casualties OR 26 (includes Guard 11) To CCS OR 25. Died OR 1.	A.I.(-) A.I.D

WAR DIARY or INTELLIGENCE SUMMARY

Army Form C. 2118.

(Erase heading not required.)

Place	Date	Hour	Summary of Events and Information	Remarks and references to Appendices
POPERINGHE ELVERDINGHE Rd A.12.c.8.1	Sept 15	6.0 pm	Casualties. O.2, O.R 9 (includes General I). To C.C.S. O.2, O.R 2. To duty O.R 1.	Mob. Refer Sheet 28 11/40000
	16	6.0 pm	Casualties. O.2, O.R 15. To C.C.S. O.2, O.R 15.	ADS
	17	6.0 pm	Lieut & Quartermaster H.G. ALDISS RAMC T.F. reported for duty in relief of Capt & Quartermaster H.E. O'KILL RAMC T.F. Lieut B.P. BURPEE M.O.R.C. (U.S.A.) joined for duty. Casualties O.2, O.R 12. To C.C.S. O.2, O.R 12.	ADS
	18	6.0 pm	Casualties O.R ix. To C.C.S. O.R 4.	
			Captain & Quartermaster H.E. O'KILL RAMC T.F. left & proceed to England to report to D.D.M.S. Northern Command for duty.	ADS
	19	6.0 pm	Received Medical transports No 6 by ADMS 50 Division the remnant of Horses & mules.	
			Casualties. O.1, O.R 9. To C.C.S. O.1, O.R 7.	ADS
	20	6.0 pm	An attack was carried out at 6.40 a.m today on wide front but all objective being found in enemy trenches protected to …. of … was the … Casualties to Brs this the H. Bat for 24 hours to 12 noon O.1 O.R 2. To C.C.S. O.R 1.	ADS
			Set 3 brand Ambulances attached to the Unit proceeded for duty to Brandhoek ADS	ADS

Army Form C. 2118.

WAR DIARY
or
INTELLIGENCE SUMMARY

(Erase heading not required.)

Instructions regarding War Diaries and Intelligence Summaries are contained in F. S. Regs., Part II. and the Staff Manual respectively. Title Pages will be prepared in manuscript.

Place	Date	Hour	Summary of Events and Information	Remarks and references to Appendices
POPERINGHE— ELVERDINGHE Rd. A.23.C.3.9.	Sept 21	6.0 p.m	Casualties this day 11 B.T. during 24 hours ending noon today 5 Officers 12. O.R. 112 Evacuated to C.C.S. Officers 12. O.R. 112	Mef Reference Sheet 28 1/40000 A)
"	22	6.0 p.m	Casualties thro' this C.M.D.S. Officers 7. O.R. 95. To C.C.S. 0.9 O.R. 94. Died O.R. 1.	A)
"	23	6.0 p.m	Casualties to Div. 0.3 O.R. 80 To CCS 0.3 O.R. 77 To duty 3. O.R.	A)
"	24	6.0 p.m	Capt. J.R.CHALMERS RAMC. T. proceeded for duty 1/m/c 2/4th London Regt. Ambulance wagons (lines) returned from duty at Divisional Advanced Dressing Station. Casualties to Div. 0.2 O.R. 3. To CCS 0.2 O.R. 30	A)
"	25	6.0 p.m	Received 'Medical' transports No. 3' by A.S.H.S. 50 Division Casualties to Div. O. nil O.R. 21. To CCS O.R. 21	A)
"	26	6.0 p.m	Horse Ambulance wagons proceeded this morning to report at 50 A.T.S. for duty at Divisional A.D.S. Attack this morning on Broenink front. Succesful All stretcher bearers proved. Casualties to Div Officers 1 today. Officers 4 O.R. 34 To CCS O. 4 O.R. 33 Received 'Operation Order No. 12' by A.S.H.S. 50 Div Received 'Administrative Instructions' issued with 50 Div order No. 60	Appendix 1. A)

WAR DIARY
or
INTELLIGENCE SUMMARY

(Erase heading not required.)

Army Form C. 2118.

Place	Date	Hour	Summary of Events and Information	Remarks and references to Appendices
POPERINGHE – ELVERDINGHE Rd.	4/8/17	6.0 p.m	Received '173 Infantry Brigade Operation order No. 42' and '173 Infantry Bde Administrative Instruction No. 1a'	Appendix 2
A.23.c.3.9			Casualties to Date. O.R. 3 O.R. 81 (including period a) To CCS. O.R. 3 A.D.S	
	28	10.0 noon	Moved over to 1/c South Midland Field Ambr complete personnel & equipment with horses. Capt J.S. WARD reported to Advanced Dressing Station DUNALLOW for duty with 2/3rd Division.	
			Capt H.E. PALMER reported for duty with this Unit. Casualties 1/58th Division through Capts H.S. Bury 28 hours ending noon today. O.R. 12 O.R. 56 To CCS O.R. 54 Died O.R. 2 A.D.S	
	29	9.0 a.m	Eq. Transport and Capt H.E. PALMER marched to join marching portion of '173 Inf Bde. front to proceed by road to rear area at RECQUES. Left to halt night file at WORMHOUDT.	
			Hut & O.H. H.G. ALDISS with 5 other ranks proceeded by motor lorry 3rd supply column. In two advance party to report in first instance area command RECQUES & thence to LOSTE BARNE to take up billets. A.D.S	
	30	6.30 p.m	Unit has transport directly proceeded by road entrained at PROVEN to proceed to PESELHOEK to AUDRIQUES for new area. Strength 2 officers 139 other ranks A.D. horses K.R.R. R.A.M.C.	

B.E.F.

SUMMARY OF MEDICAL WAR DIARIES OF 2/1st Home Counties F.A. 58th Div.

18th Corps. 5th Army. from 25/8/17.

19th Corps, 29/9/17.

Western Front Operations - Aug-Sept., 1917.

Officer Commanding - Lt. Col. A.T. Falwasser.

SUMMARISED UNDER THE FOLLOWING HEADINGS:-

Phase "D" 1 - Passchendaele Operations - "July-Nov. 1917."

(a) - Operations commencing - July 1917.

Sept. 1st-19th.   Operations R.A.M.C.   Routine at C.M.D.S.

Casualties   )   Admitted 58th Div. 1st-19th. 21 &
Casualties Gas.)   404 wounded including 1 & 109 gassed.

20th.   Operations.   Attack commenced 6.40 a.m. on whole Corps front - all objectives gained and enemy positions pentrated to depth of 1,000 yards.

21st.   Casualties.   Admitted C.M.D.S. 58th Div. up to noon 12 & 118 wounded.

22nd.   Casualties.   Admitted C.M.D.S. 58th Div. 9 & 95 wounded.
23rd.   "   "   "   "   "   3 & 80 wounded.
24th.   "   "   "   "   "   2 & 38 wounded.
25th.   "   "   "   "   "   0 & 21 wounded.

26th.   Operations.   Attack on 58th Div. front - all objectives gained.

        Casualties.) Admitted C.M.D.S. 58th Div. 4 & 34 wounded.
27th.   "   )   "   "   "   3 & 81 wounded
            "   Gas.) including 0 & 4 gassed.

B.E.F.

2/1st Home Counties F.A. 58th Div.   Western Front.
                                     September 1917.
18th Corps. 5th ARMY.

Officer Commanding - Lt.Col. A.T. FALWASSER.

19th Corps from 28th Sept. 1917.

PHASE "D" 1. - Passchendaele Operations -" July-Nov.1917."
         (a) - Operations commencing July 1st 1917.

Headquarters at A23.C.2.9. (Sheet 28).

Sept. 28th.   Casualties.   Admitted C.M.D.S. 58th Div. 0 & 56 wounded.

    29th.   Moves and Transfer.   To 19th Corps V. Army and moved
to Lostebarne.

           Appendices.   1.   A.D.M.S. 58th Div. Operation Order
                                   27. dated 26/9/1917.
                              2.   173rd Infantry Brigade Adm.
                                   Instructions 14. dated 26/9/1917.

Sept. 1st-19th. Operations R.A.M.C. Routine at C.M.D.S.
Casualties) Admitted 58th Div. 1st-19th. 21 &
Casualties Gas.) 404 wounded including 1 & 109 gassed.

20th. Operations. Attack commenced 6.40 a.m. on whole Corps front - all objectives gained and enemy positions pentrated to depth of 1,000 yards.

21st. Casualties. Admitted C.M.D.S. 58th Div. up to noon 12 & 118 wounded.

22nd. Casualties. Admitted C.M.D.S. 58th Div. 9 & 95 wounded.
23rd. " " " " " 3 & 80 wounded.
24th. " " " " " 2 & 38 wounded.
25th. " " " " " 0 & 21 wounded.

26th. Operations. Attack on 58th Div. front - all objectives gained.
Casualties.) Admitted C.M.D.S. 58th Div. 4 & 34 wounded.
27th. ") " " " 3 & 81 wounded
" Gas.) including 0 & 4 gassed.

B.E.F. 2.

2/1st Home Counties F.A. 58th Div.   Western Front.
                                      September 1917.
18th Corps. 5th ARMY.

Officer Commanding - Lt.Col. A.T. FALWASSER.

19th Corps from 28th Sept. 1917.

PHASE "D" 1. - Passchendaele Operations -" July-Nov.1917."
       (a) - Operations commencing July 1st 1917.

Headquarters at A23.C.2.9.   (Sheet 28).

Sept. 28th.   Casualties.   Admitted C.M.D.S. 58th Div. 0 & 56 wounded.

29th.   Moves and Transfer.   To 19th Corps V. Army and moved
to Lostebarne.

Appendices.   1.   A.D.M.S. 58th Div. Operation Order
                        27. dated 26/9/1917.
                   2.   173rd Infantry Brigade Adm.
                        Instructions 14. dated 26/9/1917.

S E C R E T.

Appendix 1.

Copy No. 1

O P E R A T I O N   O R D E R   No. 27.

by
Colonel J.W.H.Houghton, A.M.S.,
A.D.M.S., 58th Division.

Map Refs. CALAIS 13.
HAZEBROUCK 5A.

26/9/1917.

1. The 58th Division will be relieved by the 48th Division in the right sector of the Corps Front on the night of the 27/28th September 1917.
   On completion of relief the 58th Division (less Artillery and Pioneers) will move to the RECQUES Area.

2. The 2/3rd Home Counties Field Ambulance will be relieved on the routes of evacuation on the 28th instant by the 1/3rd South Midland Field Ambulance.
   The 2/2nd Home Counties Field Ambulance will be relieved at the Advanced Dressing Station on the 28th instant by the 1/3rd South Midland Field Ambulance.
   The 2/1st Home Counties Field Ambulance will be relieved on the 28th instant by the 1/1st South Midland Field Ambulance.
   The whole of the R.A.M.C. personnel at present administering the Corps Walking Wounded Collecting Post will be relieved by the 1/1st South Midland Field Ambulance on the 28th instant.

3. On relief the 2/2nd and 2/3rd Home Counties Field Ambulances will concentrate at GWENT FARM and will remain there until the 30th instant on which date they will entrain for the new area.
   The 2/1st H.C. Field Ambulance will remain parked at Corps Main Dressing Station until the 30th instant, on which date this Field Ambulance will entrain for the new area.
   Field Ambulances will be under orders of G.O.Cs. Brigades for the move as under.
   2/1st H.C.Field Ambulance will move with the 173rd Infantry Brigade.
   2/2nd H.C. Field Ambulance will move with the 173rd Infantry Brigade.
   2/3rd H.C. Field Ambulance will move with the 175th Infantry Brigade.

4. The Transport of the 2/1st, 2/2nd and 2/3rd Home Counties Field Ambulances will march to the new area under Brigade arrangements.
   Three lorries (1 per Field Ambulance) have been allotted and will report at GWENT FARM at 7 a.m. on the 29th instant.
   Detailed instructions as to destination will be given to the drivers.

5. Detailed orders as to entraining and marching will be issued by Brigades.

6. The Motor Ambulances of the 58th Division will move with the Division and will rejoin their respective Field Ambulances in the new area.

7. Officer Commanding 2/3rd and Officer Commanding 2/2nd Home Counties Field Ambulances will each detail one Ford Ambulance to be handed over to Officer Commanding 1/3rd South Midland Field Ambulance for use whilst in the line.

Operation Order No.27.
Sheet 2.
----

8. Officer Commanding 2/1st Home Counties Field Ambulance will be prepared to leave behind 3 Officers and sufficient personnel to maintain the Field Ambulances of the 48th Division at War Establishment.

9. All stores in excess of mobilisation equipment, oxygen cylinders etc. will be handed over to the incoming Field Ambulances, receipts taken and copies forwarded to this Office.
Wheeled stretchers will similarly be handed over.

10. On arrival in the new area the 2/2nd H.C. Field Ambulance will proceed to LICQUES and will there take over and administer the Corps Rest Station.
The 2/1st H.C. Field Ambulance will proceed to ~~GRAS PAZELLE~~ LOSTEBARNE and will there remain parked.
The 2/3rd H.C. Field Ambulance will proceed to BLANC PIGNON and will there remain parked.
Sick of the Brigades will be collected by their respective Field Ambulances and transported to the Corps Rest Station.

11. All details of relief will be arranged between Commanding Officers concerned.

12. Advanced parties (not exceeding 1 Officer and 5 men) from each Field Ambulance will be sent to take over the new sites.

13. A.D.M.S. Office will close at BRAKE CAMP on the 28th instant at 10 a.m. and will reopen at ZUTKERQUE on the same day.

14. Completion of reliefs to be wired to A.D.M.S.

15. ACKNOWLEDGE.

Issued at _____ p.m.

S.Sauray Graves. Capt
for Colonel, A.M.S.,
A.D.M.S., 58th Division.

```
Copy No. 1 to O.C., 2/1st H.C. Field Ambulance.
  "   "  2    O.C., 2/2nd H.C. Field Ambulance.
  "   "  3    O.C., 2/3rd H.C. Field Ambulance.
  "   "  4    173rd Infantry Brigade.
  "   "  5    174th Infantry Brigade.
  "   "  6    175th Infantry Brigade.
  "   "  7    A.D.M.S., 48th Division.
  "   "  8    "G" 58th Division.
  "   "  9    "Q" 58th Division.
  "   " 10    C.R.E., 58th Division.
  "   " 11    C.R.A., 58th Division.
  "   " 12    Signals 58th Division.
  "   " 13    A.P.M. 58th Division.
  "   " 14    S.S.D. 58th Division.
  "   " 15    O.C., 58th Divisional Train.
  "   " 16    D.D.M.S., XVIII Corps.
  "   " 17    D.M.S., Fifth Army.
  "   " 18    O.C., Corps Main Dressing Station.
  "   " 19    O.C., Corps Walking Wounded Collecting Post.
  "   " 20 & 21 War Diary.
  "   " 22 & 23 File.
```

Secret   A.H.A

ADMINISTRATIVE INSTRUCTIONS
ISSUED WITH
58th (LONDON) DIVISION ORDER No. 60.

1. TRAINS.

    173rd and 175th Brigade Groups will move by tactical trains on the 30th instant. One set of four tactical trains is allotted to each Brigade Group.

    For detail and accommodation of trains see Appendix 1.

2. ENTRAINING STATION.

    Not yet settled, but probably as follows:-

        Personnel Trains BRIELEN.

        Omnibus Trains   PESELHOEK.

3. DETRAINING STATION.

    Probably AUDRIQUES.

4. TIME OF ARRIVAL AT ENTRAINING STATION.

    Three hours before departure of train in case of Omnibus Trains.

    1½ hours before departure in case of personnel trains.

5. ENTRAINING AND DETRAINING OFFICERS.

    Each Brigade will appoint a Brigade Entraining and Detraining Officer.

6. Time of Departure of trains is not yet settled.

7. Duration of journey about 2½ hours.

8. SUPPLIES.

    Two days' rations will be issued to all units on the 28th for consumption on 29th and 30th. (174th Brigade has already had double issue on 25th)

    The marching portion of each Brigade will be accompanied by its A.S.C. Company.

9. LORRIES.

    Programme of lorries is attached. Appendix 2.

- 2 -

10. ADVANCE PARTIES.

Advance parties should proceed on the lorries allotted for carriage of baggage on programme. They should report in first instance to Area Commandant RECQUES.

11. NEW AREA.

Disposition of Division in new area will be as shown in Appendix 3.

12. RAILHEAD.

WATTEN. First day of drawing for 58th Division 30th Sept.

13. The 2/2nd Field Ambulance will be under the orders of the G.O.C., 173rd Inf. Bde. during the move to new Area.

Transport of 2/2nd Field Ambulance will proceed with marching portion of 173rd Brigade and personnel will be accommodated in one of the 173rd Brigade personnel trains.

The 173rd Brigade will therefore have both the 2/1st and 2/2nd Field Ambulances under their orders for the move.

14. Employment Company will travel under the orders of the G.O.C., 175th Brigade. The O.C. Employment Company will notify the 175th Brigade direct by the 27th instant numbers requiring accommodation in train.

40 men of the Signal Company will also be accommodated in train by the 175th Brigade.

15. D.A.D.O.S. will move under his own arrangements on the 28th instant.

Sd. A. McNALTY

Lt.Colonel,
A.A. & Q.M.G.,
58th Division.

26/9/17.

Copies to:-
A.D.C. to G.O.C.	D.M.G.O.	A.D.M.S.
173rd Inf. Bde.	214th M.G.Coy.	Pioneer Battn.
174th do	A.P.M.	Camp Comdt. D.H.Q.
175th do	O.C., Train	O.C., D.S.C.
B.G.R.A.	S.S.O.	O.C., 58th A.S.P.
C.R.E.	D.A.D.O.S.	Capt. L.H.Marten.
O.C., Signals	O.C. Employment Coy.	

SECRET

Appendix 2

173RD INFANTRY BRIGADE

Administrative Instruction No. 14

Issued with reference to 173rd Inf. Bde. Order No. 42

---oOo---

26th Sept. 1917.

The Brigade Group, less marching portion, will proceed by train on 30th September in accordance with attached Table "A".

The marching portion will consist of Supply Wagons and transport not detailed in Table "A". They will proceed by march route from present wagon lines on 29th September, under the command of Captain L.S.E.Page, 2/2nd London Regt.

Staging Area for transport – WORMHOUDT.

---oOo---

ENTRAINING AND DETRAINING OFFICERS.

The following officers are detailed as Brigade representatives :-

ENTRAINING
  Major G.H.Edwards, 2/3rd London Regt. at BRIELEN
    (personnel)
  Lieut. C.H.Roberts, Bde.Transport Offr., at PESELHOEK
    (transport).
    These officers will report to R.T.O. at stations named
    (a) Personnel Trains- 2 hours before departure of train.
    (b) Transport Trains- 3½ " " " "
    and will travel on the last trains.

DETRAINING.
  Major J.A.Miller, 2/2nd Lon.Regt. at AUDRIQUES.
  This officer will travel by the first train proceeding either from BRIELEN or PESELHOEK, and report to the R.T.O. at AUDRIQUES

Each unit entraining will send a representative forward to report to the Brigade representative for instructions, a quarter of an hour before his unit's arrival.. This officer will have in his possession entraining states (in triplicate) which will be handed to Brigade representative, who will pass one copy to R.T.O., forward one to H.Q., 58th Division, on completion of move, and retain the third copy.

Each unit will detail an officer to act as detraining officer, who will travel in the first train in each case.

LOADING PARTIES

As per Table "A".

HOUR OF ARRIVAL AT ENTRAINING STATIONS.

Loading parties, horses, and transport will arrive at Entraining Station 3 hours before the departure of each train. Remainder of troops 1½ hours before departure of each train.
  No horses or vehicles are to travel on Coaching Stock trains.
  Breast ropes will be required for Omnibus trains.
O.C. train will detail piquets at all stops for each end of the train to prevent troops leaving. Units will arrange for L.G.Limbers to remain near detraining station to await arrival of Lewis Guns, which are being carried on the Coaching Stock trains.
  Water carts will be entrained full.

2.

QUARTERS. The Brigade will be distributed in the new area as follows:-

    Brigade Headquarters .... NORDAUSQUES
    2/1st London Regt. .... LAPAUNE
    2/2nd London Regt. .... LOUCHES
    2/3rd London Regt. .... NORDAUSQUES
    2/4th London Regt. .... ZOUAFQUES
    173rd L.T.M.Battery .... AUTINQUES
    206th Machine Gun Coy. .... AUTINQUES
    Brigade Labour Coy. .... LAPAUNE
    504 Field Coy. R.E. .... LOUCHES

ADVANCE PARTIES. Advance billeting parties consisting of 2/Lt. C.J.Graham, 2/4th London Regt. as Brigade representative, and one officer and a small party from each battalion, will proceed by lorries on 27th inst. at 7 a.m. from DAMBRE CAMP, reporting to Area Commandant, RECQUES, on arrival.

  L.T.M.B. and 206th M.G.Co. advance parties will travel on Bde. Hd.Qtrs. lorries.

  Sufficient rations should be taken.

LORRIES. Two lorries per battalion and two for Bde. H.Q., L.T.M.B., and 206th M.G.Coy. will report at transport lines at 7 a.m. on 27th inst., and when loaded will proceed direct to the new area.

  Baggage wagons will report to units' wagon lines on the evening of the 28th inst.

  510 H.T.Coy. A.S.C. will travel with marching portion of Brigade.

RATIONS. Two days' rations will be issued to all units on 28th inst. for consumption on 29th and 30th. Rations will be delivered to units in the new area on the night of arrival for consumption the following day.

RAILHEAD. WATTEN. First day of drawing, 30th September.

H.Garraway

Captain,
Staff Captain,
173rd Infantry Brigade

SECRET.   Copy No... 23....

173RD INFANTRY BRIGADE ORDER NUMBER 42.

Reference Map Sheets:-
    BELGIUM 28 N.W.   -   1/20,000.
    HAZEBROUCK.   -   1/100,000.
    CALAIS.   -   1/10,000.

---oOo---

26th Sept. 1917.

---

1. The 58th Division (Less Artillery) is being relieved in the Line by 48th Division (Less Artillery) on night 27/28th September, 1917.

2. On completion of relief the 58th Division will concentrate in the RECQUES Area.
(Ref. Map A.2. & A.3.). 173rd Infantry Brigade moving in accordance with attached Move Tables "A" and "B".

3. Captain L.S.E. Page, 2/2nd Bn. London Regt. will be in charge of Brigade Transport.

4. During the move the Brigade Group will be composed as follows:-

    2/1st Bn. London Regt.
    2/2nd Bn. London Regt.
    2/3rd Bn. London Regt.
    2/4th Bn. London Regt.
    206th Machine Gun Coy.
    173rd L. T. M. Batty.
    504th Field Coy. R.E.

5. On arrival in RECQUES Area 58th Division will be administered by XIX Corps.

Issued to Signals at 12.30pm

A.G. Sluarman Captain,
Brigade Major,
173rd Infantry Brigade.

Copy No.
1. 2/1st Bn. London Regt.
2. 2/2nd Bn. London Regt.
3. 2/3rd Bn. London Regt.
4. 2/4th Bn. London Regt.
5. 173rd L. T. M. Batty.
6. 206th Machine Gun Coy.
7. 504th Field Coy. R. E.
8. 510th Company A.S.C.
9. 174th Infantry Brigade.
10. 175th Infantry Brigade.
11. "G" 58th Division.
12. "A" & "Q" 58th Division.
13. S. S. O.
14. Brigade Major for G.O.C.
15. Staff Captain.
16. Brigade Signalling Officer.
17. Brigade Transport Officer.
18. Brigade Intelligence.
19. War Diary.
20. War Diary.
21. File.
23. 2/1st Home Counties Fld Amb.

MOVE TABLE "A".

SERIAL NO.	DATE.	UNIT.	FROM.	TO.	REMARKS.
1.	27th. Sept.	2/3rd Bn. Lon. Regt.	REIGERSBURG.	BRAKE CAMP.	Move to be completed by 10 a.m.
2.	"	Brigade Headquarters	DAMBRE CAMP.	BRAKE CAMP.	Leave DAMBRE 4 p.m. 9.5 a.m
	"	2/1st Bn. Lon. Regt.	DAMBRE CAMP.	BRAKE CAMP.	Leave DAMBRE 4.10 p.m. 7.20
	"	2/4th Bn. Lon. Regt.	DAMBRE CAMP.	BRAKE CAMP.	Leave DAMBRE 4.25 p.m. 7.35
	"	Labour Company.	DAMBRE CAMP.	BRAKE CAMP.	March 200 yards in rear of 2/4th Bn. Lon. Regt.
	"	173rd L. T. M. Batty.	DAMBRE CAMP.	BRAKE CAMP.	Leave DAMBRE 4.40 p.m. 7.50
					INTERVALS:- 200 yards between Companies. All Units march via POTTENHOEK - X ROADS H.3.c.0.4. - CHEMIN MILITAIRE.
	27/28 Sept.	2/2nd Bn. Lon. Regt.	LINE.	REIGERSBURG.	On relief.
	"	206th Machine Gun Co.	LINE.	BRAKE CAMP.	By Bus - not to vacate positions before 8.30 p.m.
	"	2/2nd Bn. Lon. Regt. will move to BRAKE CAMP under orders to be issued later.			

MOVE TABLE "B".

SERIAL.	DATE.	UNIT.	FROM.	TO.	REMARKS.
1.	29th. Sept.	Brigade Transport (Less portion moving by train)	DAMBRE FARM.	WORMHOUDT AREA.	By March Route via VLAMERTINGHE SWITCH ROAD - WATOU - HOUTKERQUE To be clear of VLAMERTINGHE by 8.15 a.m.
2.	30th. Sept.	Brigade Group.	BRAKE CAMP.	ECRDAUSQUES AREA.	By rail.
3.	30th. Sept.	Serial Number 1.	WORMHOUDT AREA.	NORDAUSQUES AREA.	By March Route via. ZEGGERS -CAPPEL and WATTEN. Start 8 a.m.

NOTE:- In Serials 1 and 3, Brigade Transport:-

(1). Will be followed by Transport of 175th Infantry Brigade and Divisional Signal Company in that order.

(2). Further details as to time of trains, Billets etc. will be issued by Staff Captain.

SECRET.   O.42/2.

AMENDMENTS TO 173RD INFANTRY BRIGADE ORDER NUMBER 42.

Reference Para. 4 of Order No. 42.

    Add following to Brigade Group:-

        2/1st Home Counties Fld Ambulance.
        2/2nd Home Counties Fld. Ambulance.
        510th Company, A. S. C.

Reference Move Table "A" -

    Times in Serial 2, Remarks Column will read as follows:-

        For 4 p.m. read 9.5 a.m.
        For 4.10 p.m. read 9.30 a.m.
        For 4.25 p.m. read 9.35 a.m.
        For 4.40 p.m. read 9.50 a.m.

                                          for Captain,
                                          Brigade Major,
                                        173rd Infantry Brigade.

26/9/17.

To all recipients of OO 42.

Table "A"

The undermentioned Personnel, Transport and Animals will proceed by Omnibus Train from PESELHOEK STATION to AUDRIQUES at the times stated.

Date	Unit	Personnel Off.	O.Rs.	Horses	G.S. Limbered	Two wheeled carts	No. of Train	Time of departure PESELHOEK
20th Sept	173rd Bde. Headquarters	4	20	9	1	-	1	6.20 p.m.
"	Signal Section	2	48	3	1	1	1	"
"	2/1st Lon.Rgt.-Transport						1	"
	Lewis Gun Limbers		18	8	4	1		
	Cookers		12	8	4	1		
	Tool Limber	1	4	4	2	1		
	Mess Cart		2	1	-	1		
	G.S. Cart		2	2	-	1		
	Water Cart		3	2	-	1		
	Riding Horses		8	8	-	-		
	Pack Animals		7	7	-	-		
"	2/2nd Lon.Rgt.-Transport			AS	ABOVE		1	"
"	*304th Field Coy. R.E.	5	150	3	1	-	1	"
"	2/1st H.C.Field Ambulance	8	140	6	2	-	1	"
"	173rd L.T.M. Battery	5	65				1	"
	TOTAL	24	535	107	25	7		
				Handcarts and Mortars				
1st Oct.	Transport 2/3rd & 2/4th (as for 2/1st above)						2	12.30 a.m.
"	208th Machine Gun Coy.	10	170	20	7	2	2	"
"	2/2nd H.C.Field Ambulance	8	130	4	-	-	2	"
"	x 216th Machine Gun Coy.	9	150	-	-	-	2	"

NOTES:— *Find unloading party of 100 men to report to Detraining Officer on arrival at AUDRIQUES. xFind loading party of 100 men to report to Entraining Officer 3½ hours before departure

Table "A" (Contd)

DEPARTURE OF PERSONNEL TRAINS FROM VLAMERTINGHE

Date	Train	Unit	Depart VLAMERTINGHE
30th Sept	No. 1 Personnel Train	Personnel of :- 2/1st London Regt.) 2/2nd London Regt.) and Lewis Guns) 58th Div. Signal Co. (40 men))	12 noon.
30th Sept	No. 2 Personnel Train	Personnel of :- 2/3rd London Regt.) 2/4th London Regt.) and Lewis Guns) 173rd Bde. Labour Coy.)	4.20 p.m.

CONFIDENTIAL

War Diary
of
Lt-Colonel A.C. FALWASSER R.A.M.C. T.F
Commanding 2/1st Home Counties Field Ambulance

from October 1. '17   to October 31. '17

(Volume I)

WAR DIARY
or
INTELLIGENCE SUMMARY

Army Form C. 2118.

Place	Date	Hour	Summary of Events and Information	Remarks and references to Appendices
ONTREBARNE	Oct 1	6.0 pm	Transport under Capt H.F. PALMER arrived 7.0 pm yesterday (30.9.17). Remainder of Unit detrained at AUDRUICQ at 7.30 a.m today & marched to their station. Capt H.F. PALMER proceeded at 10.0 am to XVIII Corps Rest Station for duty. Unit is accommodated in stables & lofts of Chateau. When being examined two small outages have been opened as a reception place of units found for a possible maximum of 50 patients. Hospital now duly accommodation for Capt H.F. WOODS R.A.M.C. (T.C.) and Lieut P. O'BRIEN R.A.M.C. (S.R.) joined for duty. A.D.S.	M.F. Refer Sheet CALAIS, 13 F.2
"	2	6.0 pm	Lieut P. O'BRIEN proceeded for duty with 91st Division sick of 173 Inf Bde front are collected daily at 9.30 a.m by horsed ambulance wagon & admitted to the Field Ambulance up to 50 in number. Any further are transferred to 2/1/3 H.C.S. Aube (XIX C.R.S.) at LIEQUES. A.D.S.	Sheet 13 F.3
"	3	6.0 pm	Capt. J.R. CHALMERS rejoined from medical charge of 4th London Regt. Capt. H.F. WOODS proceeded for duty with 4/4th London Regt. vice Capt. J.R. CHALMERS. A.D.S.	
"	6	6.0 pm	Award of Military Medal notified in Divisional orders to the following:- Sergeant L. FARLEY A/Cpl L.P. YOUNG A/13 390 A/13 530 Pte L.M. WEBB A/13 544. A.D.S.	
"	9	6.0 pm	Capt. J.R. CHALMERS and 19 other ranks 'C' section took ambulance at 10 AM to S/Hk Army Rel. Station at 6.7 & 5.7 to relieve bat Station of 55th Divn. A.D.S.	Sheet 27

WAR DIARY or INTELLIGENCE SUMMARY

Army Form C. 2118.

Place	Date	Hour	Summary of Events and Information	Remarks and references to Appendices
OOSTERNIE	Oct-9	6.0 p.m.	Rec'd orders at 12.30 p.m. to send one section mobile & equipment to 5pth Army Rest Station to relieve that of 55th Division. This being required in addition to the personal supplied yesterday. Transport & equipment of 'C' section proceeded at 2.0 p.m.	A))
"	12	6.0 p.m.	Lieut C.E. DUNAWAY M.O.R.C. U.S.A. joined for duty from appt. Division	A))
"	13	10.30 p.m.	Capt. J.S. WARD R.A.M.C. ? Lieut P.O'BRIEN R.A.M.C. S.R. and fifteen other ranks left the evacuated sick to C.C.S. rejoined having been attached for duty to 1/3 North Midland 9 Amb. Division since 23rd ultimo.	A))
"	18	9.0 p.m.	Received Operation order No. 120 by A.S.M.C. 53rd Division :— The 53rd Division (less Artillery & Field Coys) accompanied by Divisional H.Q.Q. Column will be transferred from the RECQUES Area XIX Corps to the ST JAN TER BIEZEN area XVIII Corps. Field Ambulances will be under orders of G.O.Cs Brigades for the move to water's. If the D.A.L will move with 173 Inf Bde H.Q. ... A.S.M.S Office will close at ZUYTKERQUE at 10 a.m. on 20th inst. & will re open at POPERINGHE in the same day. Sick remaining in this Ambulance to be evacuated in accordance with instructions to the issued O.	A))
"	19	10.0 morn.	Lieut P. O'BRIEN proceed for duty to 1/3rd London Regt	
		9.0 p.m.	Received a wire from 173 Infantry Bde 'Move postponed'	A))

WAR DIARY or INTELLIGENCE SUMMARY

Army Form C. 2118.

Place	Date	Hour	Summary of Events and Information	Remarks and references to Appendices
LOISTE BARNE	Oct 22	6.0 pm	Received wire from 173 Inf Bde "The Bde will move to POPERINGHE area tomorrow 23rd."	A.??
"	23	6.0 am	Received 173 Inf Bde Administrative Instruction No.16. "The Brigade Group, less marching portion, will proceed by train on Oct 23rd" in accordance with Table.... Transport will find starting point Bde HQ. NORDAUSQUES. 1/1st H.E. Field Ambee at 10.4 a.m. 2/1st H.E. Field Ambulance will entrain with 2 bicycles supped + 6 horses at AUDRUICQ station at 12.0 midnight 23/24 & proceed by tactical train to HOPOUTRE.	
"	"	8.30 am	Transport under Capt T.S.WARD travelled to join marching portion of Bde Group. Advanced party one officer + 4 other ranks proceed by lorry carrying surplus stores.	
"	"	5.0 pm	Holding party of 4 other ranks R.A.M.C proceed to AUDRICQ station to entrain.	
"	"	7.30 pm	Remainder of Unit marched to AUDRICQ station to entrain.	A.?.?
AUDRUICQ	24	3.30 am	Entrained for HOPOUTRE (POPERINGHE).	H.of Refee A.28.a.a.8
GWENT FARM	"	11.0 am	Detrained at HOPOUTRE & marched to GWENT FARM. "The 52nd Division" will Sheet 28 Received Operation Order No 19 by A.D.M.S 58 Div "The 52nd Division..... in the line on the night 24/25 October. The ere 1/1st Fld Ambulance with that division will relieve the party of the 58th. 3 Amb at the Corpl. Main Dressing Station at DUHALLOW 2/3rd H.E. Amb at ESSEX FARM. 1 off H.E Amb will...... detail 100 bearers in numbered squads and 3 bearer sergeants to report to be C.25.d.3.0	A.?.?

WAR DIARY or INTELLIGENCE SUMMARY

Army Form C. 2118.

Place	Date	Hour	Summary of Events and Information	Remarks and references to Appendices
EWENT FARM	Oct 24	5.30 pm	Two officers & 15 other ranks proceeded to DUHALLOW for duty at Corps Main Dressing Station in relief of a similar party of 54th F. Amb. Lieut. M. AIKMAN RAMC (T.F.) joined for duty.	C.2.5, C.3.0 Sheet 20 1/40000 AD
"	Oct 25	7.30 am	Remainder of tent division in all 5 officers and 20 other ranks proceeded to DUHALLOW completed relief of 54th F. Amb. 3 dispensers & 20 bearers reported to O.C. 2/3 H.C. Field Amb. for duty in the line.	AD
DUHALLOW	26	6.0 pm	Personnel of XVIII Corps Main Dressing Station comprises one tent division of this Unit and is commanded by Lieut Col. E.B. KNOX RAMC. Corps front is held by 63rd (R.N.) Division on the right and 58th Division on the left, one Brigade of each Division being in the first line respectively.	AD
"	31	10.0 pm	Casualties of 58th Division through this Dressing Station during the period Oct 24th to 9 pm Oct 31st.	

		Admitted	To C.C.S	To duty	Died
Sick	Officers	3	3	—	—
"	Other Ranks	50	50	—	—
Wounded	Officers	17	15	1	1
"	Other Ranks	473	473	12	8

AD Lumsden L/Col RAMC T.

CONFIDENTIAL

WAR

DIARY

OF

O.C. 2/1st H.C. FIELD AMBULANCE

From Nov 1st, 1917 to Nov 30th, 1917.

MEDICAL

COMMITTEE FOR THE
MEDICAL HISTORY OF THE WAR
Date 17 JAN. 1918

WAR DIARY
or
INTELLIGENCE SUMMARY

(Erase heading not required.)

Army Form C. 2118.

Instructions regarding War Diaries and Intelligence Summaries are contained in F. S. Regs., Part II. the Staff Manual respectively. Title Pages be prepared in manuscript.

Place	Date	Hour	Summary of Events and Information	Remarks and references to Appendices
DUHALLOW	Nov 3	6.0 p.m.	Capt A.E. HUXTABLE proceeded to take medical charge of 2/11th London Regt. Divisions companies instructions such as CHDT CRE re admitted letters by o XVIII Corps based on administration of II Corps yesterday Nov 2nd.	Not offic. Sheet 28 1/40,000 C.25.A.3.0
"	7	6.0 pm	Casualties of 5th Division passed through To Capt H.D.T during the week (-) November. Officers Admitted 3 Other ranks 102 Evac to CCS 3 102 To duty 1 6	
"	12	6.0 pm	Lieut R.B. CRAIN M.O.R.C. U.S.A reported for duty. Assumed temporary command of II Corps H.D.T during absence on leave of Lieut Col E.B. KNOX R.A.M.C	
"		11.30 pm	Received Operation order No 30 by MOHS 5th Division. The 5th Division will be relieved on the night of November 16/17 .... kg. 55th Division. The Division on relief, will proceed to the PROVEN area. The 2/1st H.Q.) Ankre will be withdrawn from the Corps Main Dressing station on the 15th inst & will proceed in left heavy to PARLIAMENT CAMP near CROMBEKE (PROVEN area). The O.C 2/1st H.Q. 3/1 Ankre will be responsible for the collection & evacuation of sick of the '73 2nd Bde during	

WAR DIARY or INTELLIGENCE SUMMARY

Army Form C. 2118.

Place	Date	Hour	Summary of Events and Information	Remarks and references to Appendices
			Their stay in the PROVEN area. Detached Motor Cyclists & personnel of the Field Ambulances with the section of the permanent clearing staff at the Corps walking wounded Collecting Post who will be withdrawn later, will be returned to their respective units on relief by similar personnel. The large Motor ambulances will join their respective units by direct arrangements between the O'sC Field Ambulances with the O/C No. 3, M.A.C. Three Motor lorries one per Field Ambulance & will report at 7 a.m. on 15th inst at A.29.a.7.3. (near GWENT FARM) to convey Field Ambulance stores to new area.	Sheet 28 1/40,000
DUNHALLOW	Nov 14	10.0 p.m	Casualties of 58th Division through this C.A.D.S. during the period 8–14 November: |	Evac to C.C.S.	To duty	Died
---	---	---	---
Officers	2	—	—
Other ranks	41	30	2 | A.D.S.	
PARLIAMENT CAMP	Nov 15	6.0 p.m	1st Division proceeded from DUNHALLOW by motor lorries at 10 A.M. today to new area (PROVEN). Bearer Division & transport by route march from GWENT FARM at 1.0 p.m. A.D.S.	Hospice Noblet '19 1/40,000 X.27.a.7.9.
"	Nov 16	6.0 p.m	Unit in rest at "Alert". Sick are being collected from 173 Inf Bde front & conveyed to X.X Corps Auxiliary Rest Station PROVEN. A.D.S.	

WAR DIARY or INTELLIGENCE SUMMARY

Army Form C. 2118.

Place	Date	Hour	Summary of Events and Information	Remarks and references to Appendices
PARLIAMENT CAMP	Nov 7	9.0 p.m.	Capt. E.S. CUTHBERT reported for duty from office of DDMS IV Corps. A.S.D	
	" 18	11.0 p.m.	Lt. Col. ATTALWASSER gone on 14 days leave. I assumed command of Fd. Ambulance. — John Wood Capt. R.A.M.C.T.	
	" 18	11 p.m.	Received instructions in B.M.414 from A.D.M.S. 58th Division to send one Officer and 10 O.R. as housing party to take over camp at X.30 central C Sheet 19.	
	" 19	11.30 a.m.	1st Lieut. R.B. CRAIN M.O.R.C. U.S.A. Senior over camp at X.36 central C. from Fd. 36th Divisional personnel. J.S.W.	
	" 21	3 p.m.	Received warning Order by A.D.M.S. 58th Division No M/2/112 for one officer and four men with Stores to proceed with Lorry to near area at 7 a.m. Senle Camp on the 22nd. Met as advanced party. J.S.W	
	" 22	9 A.M	Lieut a G.M. Allison proceeded to Houtkerque. J.S.W	
	" 23	6.30 p.m	173 Inf Bde. A.I. No 18 to Road Transport to proceed starting point PENTON CAMP (Sheet 27 g.2.c.3.9) at 8.30 a.m.	
	" 24	8 A.M	Capt. E.S. CUTHBERT Distributed Road Transport as per A.I. No 18.	
	"	6.12 p.m	1st Lieut. R.B. CRAIN, M.O.R.C. U.S.A. instructions per A.D.M.S. 58th Division to M.1416.15 to Kannon 1st Officer & party from X.30 C Camp Can I.N.C.O. & 2 O.R. Senior CRAIN reported at 8 p.m. J.S.W	
	" 24	12.30 pm	Operation Order No 31 from A.D.M.S. 58th Division to move until 173 Inf Bde to New area Bruembert on the 25th inst.	HAZEBROUCK 1/100,000. CALAIS 1/100,000. J.S.W
	" 24	3 p.m	173 Inf Bde. A.I. No 19. Amdt. A.I. No. 18 re move and instructions for same to BRUNEMBERT. J.S.W	BRUNEMBERT Sheet 27 1/40,000

Army Form C. 2118.

WAR DIARY
or
INTELLIGENCE SUMMARY

(Erase heading not required.)

Instructions regarding War Diaries and Intelligence Summaries are contained in F. S. Regs., Part II. and the Staff Manual respectively. Title Pages will be prepared in manuscript.

Place	Date	Hour	Summary of Events and Information	Remarks and references to Appendices
PARLIAMENT CAMP	25/11/17	10 AM	R.A.M.C. Personnel left PARLIAMENT Camp for LART under the charge of Lieut T.S.W. C.E. DUNAWAY MORE U.S.A.	
LART	26/11/17	10 AM	Personnel Horse & Motor Transport of the Ambulance left for BRUNEMBERT under my charge completing the move at 2.30 p.m.	T.S.W.
BRUNEMBERT	26/11/17	12.30pm	Capt. E. S. CUTHBERT reported to A.D.M.S. 58th Division for duty	T.S.W.

John Moore Capt
OC 2/1 HCFA

30/11/17.

2/1st Home Counties Field Ambce.

CONFIDENTIAL

No. 6

War Diary
of
Lieut Col A.T. FALWASSER R.A.M.C. T.F
Commanding 2/1st Home Counties Field Ambce.

from Dec 1st '15   to Dec 31st '17

(Volume I)

COMMITTEE FOR THE
MEDICAL HISTORY OF THE WAR
Date —1 FEB. 1918

Army Form C. 2118.

WAR DIARY
or
INTELLIGENCE SUMMARY
(Erase heading not required.)

Place	Date	Hour	Summary of Events and Information	Remarks and references to Appendices
BRUNEMBERT	Apr 3	6.0 p.m.	Lieut. R.B. CRAIN proceeded for temporary duty in relief charge of 2/3 Lt. London Regt. Received Administrative Instructions issued with 58th Divisional Order No. 73. The personnel of 175, 174 & 173 Bde troops will move by train on 6th, 8th & 9th inst. respectively. Two covering stock trains & one ammunition train are allotted to each Bde group. Entraining Station WIZERNES Detraining Stations ELVERDINGHE & VLAMERTINGHE for covering stock & ammunition trains respectively. Marching portion of transport will move by road, one day prior to the move of the Formation to which it belongs. A.?.?	Map Ref. Sheet 13 CALAIS E.4
		6.6 p.m.	Lieut. R.B. CRAIN rejoined from temporary duty with 1/3 Lt. London Regt. Received 173 Inf Bde Order No. 49. — "The 58th Division less Artillery is to relieve the 35th Division less Artillery in the left Sector of the II Corps front.". . . . "The 173 Inf Bde Group will move to SIEGE CAMP in accordance with attached Administrative Instructions & "Move Table". Transport will be brigaded & move by road." . . . on the 7th inst. Lieut. E.C. DUNAWAY proceeded for temporary duty with 2/3rd 11 C.D. A.?.?	

WAR DIARY
or
INTELLIGENCE SUMMARY

Army Form C. 2118.

(Erase heading not required.)

Place	Date	Hour	Summary of Events and Information	Remarks and references to Appendices
BRUNEMBERT	Dec 7	6.0 pm	Transport had a limbered wagon handed it to HQ under command of Capt WARD to join working parties of Bde Transport & proceed to GWENT FARM staying at LUMBRES, ST MOMELIN, + ST JAN TER BIEZEN.	
"	8	7.0 am	Motor lorry for conveyance of stores reported at 9.30 am. H/Lieut + QM ALDISS direct to GWENT FARM	
"	"	10.0 am	R.A.M.C. personnel with 2 limbered wagons proceeded to LART to billet for the night.	
LART	"	2.30 pm	Marching portion of Unit arrived & billeted.	A.D. —
"	9	3.30 am	Two limbered wagons & riding horses proceeded to WIZERNES to obtain on supply train leaving at 10.30 am for VLAMERTINGHE.	
"	"	6.0 am	Remainder of Unit march to WIZERNES to entrain on leaving stock train at 11.30 am for ELVERDINGHE.	
GWENT FARM	"	6.30 pm	Whole Unit less marching portion of transport arrived GWENT FARM. Received Memorandum No 32 by A.D.M.S. 5th Division :— The 58th Division will relieve the 35th Division in the left sector of the II Corps front on the night of 9/10th December. The 1/3rd H.C. Amb will relieve the 105th. 3 Amb in the line on the night of 10/11th December. O.C. 1/3 H.C. Amb. will be responsible for the collection & transport of evacuation to the Advanced Dressing Stations."	A.D.—

2449 Wt. W14957/M90 750,000 1/16 J.B.C. & A. Forms/C.2118/12.

WAR DIARY or INTELLIGENCE SUMMARY

Army Form C. 2118.

Place	Date	Hour	Summary of Events and Information	Remarks and references to Appendices
GWENT FARM	Dec 10	6.0 pm	Received operation order No. 33 by A.D.M.S. 53rd Division:— "The 2/1st H.C.3. Amb. will relieve the 2/3rd H.C.3. Amb. in the line on 11th December. The O.C. 2/1st H.C.3. Amb. will be responsible for the collection & transport of casualties to the Advanced Dressing Stations CEMENT HOUSE U.29.c.2.2. and MINTY FARM C.10.c.2.3. The Rear division of 2/1st & 2/3rd H.C.3. Amb. will be kept at the disposal of the O.C. 2/1st H.C.3. Amb. All Motor & Horsed Ambulances of 2/1st H.C.3. Amb. will be placed at the disposal of O.C. 2/1st H.C.3. Amb." Handing over of transport — relief GWENT FARM at 11.0 pm. (A.1)	
ESSEX FARM	11	6.0 pm	Proceeded to ESSEX FARM at 7.0 pm. Let in right preparatory to taking over advanced posts from O.C. 2/3rd H.C.3. Amb. Visited tonight all posts on right sector of line between 7 & 10.30 a.m. and ADS at MINTY FARM & CEMENT HOUSE. Personnel of 2/3 H.C.3. Amb. relieved by 2/1st H.C.3. Amb., relief completed by 3.30 pm. Lieut. C.E. DUNAWAY U.S. M.R.C. reported for duty from 2/3rd H.C.3. Amb. & remained for duty at CEMENT HOUSE as bearer officer in effectedes. Capt. E.S. CUTHBERT rejoined for duty from office of A.D.M.S. 53rd Division & transf. to MINTY FARM as bearer officer in right sector. Horse lines of this division at GWENT FARM which is also used as a camp for bearer division of the 3 Field Amb. men stationed in line.	

Army Form C. 2118.

WAR DIARY
or
INTELLIGENCE SUMMARY
(Erase heading not required.)

Instructions regarding War Diaries and Intelligence Summaries are contained in F.S. Regs., Part II. and the Staff Manual respectively. Title Pages will be prepared in manuscript.

Place	Date	Hour	Summary of Events and Information	Remarks and references to Appendices
ESSEX FARM		6.a.m	Visited all posts on Left sector & both A.D.S.'s between 7 a.m & 10 a.m today. following table shows posts, personnel, mode of evacuation &c from forward area.	

CONEY ISLAND R.A.P. & R.ly Post. V.19.d.2.1 4 men.

PHEASANT FARM R.ly Post. 4 men.

PHEASANT TRENCH R.ly Post U.30.b.1.6 4 men.

LOUIS FARM R.A.P. U.2a.7.9

BULOW FARM Relay Bearer Post C.6.c.2.9 2 NCOs + 8 men.

HAAMIXBEEK FARM R.ly Post C.5.b.1.7 4 men.

EAGLE TRENCH R.ly Post U.28.d.8.3 1 NCO + 8 men.

Hand carriage

FERDINAND FARM R.ly Post C.5.c.0.5 4 men.

Hand carriage on wheeled stretcher.

Handwheeled trolley on rubber gauge railway.

HANLEY C.3.c.2.1 Relay Bearer Post 1 NCO + 9 men.

MINTY FARM C.18.c.3.7 A.D.S. & Bearer Bearer Post 1 NCO + 8 men.

PIG & WHISTLE R.ly Post U.28.b.3.2 1 NCO + 8 men.

CEMENT HOUSE A.D.S. & Relay Bearer Post U.29.c.2.2 1 NCO + 10 men.

RUDOLPH FARM Bearer Post C.3.c.6.4 1 NCO + 3 men.

Total Field Ambulance personnel employed. 2 Officers & 3 other ranks. 175

Army Form C. 2118.

WAR DIARY
or
INTELLIGENCE SUMMARY
(Erase heading not required.)

Instructions regarding War Diaries and Intelligence Summaries are contained in F.S. Regs., Part II. and the Staff Manual respectively. Title Pages will be prepared in manuscript.

Place	Date	Hour	Summary of Events and Information	Remarks and references to Appendices
ESSEX FARM	Dec 14	6.0 p.m.	Visited all posts in left sector today & very few casualties though fairly heavy walking cases & stretcher cases only. All found after work of 2/F. H.C. S. Amb. walk exception of senior N.C.O. at MINTY FARM & CEMENT HOUSE relieved today by similar personnel of 2/F.H? 110? Amb. Capt J. R. CHALMERS & tat 1st division of C. Section rejoined today from XIX Corps A.D.S. this Depôt. GNENDGE FARM, formerly 55th Army Rest Station. Capt GILMORE did not return with the party having been retained for duty in Office of D.D.M.S. XVIII Corps.	A.D.S.
	15	6.0 a.m.	Capt J.S. WARD proceeded to U.K. on 14 days leave. R.A.P. of left line battalion has been moved today from LOUIS FARM U.24.c.5.9 to helmet at EAGLE TRENCH U.23.6.6.3. Walking wounded & stretcher posts on adjoining nature at EAGLE TRENCH U.23.6.6.3 has been taken over as bearer post.	A.D.S.
	16	6.0 p.m.	Visited all posts in left sector between 7.30/9.30 a.m.; all quiet & in order casualties very few; no casualties in R.A.M.C. personnel.	A.D.S.
	17	6.0 p.m.	Capt J.R. CHALMERS proceeded to CEMENT HOUSE A.D.S. in relief of Lieut C.F. DUNAWAY as bearer officer; is left sector of line. 1/2 Inf Bde relieved 175 Inf Bde in the line on the night of 16/17. Lieut C.F. DUNAWAY U.S.M.C. proceeded for temporary duty on 1/16 2/n th to her Regt. Visited all posts on right sector this morning between 7 & 10 a.m	A.D.S.
	19	6.0 p.m.	Proceeded by 2nd Motor Ambulance Car to PHEASANT TRENCH U.30.d.2.6	

2449 Wt. W14957/M90 750,000 1/16 J.B.C. & A. Forms/C.2118/12.

Army Form C. 2118.

WAR DIARY
or
INTELLIGENCE SUMMARY
(Erase heading not required.)

Place	Date	Hour	Summary of Events and Information	Remarks and references to Appendices
ESSEX FARM	Dec 19	6.0 am	By road REGINA TRENCH – TRIANGLE FARM – POELCAPELLE Rd. The road is bad but is negotiable by Ford car & is a feasible alternative route of evacuation from right R.A.P.'s	A.J.T. Recd 20 S.W. 4 1/10 ono
			Capt. J.R. CHALMERS R.A.M.C. officer i/c Left Sector proceeded from CEMENT HOUSE to take up his id charge of 2/Lt. Hordern R.A. at present in Left at present in Left Sector & with Regimental Aid Post at EAGLE TRENCH U.23.f.d.3.	A.J.T.
	Dec 20	6.0 am	Visited GWENT FARM at 12 noon today with A.D.M.S. who inspected the Camp. Casualties from the line are very few owing to further lemur posts. General situation on Front is Quiet - stretcher routes of evacuation are being used without interruption.	A.J.T.
	21	6.0 pm	Visited all posts in Left Sector today, situation quiet very few casualties – evacuation proceeding in a normal manner by same routes.	A.J.T.
	22	6.0 pm	Visited all posts in Left Sector this morning. Found everything proceeding normally. A heavy enemy barrage on our front line in this Sector from 4.30 to 6.0 pm yesterday produced no casualties	A.J.T.

2449 Wt. W14957/M90 750,000 1/16 J.B.C. & A. Forms/C.2118/12.

WAR DIARY or INTELLIGENCE SUMMARY

Army Form C. 2118.

Place	Date	Hour	Summary of Events and Information	Remarks and references to Appendices
ESSEX FARM	Dec 26	6.0 pm	175 Inf Bde relieved 173 Inf Bde in the line last night. 1/1 Essex Regt in Right sector with 1/9 London Left in support, and 1/10 London Left & 1/11 London Left in Reserve. Butts with 1/11 London Left in support. (AJ)	
"	27	1.0 pm	Visited Left A.D.S. this morning, situation is generally quiet & uneventful this morning. A Lewis Gun range on Div front last night 7.05 & 8.25 p.m. & no attack followed there were no casualties. Captain E.B. JARDINE M.C. R.A.M.C (T.C) (AJ)	
"	28	6.0 pm	Relay post on Left sector 'PIG & WHISTLE' V.29.c.3.2 has today been vacated as it is required as I.P.Q for Left support Bn. A relay at U.23.c.0.0 50 yards S of cross roads at TRAFALGAR SQUARE has been taken over as relay post in its place. (AJ)	
"	29	6.0 pm	Visited Left A.D.S's & all huts on left sector today & new stoves on this line are proving normally without any difficulty. Capt- F. METCALF R.A.M.C T.F joined the Unit for duty. Capt- E.B. JARDINE assumed duty as O i/c teams on Left sector (AJ)	

Army Form C. 2118.

WAR DIARY
or
INTELLIGENCE SUMMARY
(Erase heading not required.)

Instructions regarding War Diaries and Intelligence Summaries are contained in F. S. Regs., Part II. and the Staff Manual respectively. Title Pages will be prepared in manuscript.

Place	Date	Hour	Summary of Events and Information	Remarks and references to Appendices
ESSEX FARM	Dec 30	6.0 pm	Capt. T. J. GILMORE rejoined for duty from Officer of I.S.O.M.S. II Capt. A.D.	
"	31	1.0 pm	Visited all posts in left Sector this morning. All working smoothly & no difficulties experienced in evacuating casualties. Capt. J.S. WARD rejoined from leave to U.K.	

N Dalmeter LtCl
RAMC T.
Cmdg 2/1st Home Counties Ambul

2449 Wt. W14957/M90 750,000 1/16 J.B.C. & A. Forms/C.2118/12.

CONFIDENTIAL

9/M/12

WAR DIARY

of

Lieut-Colonel A.T. FALWASSER D.S.O. R.A.M.C. T.F

Commanding 2/1st Home Counties Field Ambulance

COMMITTEE FOR THE
MEDICAL HISTORY OF THE WAR
Date -4 MAR.1918

from Jan 1st 1918   to Jan 31st 1918

(Volume 2.)

WAR DIARY or INTELLIGENCE SUMMARY

Army Form C. 2118.

Place	Date 1919	Hour	Summary of Events and Information	Remarks and references to Appendices
ESSEX FARM	Jan 1	6.0 p.m	Capt. F. METCALFE assumed duties of Bearer Officer Rifle Sector today vice Capt. E.S. CUTHBERT. Remains of 4/1st H.C.3 Amb relieved in the line by similar personnel of 4/2nd H.C. J. Ambce.	A.D.S
"	2	6.0 p.m	Visited posts in left sector today. Situation generally has been quite eventful, very few shrapnel wounds Artillery personnel, rate of evacuation steady & no difficulties experienced in evacuating. 1/5 Inf Bde relieved 175 Inf Bde in divisional front during the night 1/2 January. 2/21st London Regt with 2/2nd in support in right sector & 2/3rd London Regt with 4/4th in support in left sector.	A.D.S
"	4	6.0 p.m	Capt. E.S. CUTHBERT proceeded on leave to U.K. Visited R.A.P. v all posts in right sector this morning & generally quiet. Casualties few 3 trolley line from PHEASANT TRENCH to MINTY FARM A.D.S. was broken yesterday by shell fire at 3 points near to STEEN BEK but since repaired this temporary necessitated hand carriage stretcher wounded matters & returned are now returned. Capt. T.J. GILMORE proceeded for temporary duty as M.O. 4/c 4/1st London Regt. today.	A.D.S

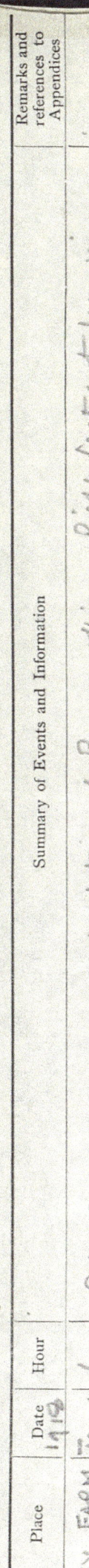

WAR DIARY
INTELLIGENCE SUMMARY

Army Form C. 2118.

Place	Date 1916	Hour	Summary of Events and Information	Remarks and references to Appendices
ESSEX FARM	Jan 6	6.0 p.m.	Received at 3 p.m. operation order No 34 by A.D.M.S. 58 Division. "The Division (less Artillery) will be relieved by the 35th Division (less Artillery) commencing on the 7th inst. On relief the Division will move to the II Corps rear area. The 2/1st H.C.D. Amb will be relieved on the 7th inst- by the 106th D. Amb. on relief the 2/1st H.C.D. Amb will march to SCHOOL CAMP L.3. c. and d. The 2/1st H.C.D. Amb will remain stored for the O.C. 2/1st H.C.D. Amb will be responsible for the collection of the kit of the 173 Bde front & their transport to the Rest Station. Detailed arrangements for the move will be made by 3. O.C. Field Ambulances concerned. Amb has been arranged for & will report as under @ GWENT FARM 9 a.m on 7th inst."	Map Ref. Sheet 27 1/40,000
"	7	6.0 p.m.	Visited posts in different sectors of line this morning. Received telephonic order of 2/1st H.C.D.Amb relieved this afternoon by 2/3rd H.C.D.Amb in the line.	
"	8	10.0 p.m.	Had it over it handed H.O.H.O.Q. Amb brigade today to O.C. 106 D Amb. 30th Div. Saw fall head forward I 8.8. Div. Saw relief of 3/5 Div. Saw chief completed at 4 p.m. Transferred HQ of relief from ESSEX FARM to GWENT FARM L3 b.f.n. & all teams found proceeded to latter place.	

WAR DIARY
INTELLIGENCE SUMMARY
(Erase heading not required.)

Army Form C. 2118.

Place	Date	Hour	Summary of Events and Information	Remarks and references to Appendices
SCHOOL CAMP 	Jan 9	6.0 p.m	Unit has had not-tat-tutorium located at II Corps Rest Station moved from SWEAT FARM at 9 am & reached SCHOOL CAMP at 11.15 a.m. Unit is accommodated in Nissen nettes huts and remaining stored bring respirable only to the collection of cook of the 173 Infantry from other troops refer to abording I had (C/J.H(C)AMb) at PROVEN.	H of Corps Rest S. 1/30 app L.A.o.d
"	10	6.0 p.m	Capt E.B. JARDINE M.C. proceeded for duty to II Corps Rest Station PROVEN.	A.D
"	13	6.0 p.m	Capt F. METCALFE proceeded at 9.30 a.m to report to ADMS 50th Division for duty.	A.D
"	14	9.0 p.m	Received the following orders by 'Q' 59 Div ' The 58th Division " be transferred to the III Corps Fifth Army on the 19th inst & will move on the " following dates to the VILLERS - BRETONNEUX area . . . 173 Bde AMIENS." " 1 train on 21st January " entraining station PROVEN detraining station " VILLERS BRETONNEUX . Advance parties will proceed on " 16th January by train, time to be notified later . . . " annual absence parties will start to D.A.G 58th Division.	H of Rest AMIENS. A.D A.D
"	15	7.0 p.m	Capt E.B. JARDINE M.C. rejoined from duty at II Corps Rest Station	A.D

Army Form C. 2118.

WAR DIARY
or
INTELLIGENCE SUMMARY
(Erase heading not required.)

Instructions regarding War Diaries and Intelligence Summaries are contained in F.S. Regs., Part II. and the Staff Manual respectively. Title Pages will be prepared in manuscript.

Place	Date	Hour	Summary of Events and Information	Remarks and references to Appendices
SCHOOL CAMP	Jan 16	6.0	Capt E.B. JARDINE and 6 other ranks proceeded by 6.10 a.m train from POPERINGHE at Advance Party to view new Area. Received Administrative Instructions for Move of 5th Division to Fifth Army area. "2/4th H.Q Amb will detrain at PROVEN at 12.30 p.m on 7 January 1918 and will detrain at VILLERS BRETONNEUX at 12.30 a.m on 7 January 1918. All Cars, ambulances & motor cycles will move to the new area by road." Received Operation Order No. 35 by ADMS III Corps Fifth Army. "The 50th Division will be transferred to the 5th Division on the 19th inst. Field Ambulances will move with Brigade Groups & at-tached affiliated. The O.C. 2/2nd H.Q Amb will be responsible for the disposal of the sick awaiting by train at VILLERS-BRETONNEUX & will arrange accordingly. Patients remaining in Field Ambulances will be evacuated to C.R.S & C.C.S. The HQrs of the ADMS will close at COUTHOVE CHATEAU on 19th inst & open at VILLERS-BRETONNEUX on 20th inst."	A.D.S
	19	6.0 p.m	Lieut R.B. CRAIN M.O.R.C USA and 19 other ranks rejoined from duty at II Corps Rest Station.	A.D.S
	20	6.0 p.m	Capt E.S. CUTHBERT rejoined from leave to U.K	A.D.S

Army Form C. 2118.

WAR DIARY
or
INTELLIGENCE SUMMARY

(Erase heading not required.)

Instructions regarding War Diaries and Intelligence Summaries are contained in F. S. Regs., Part II. and the Staff Manual respectively. Title Pages will be prepared in manuscript.

Place	Date	Hour	Summary of Events and Information	Remarks and references to Appendices
SCHOOL CAMP	Jan 21	3.0 a.m.	All transport of Unit marched from SCHOOL CAMP to PROVEN Station	A.D.S.
"	"	9.80 a.m.	Marching portion of Unit proceeded to PROVEN Station	A.D.S.
PROVEN	"	12.30 p.m.	Entrained at PROVEN Station. Strength 6 Officers 193 other ranks 64 horses 17 vehicles.	A.D.S.
LE PARCLET	22	6.0 p.m.	Detrained at VILLERS-BRETONNEUX at 3.0 a.m. this morning and marched to billeting area, about 15 kilometres, arriving at 7 a.m. Unit is accommodated in an Aerodrome Village and billets house adjoining situated at LE PARCLET. An examination for 40 sick in 2 drafts was in the village the sick will be without a hospital for the sick of the Brigade group. Capt A.E. HUXTABLE rejoined from duty with 2/1st London Regt.	A.D.S.
"	25	6.0 p.m.	Field of 73 other ranks are being allotted daily by hipped ambulance embedded to this F Amb. Cases unlikely to be fit for duty within 10 days being evacuated to No. 41 Stationary Hospital CERISY BAILLY. No. 9 Stationary Hospital CERISY BAILLY. C.O.S HARCHELPOT. Fifty other ranks proceeded today for duty as a working party at No. 34 C.C.S MARCHELPOT. Capt. E.B. JARDINE H.C. proceeded today for duty with No. 9 Labour Group at FOUCACOURT. Lieut R.R. ERAN V.S.H.O.R.C. proceeded today for duty with 75th S.T.C.	A.D.S.
"	31	6.0 p.m.	Lieut + Q.H. H.Q. ALDISS proceeded on leave to U.K.	A.D.S. Shmette Lt-Col R.A.M.C. 2/1st Home Counties Field Ambce.

Confidential

War Diary
of
Lieut. Colonel A.T. FALWASSER RAMC T
Commanding 1/1st Home Counties Field Ambulance

from February 1st 1918
to February 28th 1918

(Volume 2)

WAR DIARY or INTELLIGENCE SUMMARY

Army Form C. 2118.

Place	Date	Hour	Summary of Events and Information	Remarks and references to Appendices
LE QUESNEL	Feb 3	6.0 p.m.	Received Operation order No. 36 by A.D.M.S. 58th Division :— "The 58th Division will relieve the 30th Division in the Right Sector of the III Corps front on the night 7/8 & 8/9 inst." Ambulances (see Marching Orders) will move as ordered of the British Field Ambulances. The marching portion of the three Field Ambulances will proceed by march route to their new areas in three stages, billetting at ROYE and BUSSY en route. The wagoning portion of the 2/1st H.C. Field Amb. will move on the 4th inst. & 2/1st H.C. Field Amb. will relieve the 92nd Field Ambulance at QUIERZY on the 7th inst. Advance parties of 1 officer & 6 other ranks of each Field Ambulance will proceed by lorry with their baggage before on the 4th inst. Detailed arrangements of relief will be made. Letter to O.C. Field Ambulances enclosed.	
			Lieut. R.R. CRAIN reported for duty from 58th D.A.C. Received Administrative Instructions issued with 173rd 2/1st Bde morning order No. 3 "Advance parties will proceed on the 5th morning at following stations :— Two lorries will attend at BOVES Detraining head QUESSY detraining head to ROYES Rations for 2 days will be taken.	H.Q. 2/1st 2/1 to E 1/2000 Leavillé
				Mortiers D Mortiers C ROYES

WAR DIARY or INTELLIGENCE SUMMARY

Army Form C. 2118.

Place	Date	Hour	Summary of Events and Information	Remarks and references to Appendices
LE PARAQUET	Feb 5	6.0 am	Capt E.S. CUTHBERT and 7 other ranks proceeded in advance party at 6.45 a.m. today by road to QUIERZY.	
			Capt T.S. WARD and 27 other ranks with vehicles and 36 horses proceeded at 9.0 a.m. today by route march via ROYE and Tevoures to BUSSY & reached QUIERZY and joining advance party. A.V.	
		5.0 pm	Received 173rd Infantry Brigade Administrative Instruction No 23:— "The Brigade Group less marching portion will proceed by rail in accordance with attached Table 'A' on the 7th to meet."	
			"Table 'A'" Entraining Station VILLERS-BRETONNEUX. Detraining Station APPILLY. 2/1st H.Q. that will proceed as No 2.	
			"Personal Train departing at 1.0 pm & carrying approximately 9.0 pm"	
			"Baggage & stores of all units & the following transport will be carried on"	
			"baggage train. Infantry & transport of reserve & carrying at —) 9.0 pm 2/1st H.Q."	
			"Field Amb 2 C.C.S. baggage wagons & draught horses, riding horses"	
			Unit less Advance party & marching portion of transport marched from LE PARAQUET at 6.0 AM today & entrained at VILLERS-BRETONNEUX at 10 AM (R.A.M.C. portion) and 12 noon (A.T.O. portion with vehicles & horses).	
QUIERZY	7	10.0 pm		

WAR DIARY or INTELLIGENCE SUMMARY

Army Form C. 2118.

Place	Date	Hour	Summary of Events and Information	Remarks and references to Appendices
QUIERZY	Feb 9		These two parties detrained at APPILLY at respectively 2.30 p.m. and 2.30 p.m. and marched to QUIERZY. The site to be taken over by this Unit from 9 th. F. Amb. (30 th Divn.) was taken over by this letter Unit from a French AMBULANCE DIVISIONAIRE on 30 th ult. The accommodation consists of 3 huts (2 hospital pattern & 1 Adrian) and capable of accommodating up to a maximum of 50 patients & there is also accommodation in a re-roofed cottage for about 30 patients together with a Receiving Room, a Dressing Room, & Offices, with ration store. (AD)
		10.0 p.m	Took over at 5.0 p.m. today administration of hospital from 9 th F. Amb. with 17 patients (6 Sanitary v Hq Corps troops) Capt. J.S. WARD proceeded for duty with 2/3 rd. H.F. F. Amb. (AD)
"	10	6.0 p.m	Lieut J.B. CRAIN MORC and 20 other ranks proceeded for duty to 3 th Army Advanced Operating Centre ABBECOURT 9 F. Amb. J.A. HIGGINS MORC USA and 1 Lieut D.E. DOLOFF MORC USA rejoined from duty at No 34 C.C.S. at MARCELLEPOT on completion of which F. 3 rd Division Hq 58 th Division & this Unit took over in its entirety the F. Amb site vita little vacated by 9 th F. Amb.

Army Form C. 2118.

WAR DIARY
or
INTELLIGENCE SUMMARY
(Erase heading not required.)

Instructions regarding War Diaries and Intelligence Summaries are contained in F. S. Regs., Part II. and the Staff Manual respectively. Title Pages will be prepared in manuscript.

Place	Date	Hour	Summary of Events and Information	Remarks and references to Appendices
QUIERZY	Feb 11	10.0 p.m	Capt. E.B. JARDINE M.C rejoined from duty with 4th Labour Group.	A.D.)
"	13	6.0 p.m	Lieut D.E.DOLLOFF proceded for duty with 30 th Labour Group. Lieut J.A. HIGGINS proceded for duty at Jifft Army Kennel Operating Centre vice Lieut R.B. CRAIN rejoined for duty. Capt. E.S. CUTHBERT proceded for duty with 43rd London Regt.	A.D.)
"	14	6.0 p.m	Lieut R.B. CRAIN proceded for duty with 2/4 th London Regt.	A.D.)
"	16	6.0 p.m	Lieut & Quartermaster H.G. ALDISS rejoined from leave to U.K. Statement of divisional executions on 7 (fatals) for seven days ending 6.0 p.m.	
			Attg. Admission Standpo To CCS Discharged to duty Remaining	
			52 th Division 117 22 17 78	
			Attr Formation 72 14 17 40	
			Total 189 36 34 118	A.D.)

Army Form C. 2118.

WAR DIARY
or
INTELLIGENCE SUMMARY
(Erase heading not required.)

Instructions regarding War Diaries and Intelligence Summaries are contained in F.S. Regs., Part II. and the Staff Manual respectively. Title Pages will be prepared in manuscript.

Place	Date	Hour	Summary of Events and Information	Remarks and references to Appendices
QUIERZY	Feb 23	6.0 a.m	Statements of Admissions & Transfers & Evacuations for 7 days ending 6 p.m 22nd ing	
			Admissions & Transfers To C.C.S Discharged to duty Remaining	
			58th Division 106 51 53 30	
			Other Formations 48 12 33 43	
			Total 154 63 86 123	
			A.D.S.	
	23	6.0 p.m	Received Operation order No. 37 by A.D.M.S. 58 Division. The 175th Brigade front to be relieved by the 56th Infantry Brigade front in the LIEZ Sector. Relief than Brigade Head Quarters to be completed by 6 a.m 25th inst. The 2/2nd H.Q. 3 Amb will be relieved by the 56th 3 Amb on the 25th inst. the Officer Commanding 2/2nd H.Q. 3 Amb will hand over the A.D.S of the Relay posts in the Left Sector to the O.C. 56th 3 Amb, & the advanced dressing & Relay Posts in the Centre sector of the Divisional front. After the O/C. 2/1st H.Q. 3 Amb has the 25th inst. Relief to be completed by 6/m on the 25th inst. The 2/1st H.Q. 3 Amb on relief will march to MAREST DAMPCOURT and take over the Field Ambulance site there.	
			A.D.S.	

Place	Date	Hour	Summary of Events and Information	Remarks and references to Appendices
QUIERZY	Oct 20	10.0 pm	Received at 1.30pm Priority wire from 11th & 6th Divisions "The preparatory action that refers to the moving of personnel into a rearward battle position on receipt of further orders" orders, but will immediately stop the Divisional Left Station. A.D.S. will cease to exist as such a walking wounded collecting Post for the Right Sector of the Divisional Front is a walking wounded collecting Post for the Right Sector of the Divisional Front All sick being immediately evacuated to C.C.S. Bearers will be held in readiness to proceed at 15 minutes notice. No duty in the line. Arrangements made with No. 2a M.A.C. for necessary cars for evacuation of sick to report here on receipt of wire. Received at 7.30pm wire from D.H.Q. "Troops will now be ready to move at one hours notice instead of 15 minutes as previously ordered." Also telephone message from S.D.M.S. III Corps "Sick — Ambulance Trains not likely to be fit within 48 hours may be evacuated to C.C.S."	

A.D.Rochester Lt Col
R.A.M.C.

CONFIDENTIAL

140/849

War Diary
of
Lt. Colonel A.T. FALWASSER R.A.M.C. T.F.
Commanding 2/1st. Home Counties Field Ambulance.

COMMITTEE FOR THE
MEDICAL HISTORY OF THE WAR
Date 12 MAY 1918

from March 1st. 1918 to March 31st. 1918

(Volume II)

Vol 14

WAR DIARY or INTELLIGENCE SUMMARY

Army Form C. 2118.

Place	Date	Hour	Summary of Events and Information	Remarks and references to Appendices
QUIERZY	Feb. 1 1916	10.0 p.m.	2/1/16 Received from ADMS copy of III Corps wire "Standing by, at no known notice". Awaiting further instructions or orders. Cancelled.	
"	2	10.0 a.m.	Capt T.T. GILMORE RAMC (T.C.) 2/3rd H.C.S. Amb. posted temporarily for duty vice Capt E.B. JARDINE M.C. proceeded on leave to U.K. Statement of Sick passed thro' hands during seven days ending 6 p.m. today:—	
			Admitted Evac. to C.C.S. Died Brot. to Duty	
			H. Division 176 131 N.l 57	
			58 Division 74 59 N.l 38	
			Other Formations	
"	6	6.0 p.m.	Unit inspected by Stk. S III Corps at 3.0 p.m. today. Lieut R.B. CRAIN Ho RC USA rejoined from duty with 49th London Regt.	
"	7	7.0 p.m.	Statement of Sick passed thro' hands during seven days until 6 p.m. today:— Died Brot. to Duty	
			Admitted Evac. to C.C.S.	
			H. Division 158 73 — 52	
			58 Division 29 24 — 19	
			Other formations	

Army Form C. 2118.

WAR DIARY
or
INTELLIGENCE SUMMARY

(Erase heading not required.)

Instructions regarding War Diaries and Intelligence Summaries are contained in F. S. Regs., Part II. and the Staff Manual respectively. Title Pages will be prepared in manuscript.

Place	Date	Hour	Summary of Events and Information	Remarks and references to Appendices
RVIERZY	Feb 14	6.0 p.m	Lieut J.A.HIGGINS M.R.C. U.S.A. rejoined from 5/Flk Army Sch. of Instr. Cadre. Lieut J.A. Higgins + 3 other ranks proceeded repeatedly for a 10 days a 6 days course to the 5/Flk Army R.H.Q. School at Gt CCS HMM & the 5/Flk Army School of Instruction at PERONNE.	A.D.
	15	10.0 pm	Capt. F.J. GILMORE R.A.M.C. 1/5th H.D. but temporarily attached this unit for duty from 2nd inst proceeded for temporary duty in medical charge of 2/16 London Regt. Capt. E.SOUTHBERT R.A.M.C. rejoined from duty with 2/3rd London Regt.	A.D.
	16	7.0 pm	Statement of Sick & wounded treated thro' Unit during week ended 6 p.m. today :—	

	Admitted	Evac'd 5.C.C.S	To Capt Ref-Station	Sick & wounded to duty
Sgt Brandon Sick	127	58	35	44
Wounded	8	1	3	1
Other Formations Sick	32	12	6	7

A.D.

2449 Wt. W14957/M90 750,000 1/16 J.B.C. & A. Forms/C.2118/12.

WAR DIARY or INTELLIGENCE SUMMARY

Army Form C. 2118.

(Erase heading not required.)

Instructions regarding War Diaries and Intelligence Summaries are contained in F. S. Regs., Part II. and the Staff Manual respectively. Title Pages will be prepared in manuscript.

Place	Date	Hour	Summary of Events and Information	Remarks and references to Appendices
QUIERZY	Mch 20	2.5 p.m.	Received wire from ADMS "Prepare for attack"	A.D.S.
"	21	6.15 a.m.	Received wire from ADMS "Man battle positions".	
"	"	12.0 noon	All sick remaining in DRS have been evacuated by Motor Ambulance transport from No. 24 M.A.C. & site is being prepared with a view to opening as an Advanced Dressing Station & Gas Centre in the event of SINGENY & CHAUNY respectively becoming untenable.	
"	"	10.0 p.m.	Enemy is stated to have occupied FARGNIER & to be holding the east bank of the OISE — ST QUENTIN canal. No attack has developed against the southern portion of our line south of LA FÈRE.	A.D.S.
"	22	3.0 a.m.	Gas centre at CHAUNY closed & gas centre removed to QUIERZY. Capt. A.C. WATKIN R.A.M.C. i/c 24/11/16 Amb. who have been in charge reports still remain in charge. Enemy is stated to have crossed and still be reaching TERGNIER.	A.D.S.
"	"	7.0 a.m.	Proceeded under instructions of ADMS & established an aid post at HAREST DAMPCOURT on route of evacuation from VIRY — NOYON in anticipation of evacuation post at VIRY & selected post on CHAUNY — NOYON Rd. Placed Capt. TARDINE in charge with a small party of other ranks & 3 Motor ambulances. 1 H.S. French Division moved up this morning to counterattack between VIRY and TERGNIER.	A.D.S.

Army Form C. 2118.

WAR DIARY
or
INTELLIGENCE SUMMARY

(Erase heading not required.)

Place	Date	Hour	Summary of Events and Information	Remarks and references to Appendices
QUIERZY	Mch 22	10.0 a.m.	Capt E.B. CUTHBERT is assigned 4 hussars proceeded at 7 AM Endeavour to get in touch with N.O.s 4 2/5 & 3/4 R. horse Reports near VIRY.	A.D.S
"	"	3.0 p.m.	A few walking wounded are coming through both French + British is a larger number of stretcher cases are being dealt with at the post at HAREST DAMPCOURT	A.D.S
"	23	7.0 a.m.	153 French wounded ill ranks and 6. British all could have been dealt with since midnight. There is a French Ambulance post in this village + hundreds are made on them for evacuation of French wounded to H.Q.B. at BLERANCOURT. British wounded evacuated to A.C.C.S. at NOYON. Enemy is said to be in CHAUNY	A.D.S
"	"	12.0 noon	Capt E.S. CUTHBERT with hussars just returned + Capt E.B. JARDINE having cleared post in CHAUNY-NOYON road &c reported. All casualties from North of OISE are now coming through this post. Small parties of the enemy retail + have been advancing along N bank of OISE between CHAUNY and ABBECOURT.	A.D.S
"	"	2.0 p.m.	Proceeded to VARESNES where A.D.M.S intentions related site there for opening up a sort + party with a BESSONEAUX tent to erect in this site at VARESNES.	A.D.S

		Army Form C. 2118.

WAR DIARY
or
INTELLIGENCE SUMMARY
(Erase heading not required.)

Place	Date	Hour	Summary of Events and Information	Remarks and references to Appendices
QUIERZY	Feb 24	7.0 am	Received order to move all stores etcetera etcetera to VARESNES & there to form posts retaining only sufficient personnel vehicles to continue head post at QUIERZY. Enemy is said to be still advancing along N. bank of OISE. After cavalry are still being dealt with which appear to have been entrusted in OGNES and HERECOURT but it is impossible to obtain any clear account of the situation.	A.D.S
"	"	2.0 pm	All vehicles have proceeded to VARESNES except myself & six other ranks & all stores here have been removed leaving only sufficient dressings to maintain this post.	A.D.S
"	"	6.0 pm	Closed post by order of A.D.M.S. & proceeded with remaining personnel to VARESNES. Capt MASSEY MILES R.A.M.C. M.O. i/c London Regt. with no report of bearers remained at the post.	A.D.S
VARESNES	"	9.0 pm	Capt MASSEY MILES reports that British & French still fire were being placed all round the post & sent for instructions & was ordered him to withdraw with all personnel to VARESNES	A.D.S
"	"	11.0 pm	Capt MASSEY MILES reported with personnel.	A.D.S

Army Form C. 2118.

WAR DIARY
or
INTELLIGENCE SUMMARY
(Erase heading not required.)

Instructions regarding War Diaries and Intelligence Summaries are contained in F. S. Regs., Part II. and the Staff Manual respectively. Title Pages will be prepared in manuscript.

Place	Date	Hour	Summary of Events and Information	Remarks and references to Appendices
MARESNES	Mch 25	10.0 a.m.	Received following order from ADMS :- "Move your Field Ambulance forthwith to LA POMMERAYE Ref QUTS Q.14.A."	Closed 7.15 a.m.
LA POMMERAYE	"	11.30 a.m.	Unit marching into La Pommeraye packed & ready to move	A.D.S
"	"	2.30 p.m.	Received following order from ADMS :- "Move your Field Ambulance forthwith to NAMPCEL W.15.d Sheet 70 E."	A.D.S
NAMPCEL	"	9.0 p.m.	Billeted at NAMPCEL occupying dug-outs & elephant shelters	A.D.S
"	Mch 26	12.0 noon	Received following "Medical Arrangements" by ADMS :- 1. OC 2/1st H.C.D.Amb will open & receive casualties at NAMPCEL. These will be evacuated to Base Hospital at COMPIEGNE. OC 5a div M.T. Coy will return motor lorries as available to assist. OC 5a div M.T. Coy will supply these lorries on demand. 2. OC 2/2nd H.C.D.Amb will evacuate all casualties to NAMPCEL from which the cars will return to him. A.D.S	
"	"	"	3. 2/3rd H.C.D.Amb will remain at NAMPCEL	
"	"	2.0 p.m.	In accordance with above a hospital has been established at outskirts of village on BIERANCOURT Rd. Two operating tents & one bell tent have been erected & small shelters are also available. Arrangements have been made with OC 5D M.T.Coy	

Army Form C. 2118.

WAR DIARY
or
INTELLIGENCE SUMMARY
(Erase heading not required.)

Instructions regarding War Diaries and Intelligence Summaries are contained in F. S. Regs., Part II. and the Staff Manual respectively. Title Pages will be prepared in manuscript.

Place	Date	Hour	Summary of Events and Information	Remarks and references to Appendices
NAMPCEL	Feb 27	1.0 a.m.	to evacuate all sitting sick & wounded to Tench Hospital ROYALLIEU (COMPIEGNE) by returning empty lorries & lying sick & wounded are sent to trench hospital by Motor Ambulance	A.D.
"	"	8.5 a.m.	Received order to move all horsed transport & others not in use to HAUTEBRAYE. Casualties dealt with as yesterday	A.D.
"	Feb 28	2.0 p.m.	All horsed transport proceeded to HAUTEBRAYE & part of NAMPCEL returned & preparations made to transfer post from NAMPCEL to HAUTEBRAYE	A.D.
"	"	11.30 p.m.	All personnel & other team that employed at post proceeded to HAUTEBRAYE	A.D.
"	"		Received following order from A.D.M.S.:— "Close your Dressing Station at NAMPCEL at 12 noon 29.3.12. Move it forward to HAUTEBRAYE. Re-open as a Main Dressing Station at HAUTEBRAYE at 12 noon 29.3.12. All cases passing through the M.D.S. will be included in your AF.W.3125 as direct admissions"	A.D.
HAUTEBRAYE	Feb 29	6.0 a.m.	Capt. E.R. JARDINE M.C. returned at 9 A.M. to O.C. 2/3rd (W)D.A.H. to proceed with a party from that Unit to temporary duty at Dwan. He & R/51 men with 6 others marched to FONTENOY	A.D.
			Capt. A.F. HUXTABLE proceeded at 10 A.M. from NAMPCEL to HAUTEBRAYE, Main Dressing Station at HAUTEBRAYE in compliance with foregoing order	A.D.

WAR DIARY
or
INTELLIGENCE SUMMARY

(Erase heading not required.)

Army Form C. 2118.

Place	Date	Hour	Summary of Events and Information	Remarks and references to Appendices
HAUTEBRAYE	Mch 30	6.0 p.m.	Dressing Station at NAMPCEL closed at 12 noon and reopened here at the same hour. Remainder of personnel & vehicles with equipment proceeded by route march to HAUTEBRAYE at 2 p.m. All casualties which we evacuated from A.D.S. at BIÊCHE (2/2nd H.O.? Amb) by this point & are evacuated from here by cars & horsed vehicles of this unit to H.E. B/51 near FONTENOY. A.S.-	
	31	6.0 p.m.	All surplus stores of 3 Field Ambulances, the for which horsed transport is not available, conveyed for storage to H.Q.F.Z. B/51 until they can be collected by lorry at a later date. This is in view of probable early move of the Division to region III Corps at a point S.W. of AMIENS. Statement of Sick & wounded treated thro' this Unit during period March 21/31	

	Wounded	Sick	Total
British	241	193	434
French	142	12	154
German	16	—	16
			604

Total all nationalities all ranks

D. Luntar? Lt Col
A.D.M.S. 14th D. Amb.

Cmd'g 2/1st 14th D. Amb.

2449 Wt. W14937/Mgo 750,000 1/16 J.B.C. & A. Forms/C.2118/12.

WAR DIARY.

of

Lieut-Colonel A. T. FALWASSER. R.A.M.C.T.

Comdg. 2/1st Home Counties Fd Ambce

From 1st April 1918 to 30th April 1918

Volume II

Army Form C. 2118.

WAR DIARY
or
INTELLIGENCE SUMMARY

(Erase heading not required.)

Place	Date	Hour	Summary of Events and Information	Remarks and references to Appendices
HAUTEBRAYE	Apr 2	6.0 pm	Received verbal instructions afterwards confirmed by minute that the units under be formed would not be able to purpose of move to III Corps area	A)
		7.30 pm	Received "G" little order 9/4 (n.3) and 6/4 as starting point area near HAUTEBRAYE at 7 AM & moved to Collect at DOMMIERS tomorrow 3/4, advance billeting party to report to Staff Captain at Church DOMMIERS at 12 noon	A)
	Apr 3	9 AM	Capt. A.E. HUXTABLE + 3 Ors made billeting party proceeded from HAUTEBRAYE. Remainder of Unit left HAUTEBRAYE by march route at 9 AM via VIC-SUR-AISNE — COEUVRES — to DOMMIERS	A)
DOMMIERS		2 pm	Arrived DOMMIERS & billeted at CHONFLEUR FM	A)
	Apr 4	11 AM	Rec'd "G" little order 9/4 (n.3) and & entrain at VILLERS COTTERET at 10 midnight April 4/5. Advance party & sp/men a staff made to entrain at 10 midnight April 4/5 at LONGPORT	A)
		7.30 pm	Proceeded by march route to VILLERS COTTERET Advance party G.M. ESCUTHORT + 4 staff made proceeded at 8.0 pm to LONGPORT	A)
VILLERS COTTERET		9.30 pm	Arrived district VILLERS COTTERET. Dir. Artillery still entraining & same returns	A)
	Apr 5	1.0 am	Began entrain	
		3.30 am	Entraining completed steam left VILLERS COTTERET	A)
LONGUEAU		11.30 am	Detrained at QUAI MILITAIRE LONGUEAU that Bn D 1/100,000 H.23.c.7.° Advance party had arrived & arranged no rhendisation of Bn — Bn & Elstn	A)

Army Form C. 2118.

WAR DIARY or INTELLIGENCE SUMMARY

(Erase heading not required.)

Instructions regarding War Diaries and Intelligence Summaries are contained in F. S. Regs., Part II. and the Staff Manual respectively. Title Pages will be prepared in manuscript.

Place	Date	Hour	Summary of Events and Information	Remarks and references to Appendices
LONGUEAU	Apr 5	12.30 p.m	Handed with clear instruction & proceeded on branch to BHQ which was brought to be at CACHY - where received orders to proceed to to implement of to CITADELLE AMIENS & billet there	Meet 6.2 D 1/40000
AMIENS	"	5.0 p.m	BILLETED unit at Factory at G.32.a.6.2 & on ALBERT — AMIENS Rd in G.32.c.o.d began lines at the CITADELLE.	
"	"	10.0 p.m	Received note from A.D.M.S. 7/(?) H(?) Amb will relieve 24th D. Amb (24th Div) at fick Collecting Station BOVES at noon Apr 6th.	
Apr 6	"	10.0 a.m	Capt-Rt HUXTABLE with head-ORAIN HUPP and one tent subdivision & a large Mote Ambulance proceeded to BOVES to relieve 24th D Amb at T.7.a.2.0. Motor Ambulances T.21.c.5.0. being fixed at GENTELLES WOOD T.11.d.2.9 and at FOUENCAMPS T.21.c.5.0	A.D.)
"	"	2.0 p.m	3 HAC Cars attached for evacuation purposes to station at BOVES which is normally to 2 casualties left dead & intended as a fick collecting Station but large numbers of wounded being evacuated direct to front & British are being dealt with. Cases are being checked & transferred direct to front at NAMPS AU VAL.	A.D.)
"	Apr 7	6.0 p.m	1 CCS at NAMPS AU VAL. A Capt Main Dressing Station at the Church ST ACHEUL M.14.d.3.4 and a Cpts walking wounded Collecting Post at Salle in Rue Porte Paris AMIENS have been established today & are now sent direct to us of these posts. Received orders by A.D.M.S. to be to relieve 7th Amb in left sector of 1st section handing over to 111th Cplts Front — VILLIERS BRETONNEUX M.9 — by 4 p.m Apr 8th fick Collecting Station at BOVES & 7 Amb A.D.S Bromen Collecting Station at BOVES to 56 D Amb & wikhere on from T.11.d 29 and T.31.c.5.0	A.D.)
"	Apr 8	1.0 p.m	Handed over Post at BOVES and wikhere on from T.11.d.29 and T.31.c.5.0 Visited all RAPs & Medical posts in VILLIERS BRETONNEUX took preparatory to taking over from 7th Amb to D Amb.	A.D.)

WAR DIARY or INTELLIGENCE SUMMARY

Army Form C. 2118.

Place	Date	Hour	Summary of Events and Information	Remarks and references to Appendices
LONGUEAU	Apr 9	9 a.m.	Relief of 7th Australian Field Ambce in VILLERS BRETONNEUX sector was complete. Headqrs of Unit is established at Entrance to LONGUEAU. Site made M.D.S. & will supply 3 bearers in relays at 2 men points & also man both of Motor Ambulances required by Left & Right & 3rd ones from other Ambulances after Brigade. Refer lines of Relief and Coy trig road from G.32.a.6.2 to ÉCOLE DES FILLES MONTIÈRES, N.W. of AMIENS. Medical arrangements in forward area as follows :— Two battalions holding front line have R.A.P.s at O.36.c.2.7 and O.35.6.9.5. 3 posts of R.A.M.C. bearers are attached to latter. These posts for evacuation of persons to by road ambulance when situated in front of the lines of the R.A.P.s and evacuating casualties to A.D.S. situated in a chalk pit at O.29.a.d.5 ? evacuation by Motor Ambulance thro the village of VILLERS BRETONNEUX is impossible owing to the large amount of shell & other wreckage in the streets which causes frequent fractures of tyres. M.A.C. is provided at A.D.S. at O.29.a.6.5 & a Cell Bike & three trench stations and its personnel consists of 1 Medical Officer, 1 N.C.O. & 6 other ranks. Two large Motor Ambulances [?] at the A.D.S. evacuate casualties direct to Capt Main Dressing Station or after walking towards POIX or ST ACHEUL and AMIENS respectively. (5)	Meet 6.2D 1/100 000
"	9	10.0 p.m.	Casualties have been light. 23 cases in all passing thro' posts in 24 hours. Have been fairly busy shelling of Eastern part of VILLERS BRETONNEUX during the day & in consequence it was decided through Divisional influence women at 7 p.m. today. Evacuation from R.A.P.s to A.D.S. as now being carried out by wheeled stretchers. R.A.P. of support battalion was at O.34.6.9.7 + O.25.d.u.u.31 O.25.d.6.3. Two battalions of 17th Suffolk Regt in support lies in Pl. Schroeder + leave scouts to be attached to the R.A.P. of these battalions at T.4.9.a.0.9 and T.23.a.9.7 (5)	

Army Form C. 2118.

WAR DIARY
or
INTELLIGENCE SUMMARY
(Erase heading not required.)

Instructions regarding War Diaries and Intelligence Summaries are contained in F. S. Regs., Part II. and the Staff Manual respectively. Title Pages will be prepared in manuscript.

Place	Date	Hour	Summary of Events and Information	Remarks and references to Appendices
MONGUEAU	Apr 13	8.0 p.m	Took over posts at M.29.d.3.5 from 5th Btn. Field Ambce at a Divisional Walking Wounded Collecting Station this being in addition to occupying as a MDS reserve, Empty post & stand for Divisional Motor Thread Ambulances. Two lorries & 4 cars of No 41 Fd Ambce attached this Walking wounded post for evacuation. Evacuation from the line is proceeding normally & casualties are few in numbers	A.D.S
"	14	6.0 p.m	Capt J.M.SMEATON R.A.M.C. went out at 10 AM for division purposes & to visit at A.D.S admitted by 7th Aust Fd Amb at GENTELLES, T.12.c.q.5 in Right sheets.	A.D.S
"	15	10.t p.m	Capt J.M.SMEATON returned by order of O.C. 7th Aust Fd Amb as post at T.12.c.9.5 had been among shell & many flying shelling.	A.D.S
"	17	10.0 p.m	Heavy gas Bombardment of VILLERS BRETONNEUX area from 8 a.m to 9 a.m today continued intermittently all day. (1) Yellow Cross Shell, have fell & dealt with up to 6 p.m. and these include no reported Medical officers and 16 other ranks. Some of their shirts & letter are all emphatically sift & wear with surprising rapidly and have been sent together when at HONGRE for baths. they others have been noted only in the fog bombardment while extricating casualties from others which were full of fumes. as they were unable to see except the which they weekly removed work from front eyes attaining much pains & nausea ditto.	A.D.S

WAR DIARY or INTELLIGENCE SUMMARY

Army Form C. 2118.

Place	Date	Hour	Summary of Events and Information	Remarks and references to Appendices
LONGUEAU	Apr 10	10.0 p.m.	At other times have been evacuated to 6 p.m. today & one Battalion was taken from the line last night & was sent to billets in charge of clothing & a large proportion of men were slightly passed, being relieved by an Australian Battalion. Capt. E.S. CUTHBERT, slightly passed, was relieved at 0.29.c.d.5 by Capt T.M. SMEATON at 10 midnight. Lieut J.A. HIGGINS M.O.R.C. relieved Lieut BLAIR R.A.M.C. M.O. Jt border Regt. (posted) at 2 A.M. Lieut R.B. CRAIN M.O.R.C. relieved Capt. HARVEY HILES M.O. Jt border Regt. (posted) at 7 pm yesterday. R.A.P. in particulars we have been moved to 0.35.A.1.6 and 0.35.c.1.9 Lieut C.R. LONG M.O.R.C. relieved Lieut R.B. CRAIN M.O.R.C. (posted) at 9 am today. At 5.30 p.m today this unit relieved the 7th Australian 3 unit in the R.I.Infantry of the R.I. of 11 Capt Smit so that evacuation of casualties from whole of 2 sectors of Army 3rd are now in the hands of this unit. R.A.P.s at V.21.a.3.a V.a.b.a.7 V.2.d.9.92 have turned of heavy attacks & evacuations are carried out by Ford Car & wheeled stretches to A.D.S. at CACHY V.2.d.6.0 from A.D.S. evacuation is direct by large motor Ambulances to CHDS in the case of lying casualties & to Dist M.S.O at H.29.d.3.5 for walking cases. Army Hosp With NCO & squad in Ls established at CONTIGUES H.12.d.1.0 to be worked in conjunction.	Mont G.D. /20000

2449 Wt. W14957/M90 750,005 1/16 J.B. & A.L. Forms/C.2118/2

WAR DIARY or INTELLIGENCE SUMMARY

Army Form C. 2118.

Place	Date	Hour	Summary of Events and Information	Remarks and references to Appendices
LONGUEAU	Mar 19	9.0 p.m.	Completed handover of all posts in left (VILLIERS BRETONNEUX) subsector to 19th (?) but right subsector has been friendly quiet. Wise taking over 8th Division. Situation in right subsector	Sheet 62D 1, 20000
"	21	10.0 p.m.	Additional tanks running have been sent up to AST at CACHY and especially GENTELLES tonight in view of anticipated enemy attack tomorrow morning.	
"	22	10.0 p.m.	Attack by enemy developed at 4 AM today. Owing to heavy shelling & bridges being blown across road it became impossible to use our AFVs in CACHY itself. AFVs were withdrawn at the hour to GENTELLES & to post consisting of shelters which have been dug in front of GENTELLES WOOD T.11.d.1.9. Reinforced LONGUEAU – DOMART recommended with a view to establishing units (evacuation sheets) CACHY – GENTELLES units become impracticable.	
"	23	10.0 p.m.	Post established at 10 AM today at T.21.a.2.7 retaliatory for personnel of that front evacuation from RHQ at T.21.c.3.4 as were being shelled considerably though chance by foot Clear to T.9.9.1 at which point a large car park is established	
"	25	10.0 p.m.	A detch Lt commd. at 2 AM this morning on platoon at T.11.d.1.9 (Gentelles Wood) consisting of Sept Lt H.G. PALMER RHC & all personnel concurrently moved forward in GENTELLES T.11.d.1.9 which is being apparently quiet. No large car front of T.7.b.7.1. Hd-Qrs were still our forward to DOMART head of T.26.a.27 and to GENTELLES village	

Army Form C. 2118.

WAR DIARY
or
INTELLIGENCE SUMMARY

(Erase heading not required.)

Instructions regarding War Diaries and Intelligence Summaries are contained in F. S. Regs., Part II. and the Staff Manual respectively. Title Pages will be prepared in manuscript.

Place	Date	Hour	Summary of Events and Information	Remarks and references to Appendices
LONGUEAU	Apr 27	4.0 pm	Received O.O. No. 41 by ADMS 5th Division :— . . . on the right of 27/28 inst. the 1/1st Field Amb. on relief by Medical Personnel of Moroccan Division will proceed to LONGPRÉ . . . . will march to NEUILLY L'HÔPITAL staying for 2 nights at CROUY and AILLY LE HAUT CLOCHER	A.D.S.
"	"	12.0 midnight	Relief of Battery by French Moroccan Division started at 9.30 pm but is not yet complete	A.D.S.
"	28	4.0 AM	Relief completed. 11th Battalion have reported casualties all clear & all signals & Medical Personnel have reported. Dist Hds Collecting Station closed & now proceeding immediately to LONGPRÉ	A.D.S.
"	"	1.30 pm	Proceeded by route march with complete Unit & transport to CROUY	A.D.S.
HANGEST sur SOMME	"	10.0 pm	Arrived CROUY 5 pm & no billets available so proceeded to HANGEST sur SOMME & billeted for night.	A.D.S.
FAMECHON	29	10.0 pm	Marched from HANGEST sur SOMME at 1.30 pm arrived AILLY LE HAUT CLOCHER at 5 pm & no billets available so proceeded to FAMECHON & billeted.	A.D.S.
"	30	6.0 pm	Marched from FAMECHON at 9 AM & arrived NEUILLY L'HÔPITAL at 10.45 pm & billeted in the Château. 1/1/3/4 Fld Amb dark 30 beds will be established A.D.S. water with R.A.M.C. T. Ents. Unit. H.E. 3 Ind.	

CONFIDENTIAL

War Diary
of
Lieut Colonel A.T.FALWASSER DSO
R.A.M.C. T.F.
commanding 2/1st Home Counties Field Ambulance

from May 1st 1918 to May 1st 1919

(Volume 2)

Army Form C. 2118.

WAR DIARY
or
INTELLIGENCE SUMMARY
(Erase heading not required.)

Instructions regarding War Diaries and Intelligence Summaries are contained in F. S. Regs., Part II. and the Staff Manual respectively. Title Pages will be prepared in manuscript.

Place	Date	Hour	Summary of Events and Information	Remarks and references to Appendices
NEUILLY L'Hôpital	May 4th	10 pm	Lieut Col A T FALWASSER D.S.O. R.A.M.C. proceeded on Special leave to U.K. – date of leave revised May 1st to May 15th. Reception hospital 7.30 to be opened for sick of 173rd Infantry Brigade – Cases requiring treatment at Casualty Clearing Station were evacuated to 49 C.C.S. ST RIQUIER	ATH
	May 5th	10 pm	Capt. E.B. JARDINE M.C. R.A.M.C. detailed for temporary duty with A.D.M.S. 58th Div. Received Warning order from A.D.M.S. 58th Div. to prepare for a probable move on 7th inst to a sector on the ALBERT front	ATH
	May 6th	10 am	Received detailed instructions regarding move – destination to be MOLLIENS – au – BOIS. Transport to move on 6th inst with Transport of 173rd Infantry Brigade staging for the night 6/7 May at BOURDON Personnel to move on 7th inst entraining at LE PLESSIEL Alt	ATH
	7th	10.00am	Transport proceeded under Capt J.S. WARD R.A.M.C. in accordance with above instructions	ATH

Army Form C. 2118.

WAR DIARY
or
INTELLIGENCE SUMMARY
(Erase heading not required.)

Instructions regarding War Diaries and Intelligence Summaries are contained in F. S. Regs., Part II. and the Staff Manual respectively. Title Pages will be prepared in manuscript.

Place	Date	Hour	Summary of Events and Information	Remarks and references to Appendices
MOLLIENS AU BOIS	May 7th	7 a.m.	Reception Hospital closed at NEVILLY L'HÔPITAL at 7 a.m. Total cases dealt with during period at NEVILLY L'HÔPITAL	
			5th Div" — 2 Officers — 76.O.R	
			Other Formations — Nil — 7	
			Officers 2 Officers 63.O.R evacuated to C.C.S.	
	9 a.m	Personnel entrained at LePLESSIEL.	
		3.30 p.m.	Complete unit reported at MOLLIENS AU BOIS	
	8.30pm	Proceeded to pitch Canvas Camp in Northern portion of Wood S.W. of MOLLIENS AU BOIS.	
			Sick of 173rd Infantry Brigade to be collected by this Field Ambulance and warded to C.C.S Group at VIGNACOURT — town hall fitted in an isolated portion of the camp to accommodate incoming cases until evacuation possible	att
"	8th	10 pm	Capt J.S. Ward RAMC. proceeded on seven days special leave to U.K — period of leave 9/5/18 to 16/5/18	aSH

WAR DIARY
or
INTELLIGENCE SUMMARY

(Erase heading not required.)

Instructions regarding War Diaries and Intelligence Summaries are contained in F.S. Regs., Part II. and the Staff Manual respectively. Title Pages will be prepared in manuscript.

Place	Date	Hour	Summary of Events and Information	Remarks and references to Appendices
MOLLIENS AU BOIS	MAY 8th	10pm	Capt A.E HUSTABLE RAMCT and Capt J.S WARD RAMCT promoted to rank of Acting Major whilst commanding Sub Field Ambces dated 4th Jan 1918	att
"	10th	8 am	Two N.C.Os and twenty two men detached as a working party to the 6th London Field Ambulance - being employed at HENENCOURT on road work.	att
"	10	5 pm	Lieut R.B. CRAIN M.O.R.C. detailed for temporary duty with 3rd LONDON Regt.	att
"	12	10 am	A divisional sick collecting station opened at BEAUCOURT. Sick of the division being collected by horsed ambulances and evacuated to C.C.S Group at PERNOIS by No 10 M.A.C Cars. Accomodation for twelve cases provided.	att
"	"	11am	Lieut J.R.TRAVIS M.O.R.C reported for temporary duty from 2/3 H.C.F Amb	att

WAR DIARY or INTELLIGENCE SUMMARY

Army Form C. 2118.

Place	Date	Hour	Summary of Events and Information	Remarks and references to Appendices
ST GRATIEN	May/16	4 pm	Divisional Sick Collecting Station at BEAUCOURT closed and personnel returned by third of 4th London F. Amb.	
"			Sick Collecting Station & Field Amb site at BEAUCOURT taken over from 4th London F. Amb.	
"			Transport lines and rear headquarters established in wood Sheet 62.D B.20.d.	ADS
"		9.0 pm	Lieut ATFALWASSER RTO returned from leave to UK. Capt T.A.DICK RAMC T.F. joined for duty from No. 55 CCS & taken on the strength.	ADS
"	May/17	6.0 pm	Accommodation has been provided at BEAUCOURT for the temporary retention of 50 sick and 12 sedical cases of 58th Division. Sick of 5th Division other than of 58th Division in excess of these numbers are evacuated to CCS at PERNOIS + 2 motor ambulances of No. 10 M.A.C. are attached for that purpose.	ADS
"			Casualties from front line, sick & wounded, are being evacuated by 3/1st H.C.F. Amb with HQ of WARLOY (V.2a.a Sheet 57 D) and Advanced Dressing Station at HENENCOURT (V.27.c Sheet 57 D)	

WAR DIARY or INTELLIGENCE SUMMARY

Army Form C. 2118.

(Erase heading not required.)

Place	Date	Hour	Summary of Events and Information	Remarks and references to Appendices
ST GRATIEN	May 22	6.0 pm	3 dressing stations are in process of construction by R.A.M.C. labour with R.E. supervision in V.23.d, V.24.d, & V.30.2. Main Dressing Station is at VADENCOURT V.21.2. It is administered by 1/3rd W.R.F.A. and thence, or from A.D.S. at NENENCOURT in cases of urgency, wounded are evacuated to two of C.C.S.s at PERNOIS.	Plate 67.D
"	May 23	6.0 pm	Capt. F.A.DICK proceeded today for duty with 2/1 H.C.D. Amb. at WARLOY. 20 Iron Huts are being erected with a view to their erection in wood at short B.22.d.5.0 for the accommodation of light sick of 50 Division for whom there is no room at this Divl's post at BEAUCOURT. A.D.)	Plate 6.D
"	May 24	6.0 pm	Bivouac shelters have now been erected & 20 sick admitted	A.D.
"	May 26	6.0 pm	Capt. P.V.EARLY R.A.M.C. T.C. joined for duty taken on strength Capt. E.B.JARDINE H.C. R.A.M.C. T.C. rejoined for duty from duty with A.D.M.S. 50 Division	A.D.
"	May 27	6.0 pm	Received instructions from A.D.M.S. to return no cases other than Medical taken cases at BEAUCOURT light sick cases are still being retained however & Divl post B.22.d.5.0 accommodation being available for 45.	A.D.

2449 Wt. W14957/M90 750,000 1/16 J.B.C. & A. Forms/C.2118/12.

WAR DIARY or INTELLIGENCE SUMMARY

Army Form C. 2118.

Place	Date	Hour	Summary of Events and Information	Remarks and references to Appendices
AT QRATIEN	May 29	6.0 p.m.	"State" of women today shows 73 sick cases remaining here & at BEAUCOURT.	A)⇒
"	May 30	?	The following extract is from Divisional Routine orders dated 27.5.18 "Attachments Lieut-Colonel E.A.WRAITH DSO RAMC. assumed duties as Acting ADMS on the 25th inst. vice Lieut-Colonel (Temp.Colonel) J.W.H.HOUGHTON DSO."	A.M.S. A)⇒
"	May 30	3.0 p.m.	Attended conference at ADMS office CONTAY when various matters in connection with the relief of disposition of Medical Units in relief by 18th Division at an early date were referred to.	
"	"	7.0 p.m.	Received Operation order No. 03 by ADMS 58th Division. (See Artillery) The 58th Division (See Artillery) will be relieved in the left sector by the 18th Division (See Artillery) on the nights of May 31/June 1st and June 1/2nd. On completion of the relief the 58th Division will be in Corps reserve and will be disposed as follows DHQ HOLLIENS AU BOIS 173rd Bde SL BAZIEUX system WARLOY Cte 174th Bde AREA U.20 & 29 ? 175th Bde Area C.20 & 21. The 9th MG Bn will remain in their present site & will retain the sick collecting station BEAUCOURT. 511th Fd Amb will be responsible for the collection treatment & disposal of all sick Division in the Divisional area from 10 AM June 2nd. HDQrs 2/1st will move HDQrs of CONTAY at 10 AM June 2nd & report at MOLLIENS AU BOIS HOLLIENS AU BOIS to the new HQrs.	Med-57 D Med-62 A A)⇒

WAR DIARY or INTELLIGENCE SUMMARY

Army Form C. 2118.

Place	Date	Hour	Summary of Events and Information	Remarks and references to Appendices
ST RATIEN	Aug 31	7pm	The following Divisional Routine order dated 31.5.18 received togh. Attached. The following is extracted in place of Divisional Routine No. 1090 of 27th Aug 18 :— Lieutenant Colonel E.A. WRAITH DSO RAMC (T.F) to be ADMS 50th Division s/to be temporary Colonel, vice Lieut Colonel (T/Colonel) J.W.H. HOUGHTON DSO AMS. A.D. Delavoiter KCB RAMC T.F Copy 24th Nova Combers J. Anter	

24 CONFIDENTIAL

Original
Vol 17
40/3076.

War Diary
of
Lieut Colonel A.T. FALWASSER RAMC T.F
Commanding 2/1st Home Counties Field Ambulance

from June 1st 1915 to June 30th 1915

(Volume II)

COMMITTEE FOR THE
MEDICAL HISTORY OF THE WAR
Date 7 AUG 1918

Army Form C. 2118.

WAR DIARY
or
INTELLIGENCE SUMMARY

(Erase heading not required.)

Instructions regarding War Diaries and Intelligence Summaries are contained in F. S. Regs., Part II. and the Staff Manual respectively. Title Pages will be prepared in manuscript.

Place	Date	Hour	Summary of Events and Information	Remarks and references to Appendices
GRATIEN	June 1	6.0 p.m	Capt E.J.CUTHBERT and Capt P.V.EARLY proceeded to work collecting station at BEAUCOURT. Major A.E.HUXTABLE MC and Capt T.M.SMEATON on relief reported at IT GRATIEN. Capt C.B.JARDINE proceeded to III Corps Gas School for a 7 days course.	B.20 to Half by D A)D
	2	1.0 p.m	Capt J.A.DICK rejoined from duty with 47th MED AMB. Half unit bring two relieved last night by B/S Amb of 18 Division at the Dressing Station. HENENCOURT.	A)D
	3	6.0 p.m	Relief of all 3 Relief of Division having been completed last night 3 horse ambulances were been and bring to attend sick of 10 units of Division in transit area.	A)D
	4	8.0 p.m	Received following from A.D.M.S. "Telephone message having arrived from 'Ability' the 2/5 DAILY MAIL have known MILLIENS and Farmers.	A)D
	5	10.45 a.m	Received following memo from A.D.M.S. "Hours of frigates will take place as notified a.m. "73" Brigade will move to T.24d a.a. Antler air conces at present and to move to 173 Bde HQ at 9.AM tomorrow (date 6th). 2/5 L.F. engineers to report at 9.AM tomorrow at 2/3 HQ and details to collect men of units of 173 Bde from St MARCOU & BAZIEUX who could work moving them to fresh billets as T.24 a and b.	Sketch 57? A)D A)D

WAR DIARY
or
INTELLIGENCE SUMMARY

(Erase heading not required.)

Army Form C. 2118.

Place	Date	Hour	Summary of Events and Information	Remarks and references to Appendices
GRATION	Mar 5	7.0 p.m.	Received following note from ADMS :— "Your Sick Ambulance will be before to-morrow at 4 hours notice. No extra transport will be provided. Supplies, stores will be dumped at the Sick Collecting Station BEAUCOURT and will probably be added over to another Division. No Sick Collecting Station will be attached to the Brigade, but arrangements will be made for immediate clearing on receipt of orders." A.D.
	6	7.0 p.m.	All cases other than Sick at BEAUCOURT to be discharged to duty or evacuated, and 16 cases only have remained at this front in the next 48 hours. Inmates of these and Sick parade will be arranged on billets will to proceed at their Unit Lines. Following from ADMS:— "In the event of an urgent move of this Division." The personnel of each SSA Ambulance will be moved. It's transport of each will be separated from the personnel by road. It must be clearly understood that the transport may be separated from the Personnel travelling by train will? ? in marching order with packs. No kits will be carried on the train. ? ? will carry packs only and safe kits and men will carry their usual equipment. battalions to Brigade Headquarters will resume "Homewards respond". N.B. The item will be carried on the interior transport. Major A.E. HUXTABLE M.C. and Capt. J.M. SMEATON relieved Capt. E. SOUTHERT at Capt P.V. EARLY 3 Feb Sick at Sick Collecting Station BEAUCOURT. A.D.

WAR DIARY or INTELLIGENCE SUMMARY

Army Form C. 2118.

Place	Date	Hour	Summary of Events and Information	Remarks and references to Appendices
ST GRATIEN	January 7	3.30 pm	The G.O.C. Division inspected horse lines & vehicles of the Unit — congratulated upon the condition of the horses & the cleanliness of the turn out. (ADS)	
"	9	12.0 noon	Batteries all carried proceed from BEAUCOURT leaving only 2 officers and a few men.	
		6.0 pm	Received interesting programme for battery manoeuvre, this Unit will cooperate with '173 Bde' front in TALMAS – VILLERS BOCAGE Rd. Reconnoitred tracks to VILLER BOCAGE in rear of above advancing front (ADS)	
"	10	3.10 am	Received following wire from ADMS 'Division will be helped through by bus' to CAVILLON area west of AMIENS starting at 10 AM today.	
		6.0 am	Struck & loaded lines of tents & trench shelters and batteries standing by for bus transport.	
		7.0 pm	Received operation order No. aaa by ADMS 5th Division :- "The Division tell move to the CAVILLON area (W. of Amiens) today. Movements will be performed by bus transport by much routes. The Division will entrain by 1st Bde Groups in accordance with instructions issued … times of entraining will be '173 1st Bde Group 10 AM ….' Transport will march by Bde Groups &c... by following route HOLLIENS AU BOIS — RAINSVILLE — COISY — BOULAINVILLE — LONG-PRÉ — MONTIÈRES … Full Addresses in H.Q. area will be

WAR DIARY or INTELLIGENCE SUMMARY

Army Form C. 2118.

Place	Date	Hour	Summary of Events and Information	Remarks and references to Appendices
ST GRATIEN	June 10		Located at billets 2/1st MCD Amb DREUIL LES MOLLIENS 2/2nd ditto 2/3rd " ST PIERRE A GOUY	
"			Working party of 1 Officer + 6 men with motor ambulances will remain at sick collecting station BEAUCOURT until 12 hrs party of 1st Divison arrives on relief. The party of 2/1st MCD Amb will rejoin their unit.	
"		7.15 am	Issued orders in accordance with above for return of dismounted half Myn HUXTABLE H.C. + 2 other ranks — from BEAUCOURT and for march of dismounted personnel under Capt DICK at 9.45 AM + of horse transport at 10.15 am under Capt SMEATON. Invalided to CCS Capt E.SOUTHBERT sick P.U.O. 2 Capt P.V.EARLY sick Invalided and transferred to a unit	A)→
"	9.45 am		[struck through] Dismounted portion proceeded to VILLERS BOCAGE – TALMAS Rd to entrain	
"		10.15 am	H.T. + wheeled transport proceeded by route detailed in above O.O. of A.D.M.S.	
"		11.30 am	Myn HUXTABLE + remaining personnel from BEAUCOURT rejoined hung completed had over to 5a D. Amb of 1st Division Proceed with Motor Ambulances as a convoy to DREUIL LES MOLLIENS	A)→
DREUIL-LES MOLLIENS		1.30 pm	Arrived DREUIL without further incident + accommodation found. Village very limited in amenities	A)→ A)→

WAR DIARY or INTELLIGENCE SUMMARY

Army Form C. 2118.

Place	Date	Hour	Summary of Events and Information	Remarks and references to Appendices
BREUIL LES MEULIENS	June 10	2.50 p.m.	Dismounted portion of Unit arrived having detrained at BRIQUEMESNIL & marched from that place.	O.O. & that 62E
"	"	3.0 p.m.	Horse Transport mounted portion arrived. Received following from ADMS "The 4/1st H.F.A. Amb will move into the 173rd Bde area tomorrow 11.6.16. An Officer will be sent tonight to HQ 173rd Bde to arrange for accommodation in BOVELLES. In the event of a move the 4/1st H.F.A. Amb will move with the 173 Bde." Major HUXTABLE proceeded to HQ 173 Bde & reported in view that there was no accommodation in BOVELLES. All troops accommodation will be found at SAISSEMONT.	P.3. £
"	11	9.30 a.m.	Major HUXTABLE proceeded to MISSEMONT with Staff Capt. 173 Bde to arrange accommodation.	
"	"	1.0 p.m.	Whole unit proceeded by march route to SAISSEMONT.	
SAISSEMONT	"	3.30 p.m.	Unit arrived & billetted. Motors available for the temporary accommodation of about 20 sick of 173 Bde front. Sick to be evacuated to No.? 5 & 47 C.C.S. CROUY. Received extensive programme in event of move of Division with following arrangements made by ADMS & D.G. field Ambulances will continue in accordance with stated programme it being noticed "following troops should be fully equipped."	

WAR DIARY or INTELLIGENCE SUMMARY

Army Form C. 2118.

Place	Date	Hour	Summary of Events and Information	Remarks and references to Appendices
RAISSEMONT	June 12	6.0 p.m.	Lt. Liet. J. de R. Carles M.R.C. U.S.A. joined for duty attchd. on strength. Requested notes to refreshing troops at Rest Camp.	A.S.D
"	13	4.0 p.m.	Capt. P.V. EARLY rejoined from C.C.S.	A.S.D
"	14	2.0 p.m.	Major T.S. WARD reported from leave to United Kingdom	
		7.0 p.m.	Capt. F.A. DICK proceeded to report for duty to O.C. "A" Batn. H.Q. Capt + attchd HQ Staff	A.S.D
"	15	2.30 p.m.	Attended conference of D Adv Commanders at "ATOMS" when CAVALON informed that orders called upon in the interim tentatively of Support on the line VILLERS BRETONNEUX — McREUIL the division will relieve the 47th Division in right sector of III Corps front. Later 13/14 & 20th June orders of Jull Ambulances during tour of division in the line discussed. 2/3rd H.E.D. Ambs to relieve 5th London 3 Ambs in forward posts with HQ at (Rush-12.D.) Caravan 3/4 1/1st H.E.D. Ambs to relieve 6th London 3 Ambs at main dressing station MONTIGNY " " 3 2/1st H.E.D. Ambs to relieve 6th London 3 Ambs at MIRVAUX & rest over flow collecting station at BEAUCOURT.	
"	"	4.0 p.m.	Rec'd orders No a8 by A.D.M.S. setting the above at "Jull Ambulance bill move with orders of Adm tactical affiliated. 3/3rd – formed will proceed by bus "Transport by road" note: Transport & staff personnel of 1/1st H.E.D. Amb will be located in support at B.2.0.6. & that of 1/1st H.E.D. Amb in support at B.2.0.d. Relief of Ambs to hn bn 3 Amb at Hain Dessing Stn MONTIGNY will be completed by 12 noon 16th inst.	A.S.D

Army Form C. 2118.

WAR DIARY
or
INTELLIGENCE SUMMARY
(Erase heading not required.)

Instructions regarding War Diaries and Intelligence Summaries are contained in F. S. Regs., Part II. and the Staff Manual respectively. Title Pages will be prepared in manuscript.

Place	Date	Hour	Summary of Events and Information	Remarks and references to Appendices
LASSEMONT	June 16	10.0 a.m.	Recd. 173 Inf Bde order No 27 :— The Bde will proceed by route march to wood S.E. of MOLLIENS AU BOIS on the 17th inst. The Bde Group will entrain in the following order. (1/16, 1/16 D. Amb End-) The head of the column will halt at the back end of FERRIERES on main BRIQUEMESNIL — FERRIERES road. Transport will proceed under the Bde Transport Officer to MOLLIENS AU BOIS, forming starting point at road junction at Q.9.A.3.9 at 10 a.m. in the following order. H/of H.Q. Amb. at 10.25 a.m. (following 'B' Coy 52th H.Q. Bn., & heading 504 Field Coy R.E.)	A 17 Sheet 62 E 1/40,000
"	"	9.0 a.m.	Capt. PVEAREY proceeded to the temporary medical charge of 2/P Ldn. vice Capt. C.C. AUSTEN sick.	
			Recd. amendment to 173 Inf Bde order No 27, transport of this unit will now form column at AILLY Bridge at 11.15 a.m., D 14 inst.	A 17
"	17	9 am	Horsed transport under temporary portion of the unit proceeded under Major WARD.	A 17
"	"	2.0 pm	Proceeded by Motor Autocar to MONTIGNY B.20.C.6.0 to arrange preliminary of take over from the London 2/1 Amb. and thence to meet at B.20.C.0.6 to arrive for night.	A 17
	"	2.30 pm	Remainder of unit proceeded under Major HUXTABLE via E side on BRIQUEMESNIL — FERRIERES Rd.	A 17
	"	4.30 pm	Horsed transport & nearly portion arrived	A 17
GRATIEN hut at B.20.6.0.6	"	7.48 pm	Remainder of unit arrived having be billetted on MOLLIENS AU BOIS — BEAUCOURT Road. Putch & tents and erected bivouac.	A 17

WAR DIARY
or
INTELLIGENCE SUMMARY

Army Form C. 2118.

Place	Date	Hour	Summary of Events and Information	Remarks and references to Appendices
T GRATIEN wood	June 18	9.15 a.m.	Proceeded with reserves forward to MONTIGNY to take over Divisional Main Dressing Station for the right Sector of the III Corps front at the Rd culvert km 4 London & Astr. Thence lines & supplies forward reserves at B.20. to make Major HUXTABLE M.C.	A.D.)
MONTIGNY	"	10.0 a.m.	Take over from 4th London 3 Amb. completed.	
			A working party of two other ranks dispatched to report to O.C. 2/3 H.C.3.Amb. at FRANVILLIERS for work on mutual posts in forward area.	A.)
"	19	4.30 a.m.	A further working party of two other ranks sent to O.C. 2/3 H.C.3 Amb. at FRANVILLIERS	A.)
"	20	9.0 a.m.	Major HUXTABLE M.C. proceeded on leave to United Kingdom.	A.)
"	26	6.0 p.m.	Working parties sent to 2/3rd H.C.3.Amb. have all been returned to hypo lines in T GRATIEN wood. Generally situation on front very quiet & casualties very few averaging about 10 in 24 hrs through this dressing station.	A.)
"	29	10.0 a.m.	Attended conference of A.D.M.S. officer, 3 discussed Medical arrangements in event of a retirement. The 3 Amb working the line would continue that evacuation continue that duty of the two remaining 3 Ambs would be evening hyper sites for M.D.S. behind in echelon & in the east of the advance of M.D.S. at MONTIGNY the 1/3rd. H.C.3.Amb would be prepared to open its shelter HOUGNE AU BOIS at RAININEVILLE.	A.)
	30	10 noon	The following little casualties have passed through the M.D.S. since taking over on 18th inst.– Sgt Brown Ashin 106 Sent to CCS 80 To duty 19 Sick 3 Other Inselves. 33 623 Dead cases 3. Separate figures 7 ground cases 3. N.Y.D.N.	A.) Delemer (Adj.)

19

CONFIDENTIAL

original
JB 18
16/3/31.

July 8. 18.

War Diary
of
Lieut. Colonel A.T. FALWASSER DSO RAMC T.F
Commanding 2/1st Home Counties Field Ambulance

from July 1. 18 to July 31. 18

(Volume 2)

COMMITTEE FOR THE
MEDICAL HISTORY OF THE WAR
Date 6 SEP 1913

WAR DIARY or INTELLIGENCE SUMMARY

Army Form C. 2118.

Place	Date	Hour	Summary of Events and Information	Remarks and references to Appendices
MONTIGNY	July 2	5.30 pm	The O.C. 50 Division inspected the Dressing Station & expressed his approval of the arrangements for receiving, testing & evacuating.	A.D.7
"	3	9.0 am	Two NCOs and one man proceeded for leave duties in the line under 2/Lt K.F.G. Ant	A.D.7
"	4	10.0 am	Twenty ranks (stretcher walking cases) including a hutch in fighting kilt with retunee at 7.30 am and 9.30 am. Arrangements on sight of the Division front by number of a just there taken they objected to counter in the division being rather of every barrage which was let down on front-line & settled to us states.	A.D.7
"	5	12.0 noon	Lieut. A.F. GALLOWAY R.A.M.C. T.C. proceeded for duty as a reinforcement.	A.D.7
"	7	11.30 am	Major A.E. HUXTABLE M.C. returned from leave to United Kingdom.	A.D.7
"	8	11.0 am	Received following order from A.D.M.S. 50 Division "On receipt of message 'BATTLE STATION PRACTICE' the following procedure will be carried out by 150, 3 & 201 Ambulances (1 R.A.M.C. other ranks vacating 1 R.A.M.C. signal). No movement before 9.30 pm & no transport area no messenger before dusk. O.C. 2/3rd H.E.3 Amb. will detail 12 squads of bearers to report to O.C. 2/3rd H.E.3 Amb at C.20.t.8.2. O.C. 2/3rd H.E.3 Amb will report to A.D.M.S. at 12 noon for future details are in position by speed at daily 'BATTLE STATIONS PRACTICE COMPLETE'. On receipt of order for the office. NORMAL"	Phot. 6.D 1.A.0000

WAR DIARY
INTELLIGENCE SUMMARY

Army Form C. 2118.

Place	Date	Hour	Summary of Events and Information	Remarks and references to Appendices
HATTENCY	July 10	11.30 a.m.	"NORMAL DISPOSITIONS" detailed parties will be withdrawn after roster will be taken by 2nd Ante Commdr beyond that stated above. No	
			Lieut T. de R. COMBES HRC proceeded to A.D.S. at D.15.d.2.2 for a tour of duty & instruction.	Lieut C.D.S. A to arm.
	11	8.20 a.m.	Received wire from A.D.M.S. "BATTLE STATIONS PRACTICE" One NCO & 12 men is operating in event of being proceeded to report to O.C. 4/5th H.F.A Amb at C.20.b.2.2 at 8.40 p.m.	A.D.D
	12	9.10 a.m.	The NCO & 12 men, who proceeded as above, reported.	A.D.D
	12	11.0 a.m.	D.D.M.S. III Corps inspected the Main Dressing Station	A.D.D
	12	12.0 noon	Lieut T. de R. COMBES H.R.C. rejoined from a tour of duty & instruction at Advanced Dressing Station.	A.D.D
	15	9.0 a.m.	Lieut T. de R. COMBES M.R.C. proceeded for temporary duty in which charge of 2/6th Lenter Regt.	A.D.D
		6 p.m.	The following two Casualties details with the M.D.S. during to first 15 days of July	A.D.D

Att to front.

	Att	Evac	to duty	On St
	Off	OR	Off	OR	Off	OR	Off	OR
	19	119	2	75	15	20	2	20
59 Division	3	110	2	75	—	5	1	20
Att to front					1	5		
Total	5	105	4	115	1	26	2	A.D.D

Army Form C. 2118.

WAR DIARY
or
INTELLIGENCE SUMMARY

(Erase heading not required.)

Instructions regarding War Diaries and Intelligence Summaries are contained in F. S. Regs., Part II. and the Staff Manual respectively. Title Pages will be prepared in manuscript.

Place	Date	Hour	Summary of Events and Information	Remarks and references to Appendices
MONTIGNY	July 16	5.0 p.m.	Lieut. J. le R. COMBES returned from 6th London Regt. & proceeded for duty with O.i/c Sgd. M.C. Butts.	A)-
"	19	9.0 a.m.	Received following operation order by A.S.H.S. as shown :— "The O.C. 1/1st 1st L.F.A. will detail as Test Ambulance with 2 officers to take over the Sqdn. holding trenches CECIETE from St. MONTIGNY for 10 days. The Relief to be completed by 6 p.m. July 19th. — subsequently minuted to read 10 AM July 19th. All Kits etc. at C.W.W.C.P. will be taken over by the officer i/c 3, taking a list of same handed to the Officer.	A)-
"	19	10.0 a.m.	Major JAWARD and Lieut. A.F. GALLOWAY proceed to Corps testing trenches taken at MONTIGNY from B, 17, & 3.9 with personnel of a test detail 1.9. which is [?]ed of total detail of personnel of 10 officers and 9 other ranks in half of 50 #3 A.A. 2 plat complete at 9.45 a.m.	Sect 6LD 1/1th A.S.O. A)-
"	21	10.0 a.m.	1st Lieut. C.S. SILLIMAN MRC USA joined for duty from 30th Army Artillery School	A)-
"	23	6.0 p.m.	Capt. J.M. SMEATON proceeded to temp'y. duty with 1/1 London Regt.	A)-
"	25	7.0 a.m.	In accordance with instructions received Lieut. A.F. GALLOWAY proceeded for temp'y duty at Advanced Dressing Station at Lopan & Lances to be left in reserve. Proceeded to O.C. 1/3 M.C. Amber.	A)-

Army Form C. 2118.

WAR DIARY
or
INTELLIGENCE SUMMARY

(Erase heading not required.)

Instructions regarding War Diaries and Intelligence Summaries are contained in F. S. Regs., Part II. and the Staff Manual respectively. Title Pages will be prepared in manuscript.

Place	Date	Hour	Summary of Events and Information	Remarks and references to Appendices
MONTIGNY	July 29	10.0 p.m.	A wired with Artillery cooperation was carried out at 10 P.M. today by the 9th London Regt. against enemy trenches & posts in E.13.b.d.d. and E.15.a. and c. At a limit retaliation of this raid 106 casualties were dealt with at this HDS. In addition 106 men of Hutch Gas poisoning were passed through during 24 hrs ended 10 pm today & these casualties were retained by difficulty & wrong parties on the middle of an enemy gas shell bombardment between 11 midnight July 28 and 5 AM July 29.	Meat. 62.D 1, 40 000
	30	9.0 p.m.	Received Mobilisation order No. 40 2y AD.M.S. 50 Division :— "the tenderness between the 5th Aust Bde and the 5th Aust Bde on the right will be altered on the night of July 28/29 and July 27/28 respectively. This above that the 5th of the division to the right necessitates the handing over of R.A.P. at D.12.a.1.6.6 to the 14th Division and the taking over of R.A.P. at D.30.a.9.2 and at 7.5.1.7.6 from the 14th Aust Div Casualties of 14th division from R.A.P. at D.12.1.6.6 will be evacuated through AD.S. of this (53th.) division at D.15.d. 7.4. Purposes of sending such a slack him 67 divisions has been protested by their Main Dressing Station."	Meat. 62.D 1. 40 000
	30	12.0 noon	Received warning order by 50 Division. The 53th Division will be relieved by the 14 Division in the right sector of its Div front on the night of 43 August & in the left sector on the night of 3/4 August in order the division will forward to the CAVILLION area by train.	
	31	6.0 a.m.	Capt. W. W. WOOD R.AM.C. joined for duty from 16th Labour Group.	

2449 Wt. W14937/M90 750,000 1/16 J.B.C. & A. Forms/C.2118/12.

WAR DIARY or INTELLIGENCE SUMMARY

Army Form C. 2118.

Place	Date	Hour	Summary of Events and Information	Remarks and references to Appendices
MONTIGNY	July 31	10.0 a.m	Tabular statement of Battle Casualties treated at M.D.S. during the week :—	

	Admitted		Evacuated		To duty		Died	
	Offrs	O.R.	Offrs	O.R.	Offrs	O.R.	Offrs	O.R.
52 Division	22	415	20	367	2	44	—	4
Other formations	9	96	9	74	—	21	—	1
Total	31	511	29	441	2	65	—	5

The above figures relate to filtered "Gassed" cases.

	Admitted		Evacuated	
	Offrs	O.R.	Offrs	O.R.
52 Division	3	114	3	114
Other formations	3	17	3	17
Total	6	131	6	131

N.B.— Invaliding feel
RATE —
Aug 2/1st Home class I hab

Original
W.R. 19
140/3200

CONFIDENTIAL

War Diary
of
Lieut. Col. A.T. FALWASSER D.S.O. R.A.M.C. T.F.
C/O 2/1st Home Counties Field Ambulance

From Aug 1st 1918 to 31st 18

(Volume 2)

COMMITTEE FOR THE
MEDICAL HISTORY OF THE WAR
Date 6 OCT 1933

WAR DIARY or INTELLIGENCE SUMMARY

Army Form C. 2118.

Place	Date	Hour	Summary of Events and Information	Remarks and references to Appendices
MONTIGNY	Aug 1	8.30 a.m.	Lieut. A.F. GALLOWAY proceeded for duty to 2nd London Regt.	A.D.
"	"	9.30 a.m.	Received 'Administrative Arrangements 58th Division'. This unit will be prepared to take over the move & in the next area with # 173 Inf. Bde front and will relieve with that front at 2 A.M. on August 3rd. BEHENCOURT – BAZIEUX Rd. will defeat on HALLOY – BERTEAUCOURT Rd. and proceed to BERTEAUCOURT — there now billets vacated by 36 Inf. Bde. Hd. Qrs (with div'n).	A.D.
"	"	3.0 p.m.	Received 'Operation order No. 29 by A.D.M.S. 58 Division'. The 58th Division HdQtrs will be relieved in the centre sector of III Corps front by the 12th Division. Relief will be completed by dawn August 3rd. The division on relieved will move to the VIGNACOURT area. Divisional transport by two transports by march route. Field ambs will move with Bdes to new area & follow 2/1st HdQtrs' 173 Inf. Bde. — The 2/1st HdQtrs will be relieved by a party of the 37th Ambulance on the afternoon of 2nd August on relief the 2/1st HdQtrs will proceed to BERTEAUCOURT & take over the site of the 36th Fd Ambulance ... 2/1st HdQtrs office will close at BEAUCOURT at 10 A.M. Aug 3rd & reopen at VIGNACOURT at same hour.	A.D.
"	"	6.0 p.m.	Received 173 Inf. Bde following order.	A.D.
"	"	9.0 p.m.	Road wire from 173 Inf.Bde ..... from (Horse Transport) will proceed via HOLLIENS – VILLERS BOCAGE – TALMAS – NAOURS starting not later than 5.30 a.m. (3rd)	A.D.

Army Form C. 2118.

WAR DIARY
or
INTELLIGENCE SUMMARY
(Erase heading not required.)

Instructions regarding War Diaries and Intelligence Summaries are contained in F. S. Regs., Part II. and the Staff Manual respectively. Title Pages will be prepared in manuscript.

Place	Date	Hour	Summary of Events and Information	Remarks and references to Appendices
MONTIGNY	Aug 2	11.0 a.m.	Rec'd wire from A.D.M.S. "55 #3 Amb will take over ops holding wounded Post this morning"	A))
"	"	3.0 p.m.	Completed hand over of this Main Dressing Station to A/q 55 #3 Amb.	A))
"	"	9.30 p.m.	Completed hand over of ops holding wounded Post at MONTIGNY FARM to 55 #3 Amb.	A))
"	Aug 3	1.0 a.m.	Marched from MONTIGNY to infantry fork on BEHENCOURT – BAZIEUX R⁴ & arrived at 2 A.M.	Mar 57 E. P.30. a.9.o. A)) A))
BERTEAUCOURT	"	6.0 a.m.	Detrained & billeted	A))
"	"	10.0 a.m.	Moved tonight into Hqrs STWARD went long off with upon him at Bde.E. (Field - 62.D) at 5.30 p.m.	A))
"	"	11.0 p.m.	Received operation order No 60 by A.D.M.S. 58 Division :- "4/5 August 63 td's & march route offices commanding 2/1st & 2/2nd H.C.) Amb's will arrange direct with Bdes re times of starting. 3/1st, 3/2nd & 3/3 H.C) Amb's arrived in FRANVILLERS area will transfer in Ra event of their transport of the 3 D Amb's will proceed by road whole arrangement of their intake to O.3.C. . . . Advance billets will be sent forthwith to the road in 1./4th a.+c in . . . These will pass at QUERRIEU at 10 A.M. on the 4th inst. A.D.M.S. Office will open at QUERRIEU at 10 A.M."	A))

2449 Wt. W14957/M90 730,000 1/16 J.B.C. & A. Forms/C.2118/12.

Army Form C. 2118.

WAR DIARY
or
INTELLIGENCE SUMMARY
(Erase heading not required.)

Instructions regarding War Diaries and Intelligence Summaries are contained in F. S. Regs., Part II. and the Staff Manual respectively. Title Pages will be prepared in manuscript.

Place	Date	Hour	Summary of Events and Information	Remarks and references to Appendices
BERTEAUCOURT	Aug 4	1.15 a.m.	Received wire from 173 Bde 'Prepare to entrain a.m. 4th August'	A.1)
"		10.00 a.m.	Received 173 Inf Bde Order for move . . . . Entraining point for all units will be BERTEAUCOURT — HALLOY Rd. East of HALLOY. 2/1st H.C.3 Ambce. Entraining point (? St Pietrre end?) will entrain at 9.30 pm . . . Itinerary from ALBERT — AMIENS Rd. End of column from East & West edge of LA HOUSSOYE . . . . No transport will move independently . further instructions will be issued later today.	A.1)
"		4.0 p.m.	Received 173 Inf Bde orders for transport. Starting point road junction X.1.C.5.9 (Sheet 57E) Southern edge of HAVERNAS. Units will pass starting point as follows . . . . 2/1st H.C.3 Ambce 12.30 midnight . . . . Route HAVERNAS — FLESSELLES — VILLERS BOCAGE — MOLLIENS AU BOIS — ST GRATIEN — QUERRIEU — PONT NOYELLES . . . . Arrival of road train closely followed by advance party est. (arrived yesterday).	A.1)
REY WOOD L.19.a.7.0		5.0 a.m. 7.30 a.m.	Horse transport marching portion of Unit arrived. Received Medical Instructions by A.D.M.S. 58 Division. On the night 5/6 August the 2/1st H.C.3 Amb will take the new form ore 2/4 H.C.3 Amb, the A.D.S. I.30.a.2.2 which post on the East the new to 5/8 Division. He also 2/1st H.C.3 Amb will be responsible for the collection & evacuation of casualties from divisional sector from 10 pm August 5th and also any casualties from divisional sector passing thro' the A.D.S. 2/3 H.C.3 Amb will place at the disposal of the 2/1st H.C.3 Amb from	I.19.a.7.0 Sheet 62D

Place	Date	Hour	Summary of Events and Information	Remarks and references to Appendices
KEY WOOD	Aug 5	10.0 a.m.	from 6 p.m. Aug 7th. 3 M.O.'s 2 dert Cars & large cars 30 Bearers …… OC Ypres Hos Amb will please at disposal of …… M.O. 2 dert Cars & large cars 30 Bearers	A/S
"	"	11.0 a.m.	Attended conference at ADMS' Office & discussed Medical arrangements for operation to begin at an early date	A/S Sketch 6, D
"	"		Went on tour of cars with Major HUXTABLE to HQ of 6a.D. Arr at I.9.a.8 to get information about starting Medical arrangements in order to take over & these to ADS (Divisional train) at I.30.a.9.2	A/S
"	"	2.0 p.m.	Major HUXTABLE with Capt WOOD on test exploration of 6 point knees Proceeded to ADS to take over test forward post.	A/S
"	"	9.30 p.m.	Relief of Personnel of 50 F.Amb completed as follows. Left - RAP T.29.d.2.3, T.29.c.8.9 Right - VAUX (Artillery) Post - T.26. central Relay Post - T.30.b.9.3 Evacuation from Left - RAP to Right RAP is by hand carriage & by wheeled stretcher. From Right RAP to ADS from which to MDS Sent an Ambulance by wheeled stretcher MDS at QUERRIEU (H.10.b.1.6) is by large motor ambulance. Large hired & returning Personnel will be located at - KEY WOOD	A/S
KEY WOOD	Aug 6	9.30 a.m.	Proceeded to ADS to remain there complete medical arrangements for operation to commence on At met Major McGILLIVRAY consulted me & & we settled evacuating to be "S" Pack for "walking wounded" from T.29.c.2.9 to T.19.a.3.9 from which point wounded to be walked to C.W.W.P.2 - B.17.b.3.7 & will be convey walking wounded to C.W.W.P by III Corps detailed by 2449 Wt. W14957/M90 750,000 1/16 J.B.C. & A. Forms/C.2118/12.	A/S

WAR DIARY
or
INTELLIGENCE SUMMARY

Army Form C. 2118.

Place	Date	Hour	Summary of Events and Information	Remarks and references to Appendices
MPTHS F.M.	Aug 6	6.0 p.m.	The following casualties have passed thro' A.D.S. since take over at 9.30 pm yesterday. 52 Division 10. Other army 20. Total 70. Including Gas cases 50 gas. Other from 1 - other from 30. Total 31. Evacuation has proceeded normally & no difficulties have been encountered.	
	Aug 7	9.0 a.m.	Personnel & vehicles are the detailed from Y&L & 2/5 HLI. M.O.s have left(?). Two (?) are disposed of as follows:- One has been attached to M.O. Y and Battn in the line (a in Two(?) as in two(?)) as to supply our left in relation to Quarry R.A.P. (J.n.2.c.2.9) to attach number) as to supply our left in relation to Quarry R.A.P. (J.n.2.c.2.9) to attach to end. Y 3 Battns which have though the Battn in line after capture of first objective & the function of these Battns being to capture the second objective. Twelve stretcher squads we held at Quarry R.A.P. in reserve to reform available or tired squads & for the establishment of any relay posts which may be required forward in consequence of the advance. Major K.E. HUXTABLE M.C. is in charge in forward at the Quarry and will leave others & bearer officers after liaison officers will liquidate M.O.s and 2 (or. the R.A.P.? two & bearer officers of the Quarry R.A.P. which will become an advanced A.D.S. as the line is Medical work at Quarry R.A.P. which will become an advanced A.D.S. at the line is pass forward. Twelve stretcher squads we left in reserve at A.D.S. (Chuttitum). Stretcher squads(?) for Battle Stretches) are held as a stand reserve at H.Q. head & stretcher squads (?) And is available at QUERRIEU château. In addition 50 men of Inf. manpower Res? & Amb are held for duty at A.D.S. Four Medical Officers with O.S. in reserve at A.D.S. for duty at A.D.S. Advanced test infusion A.D.S. for duty at A.D.S. has been established in a dull pit. 150 yards S of ADS on hill side of road & one of two M.O.s has been detailed for duty here.	

WAR DIARY or INTELLIGENCE SUMMARY

Army Form C. 2118.

Place	Date	Hour	Summary of Events and Information	Remarks and references to Appendices
SMITH'S P.M.	Aug 9	6.0 a.m	All sick & walking wounded will be dealt with at this post & will be conveyed from the Rly Head Advance Dgrs to T.35.d.4.9. This Dressing Post will be staffed by 1 N.C.O. & 3 men and 3 bearers will be stationed here to convey men to the Group at B.17.d.3.9. The attack will start at 2.20 am tomorrow. Casualties Clear the A.D.S. from 6pm - 6ft. to 6pm - 7ft. 50 Division 10. Other forms 40. These figures include Gassed cases 1. Other forms 25. A.D.	Sheet (S.D.)
"	"	10.30 a.m	Attack appears to be going well — a few walking cases we slowly coming through the Quarry R.A.P. is now practically evacuated. A.D.S. A.D.	
"	"	6.0 p.m	Cases are now running to Quarry R.A.P. & front ones are running forward to destn. T.23.b.2.0. Cases are coming down in a steady stream. The attack is going well & the final objective there been gained but definite information is difficult to be certain. A.D. Cases are coming down steadily, front ones are now running to T.23.b.2.0. & to destn. T.26.d.2.3. The following cases have been dealt with since 6 AM today.	

	After Dawn	P. Rear
lying	31	32
walking	104	26
	29	6w
Total	193	62
		319

A.D.

WAR DIARY or INTELLIGENCE SUMMARY

Army Form C. 2118.

Place	Date	Hour	Summary of Events and Information	Remarks and references to Appendices
FRITHS	Aug 9	6.0 AM	The following casualties have been dealt with since 6 pm yesterday: Офф. O.Rs. Brit. 5 58 Hyde 3 30 Liffey 1 60 The casualties at first stationed at J.23.6 were all now through the place. It is stated by Lt. Col. ? that when it was apparent the KID ? stretcher bearers remaining in the ? had thrown them ? during first- in time it ? the OHLUY village had there been ? Casualties still ? only by the enemy. They shall are ambulance evacuated by the enemy the ? 3 only available in the middle of ? Casualties have been heavy during the day, experienced have been proceeding steadily through this as firing approaches. All cases we being have through ? as front at SAILLY LAURETTE. Cases dealt with since 6 AM — Офф. O.Rs. Brit. 5 35 Hyde 21 3 Liffey 3 Attack on CHIPILLY via a further portion of the enemy's line is now in progress & is reported to be going well.	
"	6.0 pm			
"	12.0 midnight		A large number of casualties are coming in as result of attack 4-5.30 pm which appears to have been successful. Troops moved to SAILLY LAURETTE which stretched forward to R.A.P.s of 17. London Regt. & K.31.a. R.A.P.s of the R.A.P.s of the ?	Ред. G.D.

WAR DIARY or INTELLIGENCE SUMMARY

Army Form C. 2118.

Place	Date	Hour	Summary of Events and Information	Remarks and references to Appendices
SMITHS FM.	Aug 10	6.0 a.m.	Battalion of 173rd Bde relieved about K.26, & (C.27) all in shell hostility very heavy but ten actually shell J.2 and 3 & 26. a. 2.3 for an extra 2 hr area of our part of SAILLY LAURETTE. Quiet until about 6 hr yesterday.	Ref - G2D
			Batter arriving Americans	AJD
			58 Div 4 5
			lying 132 53
			sitting 254 125
				Prpls 15 12
			131 American Inf Regt reported in yesterday into expected Hqrs of Company 17th Int Bde A. Staff has been made from Bn HQrs to relieve C Coy.	
			Int reports us had and the number of casualties. Co reported with DA an enemy MG with by squad with status stated are being supply till with by squad of SAILLY LAURETTE Hyrtg A localities K.26 and K.27	
			but are front of SAILLY LAURETTE to BOIS LEC CELESTINES.	AJD
			for capture of BOIS MALARD & Bois LEC CELESTINES.	
6.0 p.m.			Attack this afternoon was resumed up to noon but then the line remained and the tests report close at 3 p.m.	
			58 Div OP Americans Prpls
			lying 88 7 42 27
			sitting 20 4 22
				AJD

WAR DIARY or INTELLIGENCE SUMMARY

Army Form C. 2118.

Place	Date	Hour	Summary of Events and Information	Remarks and references to Appendices
SAILLY FM	Aug 11	6.0 am	The 58th Div was relieved in the line last night as far N as K.18 central, with a portion of the front line from this northern extremity it and K.6 central now taken over from the 18th Division making the frontage of this Div with the route of communication – 7 pm as a consequence of this side step the route of communication lies – K.16.d.2.45 — BRAY-CORBIE Rd. — T.13.c.8.1 yesterday has been K.16.d.2.45 — BRAY-CORBIE Rd. — T.13.c.5.5 — SAILLY LE SEC – ASF — BRAY-CORBIE Rd. to I.30.a.5.5 is being used. A new ASF on BRAY-CORBIE Rd. at 8AM today is hoped much to check it & V.29.c.2.2 will be maintained as long as Advanced ASF at V.29.c.2.2 will be maintained as long as our troops are in area S. of BRAY-CORBIE Rd. Cases three to 6 pm yesterday	Flash 6 D
			58 Div Ammun Rifles	
			lying 14 63 10	
			sitting 10 27 1	
			13 26	
			At 8 AM an ASF was opened at I.30.a.5.5 and the following posts were taken over from 54 F.S. Amb. (18th Div) manned by R.A.M.C.	
		6.0 pm	bearers of 58th Division — K.16.d.2.4 Advanced Coys. our front K.21.b.6.7 Advanced Coys. (hope dry) Ad L T.13.d.1.2 Main	K.17.a.9.2
			RAP of new Battery in front line at K.17.a.9.2	

WAR DIARY / INTELLIGENCE SUMMARY

Army Form C. 2118.

Place	Date	Hour	Summary of Events and Information	Remarks and references to Appendices
			RAP of support Battn. is at K.16.d.2.4. a Squad of Scouts attacked track Bttn in his support at K.16.d.2.4. carry to prevent any hostile attack on VAUX – SAILLY – CHIPILLY rode that the tanks are All fronts on ito hostile SAPs and all personnel of 5th Divison withdrawn to 1.30. a.m. which a being returned in MR of 7 tanks.	Photo 62 D
			Casualties 6 a.m. today 0.7	
			5th Div	
			Killed 10 3	
			Wounded 3 14	
			Prisoners Germans	
			7	
			2 A.D.
SMITHS FM	Aug 12	6.0 a.m	Cases thro' ADS since 6 pm yesterday Americans 9 yrs	
			5th Div 0.5 —	
			Killed 1 4 1	
			Wounded 12 25 9 A.D.
"		11AM	Visited all posts in forward sector. Casualties or few sent being evacuated without difficulty	A.D.

Army Form C. 2118.

Instructions regarding War Diaries and Intelligence Summaries are contained in F. S. Regs., Part II. and the Staff Manual respectively. Title pages will be prepared in manuscript.

WAR DIARY
or
~~INTELLIGENCE SUMMARY.~~
(Erase heading not required.)

Place	Date	Hour	Summary of Events and Information	Remarks and references to Appendices
SMITH'S FM	Aug 12	3.0 pm	All officers bearers & other RAMC personnel not now actually engaged in the line returned to their units & those of this unit to KEY WOOD I.14.a Horsed ambulance wagons also returned to I.14.a and walking wounded lorry post at I 35.d.4.9 closed and lorries now stand at A.D.S I.30.a.5.5. Rec'd operation order No 55 by ADMS 58 Division :— "The 47th Division will relieve the 58th Division .... on the night of 12/13th August. On relief the Division will be concentrated in the LAHOUSSOYE area ..... The 2/1st H.C. Fd Amb will be relieved by the 6th London F Amb at the A.D.S. J.19.c.5.9 (sic), Car posts, & Relay posts on the present 58th Div route of evacuation .... relief to be completed by 10 pm August 13th .... On relief the 2/1st H.C. Fd Amb will proceed to the wood at I.14.c & billet there." A.D.	Sheet 62D.
KEY WOOD	"	6.0 pm	Cases thro' A.D.S since 6 am today 58 Div — O. Forma[illegible] Lying 3 — 4 Sitting 2 — 10 A.D.	

D. D. & L., London, E.C.
(A10266) W1 W5300/P713 750,000 2/15 Sch. 52 Forms/C2118/16

WAR DIARY
or
INTELLIGENCE SUMMARY

Army Form C. 2118.

Place	Date	Hour	Summary of Events and Information	Remarks and references to Appendices
KEY WOOD	Aug 13	6 a.m.	Casualties thro' MG fire 6/h yesterday:- 5B [killed] 1 O.ranks [killed] 4 [wounded]	
		3.0 p.m.	MG's handed over to 6th [Bn] Border R. Mule at 10.30 am. Relief completed 2 p.m. Forward Halted Posts also handed over at KEY WOOD. All personnel of this unit is now at KEY WOOD. No casualties have been sustained by this unit during recent [operations] only one casualty (one man slightly gassed) by R.M.G. of whole division + Bty no casualty Between (on duty of some sort) men though MG's division P.Y 15 musicians 17 — — 1 — 131 115 114 w.c. [?] 54 4/31 5/31	
			Aug 6/13: MG. to have been no unusually large proportion of [Corps] [who have] but is accounted [for by] downward drift of men wounded other [?] Remainder [?] [?] heft away together afterwards.	A.D.?

WAR DIARY or INTELLIGENCE SUMMARY.

Army Form C. 2118.

Place	Date	Hour	Summary of Events and Information	Remarks and references to Appendices
KEY WOOD T.14.a	Aug 18	10.0 a.m.	Unit cleared & resting.	Place (I.D)
"	19	7.0 p.m.	Recd. instr. under No. 5a by A.T.M.S. 58 Division move to MONTIGNY & take over the site of the Cafe holding trench station from the 55th Divn. Unit to take over the cookers by 10 A.M. 20th August.	The Mst-A.D.M.S will bring new site of A.D.S. A)? A)?
"	20	8.30 a.m.	The Officers & 6 O.Rs. rank proceed to MONTIGNY B.17.k.7.0 in accordance with the foregoing.	A)?
"	"	1.45 p.m.	Remainder of unit proceed by march route to MONTIGNY.	A)?
MONTIGNY B.17.k.7.a	"	3.0 p.m.	Hostel of M.B.S. Divn Hollow at QUERRIEU Chateau - Spend a disaster on lessen for reccet operations.	A)?
"	"	5.0 p.m.	Whole unit is now at MONTIGNY with hospital divn at B.17.a.6.9	A)?
"	21	6.0 p.m.	Capt. E.B. JARDINE M.O. & 14 other ranks (out details) proceeded for duty to Corps holding trench station at BONNAY (I.17.e) in view of impending operations.	A)?

WAR DIARY
or
INTELLIGENCE SUMMARY.

(Erase heading not required.)

Army Form C. 2118.

Place	Date	Hour	Summary of Events and Information	Remarks and references to Appendices
MONTIGNY	Aug 22	7.0 pm	2nd Lieut. C.S. SILLIMAN proceed French to Bde R.G.A. attack. Capt. W.W. WOOD proceeded for duty 3 days to 58 K. Bde Leefrn. Camp. Received Medical Instructions No. 25 & Army HQRS to Omden. The 91st H.C. Amb MONTIGNY FARM will as matter to 23rd Aug be relieved by its tractors & evacuation to CRS or QCS if required from the 51st Div Vide. MONTIGNY FARM will on the 23rd inst form the 51st Rest Station. Officers duty 2/3. H.E. 9 Amb will footwalk lack case to 91 2/1st H.C. Amb all Lyng sick frames sickos tak laces sittings & lying stretcher cases remaining in 91st H.C. Amb B. 20 & Plants running on 43st H.C. Amb will be returned or evacuated & necessary it in cases required would the Lys discharge after fatal it will be handed over to 43st H.C. Amb ... Every present stretcher sick slightly wounded &c sitts, &c will be last tr 2/1st H.C. Amb & will be detained in DRS (H) & CRS (C) HCS dispersed a messing (3) Retained in provided arranged by No. 10 HAR. Additional Motor transport will be provided & requested by No. 10 H.R.P.	
	23	6.0 pm	This site has been spared today as a Divisional Rest Station. Its accommodation consists of one large building which will accommodate 80 patients and is well lit by Oil Lamps (?) W.S.	

D. D. & L., London, E.C.
(A10260) Wt W5300/8713 750,000 2/15 Sch. 52 Forms/C2118/16

WAR DIARY
INTELLIGENCE SUMMARY

Army Form C. 2118.

Place	Date	Hour	Summary of Events and Information	Remarks and references to Appendices
MONTIGNY	Aug 24	1.20 am	Received information by MOTC 58 Division in the right sector of the Corps front. The 58 Div will relieve the 47 Division in the right sector of the Corps front. The 2/1st HCE Amb will take over the medical posts on the 24th August. 2/1st HCE Amb to take this relief to be completed by 6 pm 24th August. All tour cars of 2/1st HCE Amb & large cars of 2/1st HCE Amb disposal all walking stretchers of 2/1st HCE Amb on leave of other. The 2/2nd	Field G.D.
"	"		2/1st HCE Amb. 30 tours of 2/1st HCE Amb will relieve the 2 tours of 47 Division at the HDS I.30.a.6.6. 2/1st HCE Amb will retain the Div Rest Station at MONTIGNY - MONTIGNY v will be responsible for antiseptic treatment or evacuation of sick & slightly wounded. 2/1st HCE Amb will retain areas until further orders. For collection of sick of 58 Div in back area. A.D.S.	
"	"	10.30 am	Capt TARDING RC walks to other ranks leaves a large & 1 2nd Motor ture despatched to report. HQ 2/1st HCE Amb also 6 tours of stretchers which will move into HDS. A.D.S.	
"	Aug 25	2.0 pm	Read following wire from A.D.M.S. "2/1st HCE Amb will move stock over HDS site at I.30.a.6.6. Patients be evacuated. Holding party of 1 NCO & men to be left. Army will refer as soon as possible. HFC cars will evacuate patients. Relief by 2 pm tonight". A.D.S. Issued orders for Major HUXTABLE & 6 other ranks. Afternoon advance party & long at 4 pm remainder & transport by motor route at 5.30 pm. Depart by C cars exit to F N°.10 MFC. A.D.S.	
"	"	5.30 pm	Above party recorded at 4 pm & remained at 5.30 pm. No MFC cars yet reported. Lt Capt SMEATON v 4 other ranks in charge of sick A.D.S.	

WAR DIARY
or
INTELLIGENCE SUMMARY

(Erase heading not required.)

Army Form C. 2118.

Instructions regarding War Diaries and Intelligence Summaries are contained in F. S. Regs., Part II. and the Staff Manual respectively. Title pages will be prepared in manuscript.

Place	Date	Hour	Summary of Events and Information	Remarks and references to Appendices
I.30.a.6.6	Aug 15	9.0 pm	Arrived & found that advanced party had taken over site from representatives of 2/5t He 3 Amb. at 5.30pm. M.D.S. We moved forward. Site over site of H.D.S. at I.2a.6.7.) Ascertained that nursing cars for evacuation of details from MONTIGNY.A.) been sent from to M.A.C.	Sheet 62.D A)D
"	26	6.0 pm	This site has been opened, a Divisional Sick Collecting station. Cases emerging walking cases from H.D.S. at I.2a.6 we stopped at the front used general. There we erected 2 C.G.S. transferred to R.S. FLESSELLES or retains the Sick of other formations as we visited A.D.S. & were situated at K.13.c.5.5 and M.D.S. at I.2a.6.7.) A)D	
"	27	6.0 pm	Received D.O. No.56 by A.D.M.S. 53 Division:— The 2/1st He 3 Amb. i.e. will move to MARICOURT on .... Aug 30th & will establish an H.D.S. & W.LS. Post at A.21.b.2.9. The 2/5th He 3 Amb., Knox will move to L.1.D.a.5.4 (sheet 62.D) & establish a H.D.S. It is 2/1st He 3 Amb. will establish to be completed by noon 30th inst. by our Commander a Sick Collecting Post at I.2a.6.7.) Cut-side vacated by 2/5 (He 3 Amb.) whence cases will be conveyed to Divn. Rest-Station I.30.a.6.6.	Sheet-62.D Sheet-62.D A)D
"	30	6.0 pm	Sick Collecting Post established at 10 A.M. in accordance with foregoing orders in charge with 3 men no H.E.O. o one horse & subsistence.	A)D

WAR DIARY
or
INTELLIGENCE SUMMARY.

(Erase heading not required.)

Army Form C. 2118.

Place	Date	Hour	Summary of Events and Information	Remarks and references to Appendices
L.30.c.6.6 (Sht.62D)	Aug 30	9.0 pm	Read O.O. No 27 by ADMS 58 Division :— "The 2/1st H.C.) Amb will move tomorrow 31.8.18 to HQrs at A.30.d.3.2 & HQrs. O.P. will be established there. The 1/3rd H.C.) Amb will move tomorrow 31.8.18 to take over by 4/3rd H.C.) Amb A.21.d.5.2 and will move into tents camp at L.10.c.5.3 vacated by 2/3rd H.C.) Amb The 2/1st H.C.) Amb will established there a sick collecting station & Div. Rest Station. H.C.) Amb" & will establish there a sick collecting station & Div. Rest Station. Its letter move to be completed by 5 pm."	"1st 2/1.st (H.C) Amb" "Rest H.C." ditto "Rest H.C." ditto "3rd (H.C.) Amb" (1)
"	"	7.30 pm	Issued orders for advance party of 1 Officer, 1 NCO & 3 the ranks to proceed to new site at 10.30 a.m. tomorrow & remainder of Unit by route march leaving at 1.30 pm.	(1)
"	Aug 31	10.30 am	Proceeded with above named party by Motor Ambce to L.10.a.5.3 remainder of party to proceed at 1.30 pm under command of Major HUXTABLE H.C. Some cases of Influenza (P.U.O.) of breed with Unit trans the remainder of sick disposed of as follows: those probably fit for duty to No/ Clifton Camp HEILLY the likely left ft. to C.C.S. FLESSELLES; remainder to C.C.S. (1)	
L.10.a.5.3 BRAY-MARICOURT RD	"	5.0 pm	Left of Unit with the exception of Sipping party (1 NCO & 11 men) (on new arrival Hing. ... consisting of supply damaged Adrian Nisson Huts, lgs. & ... use ... by German as billets shelter, pretty... (1)	

Army Form C. 2118.

WAR DIARY
or
INTELLIGENCE SUMMARY.
(Erase heading not required.)

Instructions regarding War Diaries and Intelligence Summaries are contained in F. S. Regs., Part II. and the Staff Manual respectively. Title pages will be prepared in manuscript.

Place	Date	Hour	Summary of Events and Information	Remarks and references to Appendices
L.10 a. 5.3	Aug 31	9.0 p.m.	RHQ. Capt W.W.WOOD proceeded for duty with 2/5.2nd London Regt. at 5 p.m. & Lieut A.F.GALLOWAY R.A.M.C. rejoined from duty with same battalion.	

A.D.Hunter Ltd
RAMC T.F
O/c 2/1st Home Counties D.Amb

14

CONFIDENTIAL

Sept 1918

original

9/R 19
140/3259

War Diary
of
Lieut Col A.T. FALWASSER D.S.O R.A.M.C. T.F.

Commanding 2/1st Home Counties Field Ambulance

from September 1st, 1918

(Volume 2)

COMMITTEE FOR THE
MEDICAL HISTORY OF THE WAR
date September 30 1918
9 NOV 1918

WAR DIARY
or
INTELLIGENCE SUMMARY
(Erase heading not required.)

Army Form C. 2118.

Place	Date	Hour	Summary of Events and Information	Remarks and references to Appendices
L.10.a.3.2	2/9/18	11 A.M.	Received Operation Order No 58 by Col. E.A. WRAITH D.S.O. A.M.S. ADMS 58th Division. The 74th Division will relieve the 58th Division in the Line. Right Section III Corps front on the night 11/12th Sept.	Map. 62.D. 1/40,000.
			1. The 2/1st will remain at present site, and continue administration of divisional sick Collecting and Rest Station	
			2. The 2/1st M.C.F.A. will return to O.C. 2/2nd M.C.F.A. The personnel and equipment on relief. O.C. 2/2nd M.C.F.A. will return to O.C. 2/1 M.C.F.A. the Loaned vehicles in the Line	
			3. 2/1st M.C.F.A. will collect from Troops of 58th Division west of line MARICOURT-MONTUBAN	
			4. R.A. All sick will be sent to 2/1st M.C.F.A. Sick collecting Station L.10 a.3.3. (A.D.)	
	6/9/18	9.30 A.M.	Received Urgent (Operation) Warning Order. The Division is probably to take over from 47th Division on the night 6/7th. The 178th Bde will take over the whole divisional front Sector west Sector line through D2d.V.5.4. and V.27.d.0.0.	62.C. 1/40,000 57.E. 1/40,000
		9.30 A.M.	O.C. 2/1 M.C.F.A. will arrange to clear all patients from your field ambulance forthwith - discharge to duty, evacuate to C.C.S. by Rest-Camps. A.D.M.S. 58th for forthwith.	
		10.15 A.M.	Reconstitution A.D.M.S. 5429 Peronne detail 80 Bearers with N.C.Os to proceed immediately after mid-day meal 15-day 15 Hdqrs 2/3 M.C.F.A. at A.21.b.9.6. They will report for duty to O.C. 2/3 M.C.F.A. Completed 2 P.M.	62.0. 1/40,000
		2 P.M.	GALLOWAY, A.J. Lieut-evacuated sick to C.C.S. A.D.M.S.	
		9.15 P.M.	Operation Order No 58 A.D.M.S. The 58th Division will relieve the 47th Division in Centre Section of III Corps front on the night 6/7th September	

Army Form C. 2118.

WAR DIARY
or
INTELLIGENCE SUMMARY.
(Erase heading not required.)

Place	Date	Hour	Summary of Events and Information	Remarks and references to Appendices
L10.a.3	2/9/16	9.15pm		b2e.1/40050
	2		The Divisional Boundaries will be East and West lines through D22.a.0.4 and D.10.a.0.6.	
	4		The 2/3rd W.C.F Ambulance will be responsible for collection and evacuation of wounded from present area and will take over the present advanced Dressing Station of 47th Division (C.20.a.9.1.) and the advanced A.D.S. at MOISLAINS (C.17.a.7.0 Reserve and cars of Divisions will be at his disposal.	
	5		The 2/1st H.C.F Ambulance will take over the present main Dressing Station of 47th Division at B.13.b.5.4 (Half MAUREPAS) and will be ready 16 noon 15th in Main Dressing Station from that point to C.20.a.9.1. at short notice.	
	7		The 2/2nd H.C.F Ambulance will proceed to the site at B.13.b.5.4 when that is vacated by 2/1st H.C.F above and form a Main Collecting Station and will be responsible for collection of sick in back areas. All moves to be completed by 12 noon September 7th.	
	9		Detailed arrangements of reliefs will be made between Officers commanding Field Ambulances concerned.	
	10		All Corps Orders will be taken over by incoming field Ambulances receipts given and copies forwarded to this Office. The A.D.M.S office will open at Quarry C.20.r at 8 a.m. Sept 7th. A.D.? SMEATON Captain left for Railhead to proceed on fourteen days leave commencing Sept 6th via Boulogne. A.D.?	

Army Form C. 2118.

WAR DIARY
or
INTELLIGENCE SUMMARY.
(Erase heading not required.)

Instructions regarding War Diaries and Intelligence Summaries are contained in F.S. Regs., Part II. and the Staff Manual respectively. Title pages will be prepared in manuscript.

Place	Date	Hour	Summary of Events and Information	Remarks and references to Appendices
MAUREPAS HALT B.13.b.5.4	4/9/18	12 a.m.	Move from L.10.a.32. to B.13.b.5.4 and taking over Main Dressing Station and staff completed at 12 a.m.	62 II 1/40.000.
		2 p.m.	Received ADMS MX.2. Recon. arranged an advance party as soon as possible to provide a Nucleus MDS at MOISLAINS near canal bank C.18.C.9.6. The remainder of party will follow at a time convenient to you. Lt.Col. FALWASSER D.S.O. RAMC and Major HUXTABLE M.C. left at 2.30 pm to take over C.18.C.9.6. and establish Main Dressing Station which was opened to receive casualties at 6 pm.	62 C 1/40000
		6 p.m.		A.D.S.
		8 p.m.	Major TOWARD left B.13.b.5.4 at 8 pm with remainder of personnel and transport completing	A.D.S.
			move at 11.45 pm.	
C.18.C.9.6.	7/9/18	7.30 p.m.	Lt. Col. FALWASSER and 2 Medical Officers and personnel with equipment to open a Main Dressing Station	A.D.S.
			at II.22.A.0.5. CURLU WOOD.	A.D.S.
		8 p.m.	MDS at II.22.A.0.5 opened to receive patients at 8 pm	
		8 pm	MDS closed at C.18.C.9.6	
			Number of Cases evacuated from 6 p.m. 7/9/18 to 5 pm 8/9/18	(-) A.D.S.
			58 Division Officers 9 OR 63 O.P.S. P.o.N O.R.S. Gas cases 0	
			from 8 pm 8/9/18 to 9/9/18 3 40 6 3 1 0	
			9/9/18 - 10/9/18 6 44 19 0 0	
			10/9/18 - 11/9/18 2 29 10 0 0	
			11/9/18 12/9/18 1 13 9 0 0	
			12/9/18 13/9/18 0 3 2 0 0	
II.22.A.0.5	13/9/18	9.a.m.	A. LISS Lt. Qr Mr returned from leave. Galloway Lt. A.T. returned from hospital	(-) A.D.S.

WAR DIARY or INTELLIGENCE SUMMARY

Army Form C. 2118.

Place	Date	Hour	Summary of Events and Information	Remarks and references to Appendices
D21.C.0.8. GUILLEMONT	14.9.18		Medical arrangements 4th Army. Operation Order No 46. The following Casualty Clearing Stations are allotted as under from midnight 13/14th inst.	62.C.1/90.070
			III Corps No 61 CCS .... MARICOURT	
			No 37 " " "	
			No 20 " " DOINGT (John Mann) and after DCC Stations at EDGE HILL	
			III NYDN. NYD Gas. S.I.W. Dysentery, Venereal, Ophthalmic, Dental and Ear, Nose & Throat Cases will be sent direct to No 41 Stationary Hospital RAYLAUM (Sheet 62.E. R.27.6.)	
			Which will be next to LUCKNOW CCS.	
			Note: Until opening of No 20 CCS will be notified later. The units deputed in the opening of Lucknow for Ambulance Trains, but it is expected that it will be ready in 48 hours.	
			No 13 ADM STORE } III Corps Dart 47, H8, 53, & 20 CCS M2	
			(MERICOURT L'ABBE)	
			No 16 ADM STORE to the Surgeon Consultr for W. Army, all indent for Oxygen will be submitted DTC SRA D'Army only	
			" " " to the Sister & Vacuum Consultr for W. Army.	
			Number of cases through Main Dressing Station during	
				Stationary Division	Walking Wounded		Sitting Cases		
				Officers	OR	Officers	OR	Officers	OR	
			From 5pm 14th Sept to 5pm 15th	Nil	3	Nil	7/8	Nil	Nil	
			From 5pm 15/9 to " 16/9	Nil	1	Nil	5	Nil	Nil	
			" 5pm " 16/9 " " 17/9	Nil	5	Nil	10	Nil	Nil	
			A.D.P.	
	17/9/18		58th Division Medical Arrangements (No 26). The O.C. 2/1st HCFA will help in the ADS E.14.A.8.8. is responsible for the evacuation of sick & wounded from the forward area. The motor ambulances attached Stretchers and Personnel Divisional HQ 2/1 HCFA will be at the disposal of the O.C. 2/1 HCFA who will be in charge of the MDS at D22.d.03.	57.C.1/40.070 62.C.1/42.070
				A.D.P.

WAR DIARY
or
INTELLIGENCE SUMMARY.

(Erase heading not required.)

Army Form C. 2118.

Place	Date	Hour	Summary of Events and Information	Remarks and references to Appendices
(Sucre bank) A22 C 0 3			Method of Evacuation from Main Dressing Station is CCS No 20 Doing by Motor Ambulance cars. Medical Officer attached to 66" Divisional R.E. and 66" A.V. M.G.C. Batt will deal Casualties passed to Sucre Casualties at M.A.S.	
			Casualties passed thru MDS 56th Division Other Formation New Corps Germans N Y S W	
			Officers O.R. Officers O.R. Officers O.R.	
			from 6pm 17/9/18 to 6pm 18/9/18 3 46 2 3 7 35 Nil Nil	
			6pm 18/9/18 to 6pm 19/9/18 32 9 Nil	
19/9/18			25 of the R.O. cases on 15, 18" occurred amongst the Artillery. GALLOWAY A+ Lieut per instruction from the ADMS reported at 10 a.m. for duty 156C CWWS.	
			Canadian Forward Itinerant MDS 58" Division Other Formation New Corps Germans N Y S W	
			Officers O.R. Officers O.R. OR13 OR11	
			from 6pm 18/9/18 to 5pm 19/9/18 3 27 2 32 7 5 4	
			6pm 19/9/18 to 5pm 20/9/18 1 17 0 8 0 2 0	
			" " 21/9/18 3 34 0 12 0 0 0	
			" " 22/9/18 1 24 1 3 0 0 0	
			" " 23/9/18 nil 0 0 0 0 0	
			24/9/18 0 0 0 0 0 0	
23/9/18	11 am		JUDKIN RJ Lieut MORC USA proceeded to 290 Bgde RFA for duty and is now o/s R.a. strength of this Unit.	
23/9/18	11 am		Warning order that the Division will probably be relieved on the nights 22/23rd inst — for period Field Ambulance will proceed as under :— 2/1st NCFA 15 are relieved by 173rd Inf Brigade. Field Ambulance will collect over of the Brigade, and will arrange accommodation for 20 cases of sickness likely to some to be far within four days. All personnel and equipment attached or on loan to Fd. 2/3 Wx F.A. will be returned to 15 of Red Ambulance.	

Army Form C. 2118.

WAR DIARY
or
INTELLIGENCE SUMMARY.
(Erase heading not required.)

Instructions regarding War Diaries and Intelligence Summaries are contained in F. S. Regs., Part II. and the Staff Manual respectively. Title pages will be prepared in manuscript.

Place	Date	Hour	Summary of Events and Information	Remarks and references to Appendices
GURLU both D22.c.6.3	23.9.18	11 AM	Warning Order No 2. The 58th Division will be relieved on the night 23/24th inst by 12th Division Field Ambulance will soon unit 173rd Infantry Brigade. Lorries will be provided for personnel of Field Ambulance as under:— 2/1st H.C.F.A plus 50 bearers of 2/2nd H.C.F.A embus midday 24th; instr. on the LIERAMONT-VILLERS FAUCON Rd Concentration 250. 2/2nd Ambulance Site N as Area relieved by 173rd Inf Brigade HARDICOURT or MONTAUBAN. Transport will so far as possible proceed with Brigade Groups. Previous Warning Order is Cancelled.	
	23.9.18	12:45 pm	B/favention order No 60. by A.D.M.S. 58th Div unit be relieved by the 12th Division in the line on the night of 23/24th Sept. 1918. The 3/3rd H.C.F.A will be relieved by the 36th Fd Ambulance. Relief is to be completed by 10 pm 23/9/18. Arrangements for relief will be made similar between the OC 2/3rd H.C.F.A & OC 36th Fd Ambr. All personal stores and Ambulances leaves 15 Fd 2/1st H.C.F.A by the 2/1st & 2/2nd H.C.F.A.D will be returned by 8 pm 23/9/18 to their respective units. Corps stores will be disposed of in accordance with D.D.M.S instruction dated 21/9/18. Field Ambulances will move to new sites in accordance with A.D.M.S warning order No 2 & embussing Programme here to attached. Completion of relief of 2/3rd H.C.F.A & arrival reports giving exact location of same field Ambulance in new area will be forwarded to A.D.M.S as soon as possible. Medical Instructions No 1 in connection with III Corps G.O No 82's dated 21/9/18. Attached thereto:— II Corps Stores Sufficient Blankets, Stretchers & Marquees of Corps Stores at Divisions. Dy Efance. etc Airraines may be retained if required in establishing D.Rs Rest Stations	

WAR DIARY
or
INTELLIGENCE SUMMARY.

Army Form C. 2118.

Place	Date	Hour	Summary of Events and Information	Remarks and references to Appendices
SURLUQUE DAGOB	23/9/16		Corps Stores. Corps store surplus to requirements will be returned to Corps K.S. Station.	A/1
			Instructions from ADMS. Reference DMS No B25. dated 21/9/16 number 15 The Officer i/c crown in pouches	
			List of Corps Stores :— (a) Retained (b) Returned to C.W.C. Station.	A/2
	24/9/16		All corps stores dealt by 2/1/11 & 2 a returned to C.W.C. Station.	A/3
	23/9/16	5.50pm	Inf. Bde. Order No. 56 received 4.50pm. The Brigade Group will move to MONTAUBAN area. Personnel will move by bus transport by road. Approach march & entraining point in VILLERS FAUCON - NURLU R³⁴. Will be carried out under instructions to be issued by the Staff Captain. Time of entraining will be 12 noon. Transport & Brigade Group will move at 6am. Route via COMBLES and BOULEMONT. an interval 5cm. Gap will be maintained during the march between 15 Transport & cook carts. Brigade hdqrs will close at the Quarry D.15.a at 10am 24pm 24"	57 C, B26 B2C A/2
	23/9/16	9.45pm	Instructions for move of 173 Inf. Bde. Group in accordance with 173 Bde. Order No 56. 2/L K. & G. will form Corps works at E.15.a.0.2. on march to entraining point at 1.30pm. Entraining Point will be in the MONTAUBAN - MAMETZ area heavily entrained at Embrace & MAMETZ.	57C B2C 57A B2C A/5

WAR DIARY or INTELLIGENCE SUMMARY

Army Form C. 2118.

Place	Date	Hour	Summary of Events and Information	Remarks and references to Appendices
			Mon 1 TC Transport by Road. Starting point mile to the hand junction on NOISLAINS-BOUCHAVESNES Rd at C.15.C.0.6. 2/1 MCFA mile from this point at 12.20 a.m. Route COMBLES – GUILLEMONT. Destination S.26.d.	S2D/14,000.
GUILLEMONT B.22.C.0.3.	24/9/16	9.45 am	Transport under the charge of Major J.S. WARD left at 9.45 a.m. and arrived MONTABAN S.26.d. 2.30 pm. Personnel under the charge of Major A.K. HUXTABLE M.C. left D.22.C.0.3. for entraining point and arrived at B.26.d. 6 pm. Movement completed at 6 pm.	A.D. A.D.
	24/9/16	11 pm	GALLOWAY reported from Corps H.Q. S.26.d. 11 pm.	A.D. A.D.
MONTABAN	25/9/16	7.15 am	JARDINE, E.B. (Capt.) M.C. in DANCO under instructions from ADMS proceeded to 2/2 MCFA. 15.40 to AUBIGNY by Ambulance of 2/2 MCFA via St POL-ARRAS Rd. report 15 MAAS 51st Div. for purpose of briefing.	A.D.
	24/9/16	9.30 pm	Received A.531. 2/1 MCFA will move tomorrow 25 RIBEMONT view to entraining 26th. To ADMS, from 57th Division. To O.C. 2/1 MCFA forwarded for your compliance. On arrival you will communicate with Mayor of Bougun to which application also report Completion of move 5 th officer.	A.D. A.D.
	24/9/16 25/9/16	8.30 pm 12.30 pm 7 pm	Warning order. 173 Inf Brig will entrain on 26th mon. at MERICOURT L'ABBAYE. Personnel & Transport left S.26.d. arrived RIBEMONT 3 pm. SMEATON Capt. rejoined unit from leave.	A.D. A.D.

WAR DIARY
INTELLIGENCE SUMMARY

Army Form C. 2118.

Place	Date	Hour	Summary of Events and Information	Remarks and references to Appendices
RIBEMONT	20/9/16	5.30 am	Transport left for entraining station MÉRICOURT L'ABBAYÉ. Personnel left at 6.45 a.m. Arrived ACQ 5.30 pm Arrived LE PENDU at 6.30 pm, 7.10.3.8.	LENS 11. S.I.C. 1/40,000
LE PENDU Camp F.1.a.3.9	Sept 27	10.0 am	Interviewed by ADMS VIII Corps about the relief of nearly div and that the Unit will use the Dressing Station & forward indirect posts taking them over from 72 (?) but on right & from 7a.7th.3 Amb on left.	LE PENDU -S.I.C. 1/40,000 A.D.3
"	"	2.0 pm	Proceeded by car with Major HUXTABLE M.C. a.d WARD to AIX NOULETTE (R. 12. a. v. 5.) to HQ of 7a 7 Amb and to FOSSE 10 Main Dressing Station (R.B Central) HQ of 7a 7 Amb to gather information about A.D.Ss & forward posts on R, & life tickets of Bde Front repeatedly and made necessary arrangements with these units re. advanced parties & final take-over.	Sheet 44 B 1/40,000
"	"	11.0 am	Attended conference at ADMS' office VILLERS CHATEL (Y. 19. 25) VIII Corps Sist Army in this new area.	Sheet 44 B A.D.3
"	"	2.0 pm	Major J.S. WARD & d officer ranks proceeded in advance party to HQ RAP & thence to Right A.D.S. & forward posts	A.D.3

Army Form C. 2118.

WAR DIARY
or
INTELLIGENCE SUMMARY.
(Erase heading not required.)

Place	Date	Hour	Summary of Events and Information	Remarks and references to Appendices
LE RENDU CAMP F.1.a.3.9	14/9/29	6.0 pm	Recd. Opers: order No. 61 by ADMS 58 Division :— The 58th Division will relieve the 24th Division in the effects of the VIII Corps front on 29th, 29th & 30th September. The 9/, 10/, 11/ & 12/ Ants will relieve the 3/rd, 4/st & 5th Ants & establish parts at AIX NOULETTE respectively in right sub-sector of divisional front (including ADS M.26.d.9.1 and WWCP H.23.6.7.1) will be taken over from 7/1st & Ants by 4 pm on 29th Sept. The ADS H.11.c.3.7 WWCP H.9.6.1.2 and posts in left + centre subsectors of divisional front from the 74/st & Ants by noon 30th Sept. The 9/21st He & Ants will relieve the 7/st & Ants at the MDS (FOSSE 10) R.8 central on 30th Sept. The 4/3rd He & Ants will relieve the 73rd & Ants at the DRS (GRAND SERVINS) Q.31.a.2.5 on 30th Sept. D.S.C. 2/1st & 2/3rd He & Ants will each place at disposal of O.C. 9/4st He & Ants 50 Bearers & large Motor Amls & all Sand Cars, all wheeled stretchers. ADMS Office will close at VILLERS CHATEL at 4 pm on 30 Sept and reopen at SAINS-EN-GOHELLE at the same hour.	Ref Sheet 1/40,000 Ref Sheets 44 B & 44 A ADS
"	Sept 29	10.0 am	Whole unit with Transport marched (less advance party already proceeded) via VILLERS-AU-BOIS — GOUY SERVINS — BOUVIGNY-BOYEFFLES to AIX NOULETTE. Major HUXTABLE R.C. with Capt. JARDINE R.C. and 10 other ranks being the party at BOUVIGNY-BOYEFFLES to report to 7/a & Ant at FOSSE 10 as advance party for 9/1st He & Ant through party to revert to 7/a & Ant at FOSSE 10 ADS	

WAR DIARY
INTELLIGENCE SUMMARY

Army Form C. 2118.

Place	Date	Hour	Summary of Events and Information	Remarks and references to Appendices
AIX NOULETTE	Sept 29	4.10 pm	Relief of 2nd/1st Hut at ADS & Advanced posts C.I were taken over as follows:	Map Ref:
			Advanced Dressing Station Cholis Post ANGRES H.33.a.1.9	B.4
			Collecting Post, Advanced Car Post White Chateau LIEVIN H.29.c.7.1	44.B
			Relay Post & forward orderlies Green House M.23.d.4.3	44.A
			Quarry R.A.P. H.29.c.6.6	
			Viery R.A.P. M.17.c.6.4	
			One large Motor Ambulance stands at White Chateau LIEVIN and two at ADS Cholis Post ANGRES	ADS
	Sept 30	6 pm	Remainder of Battery to relieve remained of 2/1st. Ambce. left ADS & stretcher bearer posts proceeded at 9 AM today & relief was completed at 10.30 AM.	
			Posts taken over are:	
			Car Post & walking wounded Collecting Post FOSSE 11 M.2.E.1.2	
			Advanced Dressing Station CITE ST PIERRE M.11.a.9.5	H.11.c.B.9
			Junction Post R.A.P. M.11.a.9.5	
			Hartz Post R.A.P. M.6.d.3.4	
			Large Motor Ambulance stand by day at FOSSE 11 & forward at dusk to ADS CITE ST PIERRE returning to FOSSE 11 at dawn.	
			Station at FOSSE 10 R.O. (situated three miles behind ADS) Routes K.19.c	

original

Oct. 19th 16

CONFIDENTIAL

War Diary

of

Lieut Colonel A.T. FALWASSER D.S.O. R.A.M.C. T.F.
Commanding 2/1st Home Counties Field Ambulance

(Volume 2)

from October 1. 18 to October 31. 18

WAR DIARY or INTELLIGENCE SUMMARY

Army Form C. 2118.

Place	Date	Hour	Summary of Events and Information	Remarks and references to Appendices
AIX NOULETTE R.22.a.2.5	19.1.17	12.00	Medical arrangements in forward area at divisional front are as follows:—	Sheet 44 B 1/40000
			Right A.D.S. at ANGRES M.33.a.1.9. advanced Coy front at LIEVIN M.29.b.7.1. Advanced post for head casualties at CROCUS HOUSE M.23.d.4.8. R.A.P. at the Quarry M.29.c.6.6. Major J.E. WARD is in charge of A.D.S. & all walking party in this Sector.	Sheet 44 A 1/40000
			Left A.D.S. CITÉ ST PIERRE H.11.c.8.9. R.A.P.s are situated at H.17.c.6.4, H.12.a.7.5, & M.6.d.3.4. Evacuation from the first named is by wheeled stretchers to A.D.S. & from the two latter by both trolly on Decauville railway to A.D.S. Cars stand at A.D.S. by night but during daylight remain at FOSSE 11 H.5.6.1.2. and evacuation by day from A.D.S. to trolly point is by hand trolly. Cars from Left A.D.S. are evacuated to M.D.S. (Christ Ch. Annex) at FOSSE 10 (R.B. Central) thence to C.C.S. group at RUITZ. The whole line is at present very quiet & practically no casualties are occurring.	Sheet 44 B
			Major A.E. HUXTABLE HC with Col. E.B. JARDINE is in charge A.D.S. of Left A.D.S. elects Stine.	

Army Form C. 2118.

WAR DIARY
or
INTELLIGENCE SUMMARY
(Erase heading not required.)

Place	Date	Hour	Summary of Events and Information	Remarks and references to Appendices
AIX NOULETTE	Oct 3	1800	The line has gone forward about 3000 yards during last 36 hours & a counter attack but greater advance has been made by the Division on our left (15th) LENS is now clear of the enemy & RAPs have consequently been advanced to H.33.d.7.3, N.1.d and N.7.d in left sector & to N.19.a on Rt sector of the Main Dressing relay posts have been established. Large Motor Ambulances were used in daylight from ADS M.11.c.3.9 & 2nd Ambulance work forward to M.12.a.9.5. Casualties thro' posts during last 24 hours 3 2 Officers 46 other ranks including Gassed 17 other ranks.	
	Oct 4	2000	Owing to advance & consequent shortening of one front the Rt Bde has been engaged out between its centre Bde & the Rt. Bde on our right the Rt ADS at ANGRES has consequently been closed today & Rt posts on Rt letri have been closed, relay parties only being left at CROCUS HOUSE and White Chateau LIEVIN. Major WARD has returned to H.Qrs of unit. RAPs in left sector have all been advanced to H.33.a and at N.1.d & N.a.c. The evening relay posts being established ADS has been advanced from M.11.c.3.9 to N.1.d.9.0 from which point 2nd Ambulance evacuate back to Motor Car post at M.12.a.9.5. Casualties through posts during past 24 hours 3 Officers 36 other ranks.	AD

WAR DIARY or INTELLIGENCE SUMMARY

Army Form C. 2118.

Place	Date	Hour	Summary of Events and Information	Remarks and references to Appendices
AIX NOULETTE	Oct 6	1900	As there is considerable shelling of LA BASSÉE Rd in neighbourhood of MSM Fort Aubers it has been withdrawn from there about 1½ mile east of Mn a.9.6 & evacuation of this point from ADS at N.1.d.7.9. is by push trolley on decauville railway to by wheeled stretcher. Stretcher privately is country. Casualties for 10 others made only in past 24 hours.	Hospital A.95 A.D.S
"	Oct 9	1000	Trouble through LENS connecting BETHUNE — LIENS — CARVIN Rd. have been reconnoitered today & were found to be passable for Ford cars though bad. A site which in its event of a forward move would be suitable for an ADS has been located at N.15.c.1.5 on CARVIN Rd & a party posted there to procure it.	A.D.S
"	Oct 11	0900	Recd. warning order from Division that an eighth 12/13th Division tomorrow will be attached to the right to SALLAUMINES — MONTIGNY Rd taking over the shelter from a Brigade of 11th Division.	A.D.S
"	"	2200	In consequence of above warning order & as LOISON in our front and SALLAUMINES on our right rear were reported & telephone reports of evacuation ADS were opened tonight at N.15.c.1.5 and R1. ADS at N.1.d.7.1 was closed & vacated crews to large our stand at ADS & transferred & then on large cars to M.D.S.	A.D.S

WAR DIARY
or
INTELLIGENCE SUMMARY

Army Form C. 2118.

Place	Date	Hour	Summary of Events and Information	Remarks and references to Appendices
AIX NOULETTE	Oct 12	0900	Recd. oper. order No 6 to A.D.M.S. :— "Field Ambulances will move as under :— 2/1st. H.Q.& A.M. (H.Q. & Transport) will move to Petit Château. M. 22.6.2.7. 2/1st. H.Q.& A.M. to St. PIERRE the new A.D.S. site – also JUNCTION Post M.12.a.9.5 and will establish: HQ. & all A.D.S sites ST PIERRE – 2/3rd. H.Q.& Amb. will move to Zone 10 (site of M.B.S.) & establish Divisional Rest Station there. Above moves to be completed by 1200 hours 13th October."	Medl. A44. A.D.J.
"	"	1600	Lieut. A.F. GALLOWAY rejoined from duty at No.7 C.C.R.	A.D.J.
KIEVIN	Oct. 13	1200	H.Q. & Transport of Unit moved here at 1130 hours today. Line had been advanced considerably during past 24 hours. A.D.S. remained at N.15.C.15 & but R.A.P.s have all moved forward & Fd ambulances stand at N.10 & and N.11 & evacuate to M.B.S. left influence long hay truck forward to A.D.S. & erecting Horse to M.B.S. Horsed ambulances are also posted forward on the LENS–CARVIN and the LENS–LOISON Rds and a left & Right rate of evacuation time had to be established every little ferry no bridge across to HAUTE DEULE exept at N.21.a.8.9. (Casualties thro' A.D.S. during past 24 hours — 37)	A.D.J.

WAR DIARY
or
INTELLIGENCE SUMMARY.

Army Form C. 2118.

Place	Date	Hour	Summary of Events and Information	Remarks and references to Appendices
LIEVIN	Oct 14	1800	Major J.S. WARD and Capt H. E.B. JARDINE H.C. proceeded on leave to UK. Advanced Dressing Station closed at N.15.c.1.5 and opened at 1200 hrs at FOUQUIERES O.15.c.3.1. R.A.P. lines presently been advanced & fwd ambulances stand at O.23.a.2.2 and O.9.b.5.6.	Next-etc.A
"	15	2100	Rec'd operation order No 63 by A.D.M.S. 58 Division :— The 1/2nd H.F.D Amb. (Heir Dressing Station) will move on 17 October to FOUQUIERES O.21.a.4.5. Horse to be completed by 1200 hrs. OC 1/2nd H.F.D Amb. will arrange with O.C. 2/1st H.F.D Amb for its reception. Transport disposal of my cavalier during the move on the morning of the 17th inst.	A.D —
"	"	2300	Rec'd minute from A.D.M.S. "your H.Q. & Transport lines will move to FOUQUIERES area tomorrow October 16th."	A.D —
MONTIGNY	16	2100	Unit with Transport left LIEVIN at 1030 hrs & arrived MONTIGNY 1345. A.D.S. closed at O.21.a.4.5 at 1200 hrs and opened at COURRIÈRES at the same time I.35.d.6.3.	Q.23.a.1.3 A.D —
"	17	2100	A.D.S. moved forward from COURRIÈRES to OIGNIES J.27.c.6.9 at 1050 hrs today.	A.D —

Army Form C. 2118.

WAR DIARY
or
INTELLIGENCE SUMMARY.
(Erase heading not required.)

Place	Date	Hour	Summary of Events and Information	Remarks and references to Appendices
MONTIGNY	6.11.18	11.15	Recd Opn order No 6.14 by "ADMS" 51st Division. — The following named will take the place as under:— 2/1st (W.R.)Amb will move today to "OSTRICOURT" or MONCHEAUX	
OSTRICOURT	"	17.00	Arrived having left MONTIGNY at 13.00 hours. ADMS moved at 08.00 hours from CIGNIES to MONCHEAUX	P.6.6.3.5 (A.D.)
"	"	"	Recd following order from ADMS "You will move tomorrow morning to MONCHEAUX or district. The 1/1st (W.R.)Amb (H.D.S.) will take over your present site at OSTRICOURT."	(A.D.)
MONS EN PÉVÈLE	7.11.18	15.30	Arrived at 15.00 having left OSTRICOURT at 09.00 hours	(A.D.)
"	"	17.00	Recd following order from ADMS "The following moves will take place as under:— 2/1st (W.R.)Amb will move tomorrow 20— to area E of BERSÉE site the personnel & details to this office. 1/1st (W.R.)Amb will move tomorrow to MONS & take over site vacated by 2/1st (W.R.)Amb. 2/3rd (W.R.)Amb will move tomorrow to OSTRICOURT & be vacated by 1/2nd (W.R.)Amb."	(A.D.)
"	"	"	ADS shed today at MONS at 15.00 hours & opened at the same hour at AUCHY (G.2.a.6.a)	Herd 44 (A.D.)
AUCHY	8.11.18	10.30	Arrived having left MONS at 08.30 hours ADS closed at AUCHY & opened at NOMAIN	1/1 approx. (A.D.)

WAR DIARY / INTELLIGENCE SUMMARY

Army Form C. 2118.

Place	Date	Hour	Summary of Events and Information	Remarks and references to Appendices
AUCHY	20/10	10.00	Recd. Oper. order No. 65 by A.T.O.S. 58 Division:— "The 2/1st H.C.Ans will move tomorrow 21st inst. the 1/1st H.C.Amb (M.D.S.) will move tomorrow to VERT BOIS (G.14.a.5) the 2/3rd H.C.Amb (B.R.S) will move tomorrow to BERSÉE". A.D.M.S. advanced at 16.00 hours from NOMAIN to AIX BAS H.6.a.central hence our post still remained at NOMAIN owing to roads and main entrance atteint H.10. central not being trafficable for large motor ambulances.	The 2/1st H.C.Amb. (G.14.a.5.) Sheet 44 A.)) A.))
LANNAY H.2.c.7.7	21	22.00	H.Q. of unit & transport arrived LANNAY 16.30 hours from AUCHY. A.D.S. moved at 14.30 hours from AIX BAS to RONCY I.5.a.5.6. bye & took motor ambulance evacuated from this point these RUMÉGIES – MOUCHIN – cross roads at H.7.t.5.3. – NOMAIN to Ham Dressing Station at VERT BOIS G.14.a.4.) Divisional H.Q. advanced to MOUCHIN today. Casualties thro' A.D.S. during past 24 hours – 1 Officer 10 other ranks. A.))
"	"	21.00	Heavy shelling with little H.E. & Gas of RONCY during last night & direct hits on building occupied by A.D.S. thereat but in consequence only 4 + 1 car only retained at RONCY remainder being sent down to Bearg at RUMÉGIES G.I.13.t.7.4. Considerable attention met with today at MAULDE in [illegible] and casualties now numbering 50. A.))

Army Form C. 2118.

WAR DIARY
or
INTELLIGENCE SUMMARY.
(Erase heading not required.)

Instructions regarding War Diaries and Intelligence Summaries are contained in F. S. Regs., Part II. and the Staff Manual respectively. Title pages will be prepared in manuscript.

Place	Date	Hour	Summary of Events and Information	Remarks and references to Appendices
LANNAY H.3.c.7.7	Feb-23	2200	Enemy shells shelling HQs etc around HQF during last night + this morning. HQF withdrawn from RONEY at 130 hours to RUMEGIES. I.13.6.7.9.4. Nil at RONEY being retained only as an advanced post for casualties amongst RMC Band etc units troops still holding Rear area, not known.	Mud + wet 1.40000
"	27	18.00	Situation remains unchanged at HQF still forward posts remain the same. Casualties we hear & have managed to do daily during past few days AD	
"	29	11.00	Situation unchanged. Still posts remain unaltered. Casualties few, 3 other ranks during past 48 hours. AD	
"	31	2000	Situation unchanged, all Regimental Aid Posts & Field Ambulance posts remain before. Casualties we hear in number 1 Offr & 18 other ranks only during past 48 hours.	

A.D.Dwadee KCB
RMC TF
2/Lt HCD Auk

Original
Vol 22
no/3401

Copy posted 14
March 1916

War Diary
of
Lieut Colonel A.T. FALWASSER D.S.O. R.A.M.C. T.F.
Commanding 2/1st Home Counties Field Ambulance

from November 1st 1918 to November 30th 1918

(Volume 2)

Army Form C. 2118.

WAR DIARY
or
INTELLIGENCE SUMMARY.
(Erase heading not required.)

Instructions regarding War Diaries and Intelligence Summaries are contained in F. S. Regs., Part II. and the Staff Manual respectively. Title pages will be prepared in manuscript.

Place	Date	Hour	Summary of Events and Information	Remarks and references to Appendices
	1918			
LAUNAY (H.3.c.7.?)	Nov 2	12.00	Major J.S.WARD and Capt. E.B.JARDINE M.C. returned today from leave to U.K. Situation in divisional front unchanged & all Regimental Medical & Field Amb posts remain the same. Condition very fair in winter.	Nov-44 L.40000 A.5
	Nov 3	08.00	Lieut Col A.T.FALWASSER D.S.O. proceeded on 14 days leave to United Kingdom	OLH
	Nov 4	12.00	Major J.S.WARD proceeded to A.D.S. to take command of A.D.S. at I.13 b.9.4. Shut 4.4 L/4000 & all forward posts	ASH
	Nov 8	12.00	A.D.S. opened at ROISY 15.a.b.5. Shut 4.4 at 5 p.m. Received Operation orders from A.D.M.S. 58th Divn for Headquarters of this unit to move to ROISY on 9th inst. Transport to proceed as well	ASH
L.E.G.I.S K.1.a.5.5.	Nov 9	12.00	Orders to proceed to ROISY cancelled and orders received to Headquarters Transport and A.D.S. staff to proceed to L.E.G.I.S. Move to be complete by 1800 hrs 9/11/18	Shut 4.4 L.40000
PERUWELZ L.3.a.5.6	Nov 10	10.00	A.D.S. moved forward to BASECLES - Headquarters and Transport proceeded to PERUWELZ - move complete by 1800 hrs	ASH

Army Form C. 2118.

WAR DIARY
or
INTELLIGENCE SUMMARY.
(Erase heading not required.)

Instructions regarding War Diaries and Intelligence Summaries are contained in F. S. Regs., Part II. and the Staff Manual respectively. Title pages will be prepared in manuscript.

Place	Date	Hour	Summary of Events and Information	Remarks and references to Appendices
QUEVAUCAMPS A 23 c 9.8	Nov 11th	09.00	ADS opened at BELOEIL. Headquarters and transport moved to QUEVAUCAMPS – Ambulance commenced at 11 am – orders given for all troops to stand fast till further orders. AH	Sketch 45° 1:40,000
BELOEIL R.3.d.4.8	Nov 12	12.00	Headquarters and Transport moved forward to join ADS staff at BELOEIL	Sketch 45° 1:40,000
			Lieut A GALLOWAY RAMC proceeded on 14 days leave to UK AH	
BELOEIL	Nov 14th	13.00	LYONS C.Y. 1st LIEUT M.R.C. posted to this unit for duty AH	
	Nov 20	09.00	JARDINE E.B. Captain RAMC attached to CRE 56th Division for duty. seven days on Temp. duty AH	
	Nov 22	06.00	LYONS C.Y. 1 LIEUT. M.R.C. proceeded to ADMS 56th Division returning 11.1642 AH	
	Nov 22	23.00	Lieut Col ATFALWASSER D.S.O returned from leave 15 units kingdom AH	
BELOEIL	Nov 26	16.00	Received verbal arrangements NO 31 from ADMS. 2/Lt. H.C.7.A will move to BONSECOURS tomorrow Nov 27th. The divisional Rest Station will be established at BONSECOURS. tw. 1st 2/3rd H.C.7.A PERUWELZ will continue to admit and dispose of all special cases (including venereal and Scabies). Sick hitherto collected by the 2/1 N.& 2/1 Wot will from 15.27 hrs be collected by the 2/2nd N.C.7.A.	Sketch 45° 1:40,000

WAR DIARY
or
INTELLIGENCE SUMMARY.

(Erase heading not required.)

Army Form C. 2118.

Place	Date	Hour	Summary of Events and Information	Remarks and references to Appendices
BELLEUL	27.6.0	09.00	31st Battalion with Transport moved to BONSECOURS	Awy 44 1.40.000
BONSECOURS L 10.c.4.8		12.30	Arrived at BONSECOURS	
		14.00	Divisional REST Station opened at BONSECOURS to receive patients (sick) from Division	
"	30 Wed	1900	Major J.S. WARD left Unit today to proceed to England on 21st leave for 14 days special leave. Lieut A.F. GALLOWAY rejoined Unit from 14 days ordinary leave to England.	M J Schneider K/QR R.A.M.C. T/O

CONFIDENTIAL

Vol 23

War Diary of
Lt. Colonel A. FALWASSER D.S.O.
R.A.M.C. T.F.
Commanding 2/1st Home Counties Field Ambulance

(Volumes 2)

Army Form C. 2118.

WAR DIARY
or
INTELLIGENCE SUMMARY.
(Erase heading not required.)

Instructions regarding War Diaries and Intelligence Summaries are contained in F. S. Regs., Part II. and the Staff Manual respectively. Title pages will be prepared in manuscript.

Place	Date	Hour	Summary of Events and Information	Remarks and references to Appendices
	1917			
RONCEURS	Dec 1	1900	The following were at present remain in this – the 52th Divisional Rest Station other ranks	H.A. Rifles Rest-line L.10.c.3.9
			Officers 2	
			52 Division — 75	
			Other formations — 4	
				A))
	4	1900	Major M.E. HUXTABLE M.C. left Rest Stat'y to proceed on 14 days leave to England.	A))
	7	1800	Capt E.B. JARDINE M.C. rejoined and taking duty from temporary duty in H.D. 4a 52th Div RE.	A))
	9	1200	The following cases have been dealt with in Div'l Rest Station during past week	A))

	Received O.R	Admitted O.R	Evacuated O.R	To Duty O.R	Remaining O.R
52 Div.	0 · 75	0 · 130	0 · 35	0 · 60	0 · 122
Other formations	— · 4	1 · 20	1 · 5	1 · 10	1 · 17
Total	2 · 79	6 · 150	1 · 39	3 · 70	4 · 139

A))

Army Form C. 2118.

WAR DIARY
or
INTELLIGENCE SUMMARY.
(Erase heading not required.)

Place	Date	Hour	Summary of Events and Information	Remarks and references to Appendices
RONSSOURS	Dec 14	1300	Two other ranks and nurse left the Unit today being the first members of this Unit to be demobilised.	Map Ref see sheet 44 L.10.c.3.9
"	15	1800	Cases dealt with in 52nd Divisional Rest Station during past week:—	
			Received Admitted Evacuated To Duty Remaining	
			O . ORs O . ORs O . ORs O . ORs O . ORs	
			52nd Div. 3 . 122 2 . 112 0 . 35 5 . 108 0 . 91	
			Attachd 1 . 17 2 . 23 1 . 7 1 . 17 1 . 26	
			Total 4 . 139 4 . 135 1 . 42 6 . 125 1 . 117	A))
"	17	1200	Major J.F.WARD reported to Unit from officers leave to U.K. at 23.57 hours yesterday.	A))
"	22	1800	Cases dealt with in 52nd Div. Rest Station during past week:—	
			Received Admitted Evacuated To Duty Remaining	
			O . ORs O . ORs O . ORs O . ORs O . ORs	
			52nd Div. 1 . 91 1 . 75 1 . 27 0 . 73 1 . 66	
			Attachd 1 . 26 1 . 16 1 . 4 1 . 24 1 . 14	
			Total 1 . 117 1 . 91 1 . 31 1 . 97 1 . 80	A))

Army Form C. 2118.

WAR DIARY
or
INTELLIGENCE SUMMARY.

(Erase heading not required.)

Place	Date	Hour	Summary of Events and Information	Remarks and references to Appendices
RONFÉCOURT	Dec 1918		Major A.E. HUXTABLE R.C. returned back from leave to United Kingdom. ADS	Ref Ref Check as L.10.23.9
	29	1200	The following troops were left with us Sinaina Field station during past week :-	

	Received		Admitted		Evacuated		To duty		Remaining	
	O.	O.Rs	O.	O.Rs	O.	O.Rs	O.	O.Rs	O.	O.Rs
54 Division	-	16	1	30	-	16	1	56	-	24
Other Formations	-	14	-	13	1	2	-	14	-	11
Total	1	30	1	43	1	18	1	70	-	35

ADS

ADDubester R.C.
Rene T.F.
C. off. y 1st How Centers, T.H.

CONFIDENTIAL

58 DIN
Box 2864

War Diary
of
Lieut Colonel A.T. FALWASSER DSO RAMC T.F.
Commanding 2/1st Home Counties Field Ambulance

from Jan 1st 1919 to Jan 31st 1919

(Volume 3)

Army Form C. 2118.

WAR DIARY
or
INTELLIGENCE SUMMARY.
(Erase heading not required.)

Instructions regarding War Diaries and Intelligence Summaries are contained in F. S. Regs., Part II. and the Staff Manual respectively. Title pages will be prepared in manuscript.

Place	Date	Hour	Summary of Events and Information	Remarks and references to Appendices
BONSECOURS	1919 Jan 1	1800	Lieut A.F. GALLOWAY evacuated sick today to No. 41 C.C.S.	N.I.D
"	5	1300	Capt. E.B. JARDINE M.C. proceeded on 8 days leave to PARIS. Sick de lt with during past week in Divisional Rest Station:—	

	Remained		Admitted		Evacuated		To duty		Remaining	
	O	ORs	O	ORs	O	ORs	O	ORs	O	ORs
To Div	1	24	—	48	—	23	—	26	0	23
Other Army	—	11	2	22	1	9	1	13	1	11
Total	1	35	2	70	1	32	1	39	1	34

ADS

| " | 11 | 1300 | Capt. & Quartermaster H.G. ADISS proceeded on 14 days leave to United Kingdom. | ADS |

Army Form C. 2118.

WAR DIARY
or
INTELLIGENCE SUMMARY.

(Erase heading not required.)

Place	Date	Hour	Summary of Events and Information	Remarks and references to Appendices
BONSECOURS	Jan 12	13:00	Statement of sick to all ranks at Divisional Rest Station during week ending noon today: —	Map Ref. Sheet 44 L.16.c.3.9

Statement of sick to all ranks at Divisional Rest Station during week ending noon today: —

	Remained		Admitted		Evacuated		To duty		Remaining	
	O	O.Rs	O	O.Rs	O	O.Rs	O	O.Rs	O	O.Rs
50 Div	—	23	4	64	4	22	1	17	1	48
Other Forma.	1	11	—	13	—	3	—	11	1	10
Total	1	34	4	77	4	25	1	28	1	58

| | 14 | 18:00 | Capt. E.B. JARDINE M.O. returned unit from leave to PARIS | A.D. |
| | 14 | 13:10 | Statement of sick dealt with at Brig. Rest Station during week ending noon today: — | A.D. |

	Remained		Admitted		Evacuated		To duty		Remaining	
	O	O.Rs	O	O.Rs	O	O.Rs	O	O.Rs	O	O.Rs
50 Div	1	48	1	55	1	31	1	37	—	35
Other Forma.	—	10	—	9	—	5	—	11	1	3
Total	1	58	1	64	1	36	1	48	1	38

A.D.

Army Form C. 2118.

WAR DIARY
or
INTELLIGENCE SUMMARY.
(Erase heading not required.)

Place	Date	Hour	Summary of Events and Information	Remarks and references to Appendices
RONTÉCOURT	1919 Nov 25	1200	Capt E.R.TARDIVE M.C proceeded today for duty in medical charge of 55th Divl. R.E.	Map Ref Sheet 57c L.10.c.3.9 (A.D.)
	26	1200	Statement of sick dealt with at Divisional Rest Station during week ending 1200 hours today:-	

	Received		Admitted		Evacuated		To duty		Remaining	
	O	ORs	O	ORs	O	ORs	O	ORs	O	ORs
55 Div	1	30	1	49	1	27	1	27	1	29
Other form.	—	3	—	10	—	1	—	4	—	8
Total	1	39	1	59	1	28	1	31	1	37

Capt. T.M.SHEATON left the Unit today to proceed on 14 days leave to United Kingdom. (A.D.)

A.D.Snider Lt.Col
R.M.C. T.F

Library

War Diary
of
Lieut Colonel A.T.FALWASSER DSO.
R.A.M.C. T.F

Commanding 2/1st. Home Counties Field Ambulance

from Feb 1st 1919 to Feb 28th 1919.

(Volume 3)

Army Form C. 2118.

WAR DIARY
or
INTELLIGENCE SUMMARY.

(Erase heading not required.)

Instructions regarding War Diaries and Intelligence Summaries are contained in F. S. Regs. Part II. and the Staff Manual respectively. Title pages will be prepared in manuscript.

Place	Date	Hour	Summary of Events and Information	Remarks and references to Appendices
BONSECOURS	Feb 2	1200	Statement of sick taken in 55th Divisional Rest Station during week ended noon today:—	Hd. Qs. Rest sta. L.15.c.3.9

	Received		Admitted		Evacuated		To duty		Remaining	
	O	ORs	O	ORs	O	ORs	O	ORs	O	ORs
55th Division	1	29	3	39	1	24	1	22	2	22
Other forms	—	8	1	9	—	8	1	3	1	76
Total	1	37	3	48	1	32	1	25	2	28

| | 7 | 1200 | Capt. & Quartermaster H.G. ALDISS reported to unit today from leave to the United Kingdom. His leave having been extended by high authority from 26.1.19 to 5.2.19 | AD |
| | 8 | 1200 | An attempt to disinfect of 10 other ranks per week from this Unit has been received. Four other ranks & inmates have been disinfected up to date. | AD |

WAR DIARY
or
INTELLIGENCE SUMMARY.

Army Form C. 2118.

Place	Date	Hour	Summary of Events and Information	Remarks and references to Appendices
BONE BEOURS	Feb 15	1800	Capt. E.B. HARDING M.C. rejoined the Uny from duty with 57th Sanf R.E. & posted for duty to 12th London Regt.	Nof Rt stat at h.10.2.39 A.1.?
"	16	1200	Detachment of sick will walk in 59th. Several had Malaria during 14 days aly room today	

	Received		Admitted		Evacuated		To duty		Remaining	
	O	OR	O	OR	O	OR	O	OR	O	OR
57th Div	0	2	—	44	½	45	½	243 28?	0	13
Other forces	1	6	1	40	1	12	1	17	1	17
Total	2	258	1	121	1	59	2	60	1	30

A.1.?

| " | 20 | 1800 | An other ranks RAMC & 7 PB personnel stuck and 1 RAMC MT have been demobilized up to date & have been despatched to base for return to England. New establishment of Field Ambulance whole & section had been received which has been reorganized on the basis | A.1.? |

WAR DIARY
or
INTELLIGENCE SUMMARY.
(Erase heading not required.)

Army Form C. 2118.

Instructions regarding War Diaries and Intelligence Summaries are contained in F. S. Regs., Part II. and the Staff Manual respectively. Title pages will be prepared in manuscript.

Place	Date	Hour	Summary of Events and Information	Remarks and references to Appendices
RONCOURT	26.23	12n.c	"Observed it took from through Amiens ReStation during week ending now today:—	Hop Rft Strike not L.10.C.57

	Received		Hospital		Evacuated		To duty		Running	
	O	OR	O	OR	O	OR	O	OR	O	OR
52 Div	—	13	—	65	3	45	1	14	—	19
Other Forms	1	17	2	25	2	26	—	6	1	10
Total	1	30	6	90	5	71	1	20	1	29

A.D.
26	1900	Day without anything known about 'Z' incorporated today to 52nd Highlanders for inclusion in the diary entry work
27	1900	Received intimation today that Capt. E.B. JARDINE MC is to proceed to England forthwith to identifying stan A.D
28	1900	Capt. E.B JARDINE MB signed for duty with that kinda left in view of intimation received for his duties at an early date A.D.Delivering L.Col

Original.

No.1.1919.

WO 26
140/3556

CONFIDENTIAL.

WAR DIARY.

of

2/1st Home Counties Field Ambulance. R.A.M.C. T.F.

From 1st March 1919.   To 31st March 1919.

17 JUL 1919

Volume II

WAR DIARY
or
INTELLIGENCE SUMMARY.
(Erase heading not required.)

Army Form C. 2118.

Place	Date	Hour	Summary of Events and Information	Remarks and references to Appendices
BONTECOURT	1917			
	Nov 1	1300	Capt E.R. JARDINE M.C. proceeded today to I Corps Convalescent Camp TOURNAI en route for England to be demobilized.	Hy. Ref Nov 44 5.10.9.3.9
			Capt J.M. SMEATON is struck off the strength of the Unit having been absent from the United Kingdom for over 30 days. A)I)	
	2	1300	Parasitic mice into force today throughout B.E.F. Unit being Inspected no less than 2300 Rumo yesterday. Statistic of sick dealt with in A.R.S. during 7 days ended more leave today:-	

	Remained		Admitted		Evacuated		To duty		Remaining	
	O	O.R	O	O.R	O	O.R	O	O.R	O	O.R
Officers	—	19	1	64	1	49	1	13	1	21
Other Ranks	—	10	1	22	1	21	1	9	1	2
Total	—	29	2	86	2	70	1	22	—	23

Major A.E. HUXTABLE and Capt J.S. WARD left unit today to proceed to I Corps Convalescent Camp for ten hourly storm Lieut A.F. GALLOWAY proceeded on special leave for 4 days to England A)I)

Army Form C. 2118.

WAR DIARY
or
INTELLIGENCE SUMMARY.
(Erase heading not required.)

Instructions regarding War Diaries and Intelligence Summaries are contained in F. S. Regs., Part II. and the Staff Manual respectively. Title pages will be prepared in manuscript.

Place	Date	Hour	Summary of Events and Information	Remarks and references to Appendices
Bonsecours	March 2nd	10.00	Capt. G.W.M. ANDREW from 2/3rd Home Counties F. Amb. joined this unit for duty and taken on strength.	Hd. Qrs. Shell Left K.10.a.3.9. A.D.S.
"	3rd	10.00	Capt. W.B. MACLEAN M.R.C. U.S.A. from 2/1st London left posted today for duty. Struck off strength.	A.D.S.
"	4th	12.00	Recd R.A.M.C. order No. 71 by A.D.M.S. to swiss :- The 2/1 1/1 C.F. Amb. will move to CHAPELLE À OIE on to March. Move to be completed by noon 2nd to March. The Bn. of Rest Station (Off. 1/1 1/1 C.F. Amb. will close at BONSECOURS and open on 6th March and reopen at CHAPELLE À WATTINES (Off. 1/1 1/2 Amb.) at same hour. Details remaining in 2/1 1/1 C.F. Amb. will be transfer to C.C.S. at Pte 3. returned at strength.	A.D.S.
"	"	11.00	Visited CHAPELLE À OIE to obtain accommodation. The billets is very sparse & the village by itself generally seemed to be unit with several batteries stationed near. (K.10.)	A.D.S.

WAR DIARY or INTELLIGENCE SUMMARY

Army Form C. 2118.

Place	Date	Hour	Summary of Events and Information	Remarks and references to Appendices
BONSECOURS	Feb 2nd 1916	8:30	Advance party of 5 other ranks proceeded to CHAPELLE À OIE Capt. J.M. SMEATON reported sick, leave [illeg] [illeg].	A.D.)
"	"	6:00	Class III R.E. all sick cases remaining here moved to C.C.S.	A.D.)
"	"	10:00	After 1st Sqn of 10 other ranks proceeded to CHAPELLE À OIE and returned ranks of [illeg] departed the lines via [illeg] (L.D. & H.B.) deemed "X" provided by road to BOULOGNE for return to England, and 2 riding horses to ft. M.V. Return for [illeg] duty.	A.D.)
"	"	18:00	Bn. ordered to put a additional draught horses for [illeg] teamers.	A.D.)
"	"	10:30	Unit proceeded by march route to CHAPELLE À OIE. Civilian remain at BONSECOURS & will be sent on tomorrow [illeg] in [illeg] of [illeg] [illeg] [illeg] [illeg] of horses remaining with unit 13 riding and 7 draught only	A.D.)
CHAPELLE À OIE	"	14:00	Unit arrived & billeted in Chateau on outskirts of Commune of BUEGNY at CHAPELLE À OIE.	A.D.)
"	3rd Feb	11:00	Handed over today BREWETT [?] Infant M/c re 1 Unit to offr C.N.M. ANDREW on view of my departure tomorrow for England for duties not released [?] [illeg] [illeg] to other ranks not released & A.D.S. reg't. Bearer for duty.	A.D.)

WAR DIARY
or
INTELLIGENCE SUMMARY

Army Form C. 2118.

(Erase heading not required.)

Instructions regarding War Diaries and Intelligence Summaries are contained in F. S. Regs., Part II. and the Staff Manual respectively. Title pages will be prepared in manuscript.

Place	Date	Hour	Summary of Events and Information	Remarks and references to Appendices
			[Handwritten war diary entries, largely illegible. Dates appear to be in March 1919, referencing locations such as LEUZE, TOURNAI, and mentions of 51 C.C.S., officers including Lt Col A.J. Falwasser, Major Greaves DSO MC, and various troop movements and hospital/demobilization activities.]	

WAR DIARY
or
INTELLIGENCE SUMMARY
(Erase heading not required.)

Army Form C. 2118.

Place	Date 1919	Hour	Summary of Events and Information	Remarks and references to Appendices
CHAPELLE à OIE	May 17	17.00	Vehicles in Park at LEUZE in good clean condition, serviceable stores to be sorted. Equipment & Armlets to be regimentally examined, Brass Polish.	
"	18"	18.00	M.E. Camp. Rec'd WRO/SW.C. to supply 2 yr. Australian papers supplied than number EM7/43753 enable ATS 54. I OR. Ordered to report STASNOS 29" OWN: have completed nearing & have Regd. y" have sold LEUZE for entraining. Only state war at N.O. Each on our store and other lorries in parks at dump at LEUZE.	E. Stratford Capt
"	19"	18.00	Supplies Stationary despatch STASNOS 38" DIV for Dupan	S.S.R
"	28/29	18.00	Nil.	S.S.R
"	29"	18.00	G.O.Remarks & Concentration Camp for demobilization	S.S.R
"	29/30	17.00	Nil.	S.S.R
"	30"	14.00	Re O/Remarks to Concentration Camp for demobilization Unit reduced to Cadre establishment	S.S.R
			Unit remains at CHAPELLE à OIE.	

CONFIDENTIAL.

WAR DIARY.

of

2/1st HOME COUNTIES Fd. Ambce R.A.M.C. T.F.

From 1st April 1919. to 30th April 1919.

Army Form C. 2118.

WAR DIARY
or
INTELLIGENCE SUMMARY.
(Erase heading not required.)

Place	Date	Hour	Summary of Events and Information	Remarks and references to Appendices
CHAPELLE d'OIE BELGIUM	1.4.19 2.4.19		Nil	
	3.4.19		Capt W R Maclean MRC USA proceeded to L H A BEF for return to USA	
	4.4.19 5.4.19		Nil	
	6.4.19		Capt J M Anderson RAMC TC proceeded to UK for demobilisation on 7.4.19	
	7.4.19 to 20.4.19		Nil	
			The unit remains at Cadre strength and stationed at CHAPELLE d'OIE Belgium	

Harry Harrison
Major RAMC
2/1st Home Counties Field Ambulance

CONFIDENTIAL.

War Diary
of

2/1st HOME COUNTIES FIELD AMBULANCE
R.A.M.C.(T.F.)

From 1-5-1919   To. 31. 5-1919

(Volume 11)

Army Form C. 2118.

WAR DIARY
or
INTELLIGENCE SUMMARY.
(Erase heading not required.)

Instructions regarding War Diaries and Intelligence Summaries are contained in F.S. Regs., Part II. and the Staff Manual respectively. Title pages will be prepared in manuscript.

Place	Date	Hour	Summary of Events and Information	Remarks and references to Appendices
CHAPELLE A OIE BELGIUM	4.5.19		Major S.S. Greaves. R.A.M.C. T.F. D.S.O. M.C. proceeds for demobilisation on 4-5-19. Relinquished command of 2/1st Home Counties Fd Ambce on 4-5-19 also acting Rank of Major from 4-5-19.	JMS
	4.5.19		Capt. G.W.M. Andrew R.A.M.C. T.F. assumed command of unit on 4-5-19.	JMS
	12.5.19		4. O.Rs. R.A.M.C. proceed to dispersal station for demob on 12-5-19.	JMS
	13.5.19		Capt. G.W.M. Andrew R.A.M.C. T.F. relinquishes Command of unit on 13.5.19. and posted to No.1. A.C.D.	JMS
	13.5.19		Capt. A.Q.M. H.G. Aldis R.A.M.C. T.F. assumed Command of unit on 13-5-19.	JMS
	13.5.19		Strength o/c of Unit "No. A. 724" Check on 13.5.19.	JMS
	20.5.19		2. O.Rs. proceed to dispersal station for demob on 20.5.19.	JMS
	22.5.19		5. O.Rs. do do do 22.5.19.	JMS
	24.5.19		9. O.Rs do do do 24.5.19.	JMS
	26.5.19		Capt & Q.M.S. T.M. Alessio R.A.M.C. T.F. reports for duty from Base 26.5.19 and assumes Command of unit on 28.5.19. VICE. Capt & Q.M. H.G. Aldis "awaiting demob"	JMS

Army Form C. 2118.

WAR DIARY
or
INTELLIGENCE SUMMARY.
(Erase heading not required.)

Instructions regarding War Diaries and Intelligence Summaries are contained in F. S. Regs., Part II. and the Staff Manual respectively. Title pages will be prepared in manuscript.

Place	Date	Hour	Summary of Events and Information	Remarks and references to Appendices
CHAPELLE-À-OIE. BELGIUM	31/5/19		Capt & Q.M. H.Q. Aldis R.A.M.C. T.F. proceeded for demob. on 31.5.19.	End
	31/5/19		5. O.R. proceeded to dispersal station for demob on 31.5.19.	End

Jno. M. Stevens
Capt RAMC
Cmdg 2/1 St Home Counties Flanders
RAMC. T.F.

WO 29.
Cense
6/3585-

13 AUG 1919

CONFIDENTIAL

War Diary

of

2/1st Home Counties Field Ambulance.

R.A.M.C. (T.F.)

From 1-6-1919   To 13-6-1919

(Volume II)

Army Form C. 2118.

WAR DIARY
or
INTELLIGENCE SUMMARY.
(Erase heading not required.)

Instructions regarding War Diaries and Intelligence
Summaries are contained in F. S. Regs., Part II.
and the Staff Manual respectively. Title pages
will be prepared in manuscript.

Place	Date	Hour	Summary of Events and Information	Remarks and references to Appendices
LENZE	3.6.19		The Unit moved from Chapelle-a-oie to LENZE on 3.6.19.	
	7.6.19		16. ORs. proceeded to demob on 7-6-19.	
			The Equipment guard of 15. ORs and 1 officer entrained with Equipment and Vehicles at 22.00 hours on 10-6-19 at LENZE, Belgium en route for Antwerp.	
ANTWERP	13.6/19		The Equipment guard of 1 Officer & 13. other Ranks with Equipment & Vehicles entrained for U.K.	

13-6-19.

Thos L Stevens
Major R.A.M.C.
Comdg 2/1st Home Counties Fd Amb.
R.A.M.C. T.F.

www.ingramcontent.com/pod-product-compliance
Lightning Source LLC
Chambersburg PA
CBHW080908230426
43664CB00016B/2758